MAN VERSUS MACHINE

W9-CCW-772

WRITER: **NATHAN EDMONDSON**

ARTIST: **MIKE PERKINS**

COLOR ARTIST: **ANDY TROY**

LETTERER: **VC'S JOE SABINO**

COVER ART: **MIKE PERKINS** & **ANDY TROY** (#6-8, #10) ; AND
MIKE PERKINS, BUTCH GUICE & **ANDY TROY** (#9)

EDITOR: **JAKE THOMAS**

EXECUTIVE EDITOR: **TOM BREVOORT**

COLLECTION EDITOR: **MARK D. BEAZLEY**
ASSISTANT EDITOR: **SARAH BRUNSTAD**
ASSOCIATE MANAGING EDITOR: **ALEX STARBUCK**
EDITOR, SPECIAL PROJECTS: **JENNIFER GRÜNWALD**
SENIOR EDITOR, SPECIAL PROJECTS: **JEFF YOUNGQUIST**
BOOK DESIGNER: **ADAM DEL RE**
SVP PRINT, SALES & MARKETING: **DAVID GABRIEL**

EDITOR IN CHIEF: **AXEL ALONSO**
CHIEF CREATIVE OFFICER: **JOE QUESADA**
PUBLISHER: **DAN BUCKLEY**
EXECUTIVE PRODUCER: **ALAN FINE**

DEATHLOK VOL. 2: MAN VERSUS MACHINE. Contains material originally published in magazine form as DEATHLOK #6-10. First printing 2015. ISBN# 978-0-7851-9279-4. Published by MARVEL WORLDWIDE, INC., a subsidiary of MARVEL ENTERTAINMENT, LLC. OFFICE OF PUBLICATION: 135 West 50th Street, New York, NY 10020. Copyright © 2015 MARVEL No similarity between any of the names, characters, persons, and/ or institutions in this magazine with those of any living or dead person or institution is intended, and any such similarity which may exist is purely coincidental. **Printed in Canada.** ALAN FINE, President, Marvel Entertainment; DAN BUCKLEY, President, TV, Publishing and Brand Management; JOE QUESADA, Chief Creative Officer; TOM BREVOORT, SVP of Publishing; DAVID BOGART, SVP of Operations & Procurement, Publishing; C.B. CEBULSKI, VP of International Development & Brand Management; DAVID GABRIEL, SVP Print, Sales & Marketing; JIM O'KEEFE, VP of Operations & Logistics; DAN CARR, Executive Director of Publishing Technology; SUSAN CRESPI, Editorial Operations Manager; ALEX MORALES, Publishing Operations Manager; STAN LEE, Chairman Emeritus. For information regarding advertising in Marvel Comics or on Marvel.com, please contact Jonathan Rheingold, VP of Custom Solutions & Ad Sales, at jrheingold@marvel.com. For Marvel subscription inquiries, please call 800-217-9158. **Manufactured between 7/31/2015 and 9/7/2015 by SOLISCO PRINTERS, SCOTT, QC, CANADA.**

>>> BEFORE: HENRY HAYES WAS A COMBAT MEDIC, INJURED IN BATTLE.

BUT HE WAS GIVEN A NEW LEASE ON LIFE THROUGH PROSTHETICS MADE BY BIOTEK...

>>> NOW: HENRY WORKS FOR MEDICS WITHOUT BORDERS, GOING INTO WAR ZONES TO HELP PROVIDE AID AND RELIEF. OR SO HE THOUGHT...

WITHOUT HIS KNOWLEDGE, HENRY WAS TURNED INTO DEATHLOK, A CYBORG ASSET FOR A MYSTERIOUS ORGANIZATION'S DEADLY COVERT OPERATIONS. IMPLANTED FALSE MEMORIES ALLOWED HAYES TO BELIEVE HE WAS HELPING PEOPLE, BUT SINCE BEING SHOT BY THE A.I.M.-HIRED MERCENARY DOMINO, HENRY HAS BEEN ABLE TO RETAIN MEMORIES OF HIS INVOLUNTARY ATTACKS. NOW, DEATHLOK DEMANDS TO KNOW: JUST WHAT THE HELL IS HE?

MEANWHILE, S.H.I.E.L.D. AGENT ANDREA HOPE, IN PURSUIT OF THE ORGANIZATION BEHIND DEATHLOK, WAS DRUGGED AND TAKEN, ALONG WITH HAYES'S DAUGHTER ARIA. WHILE ARIA AWOKE AT HOME WITH HER OWN IMPLANTED FALSE MEMORIES, HOPE'S WHEREABOUTS ARE CURRENTLY UNKNOWN.

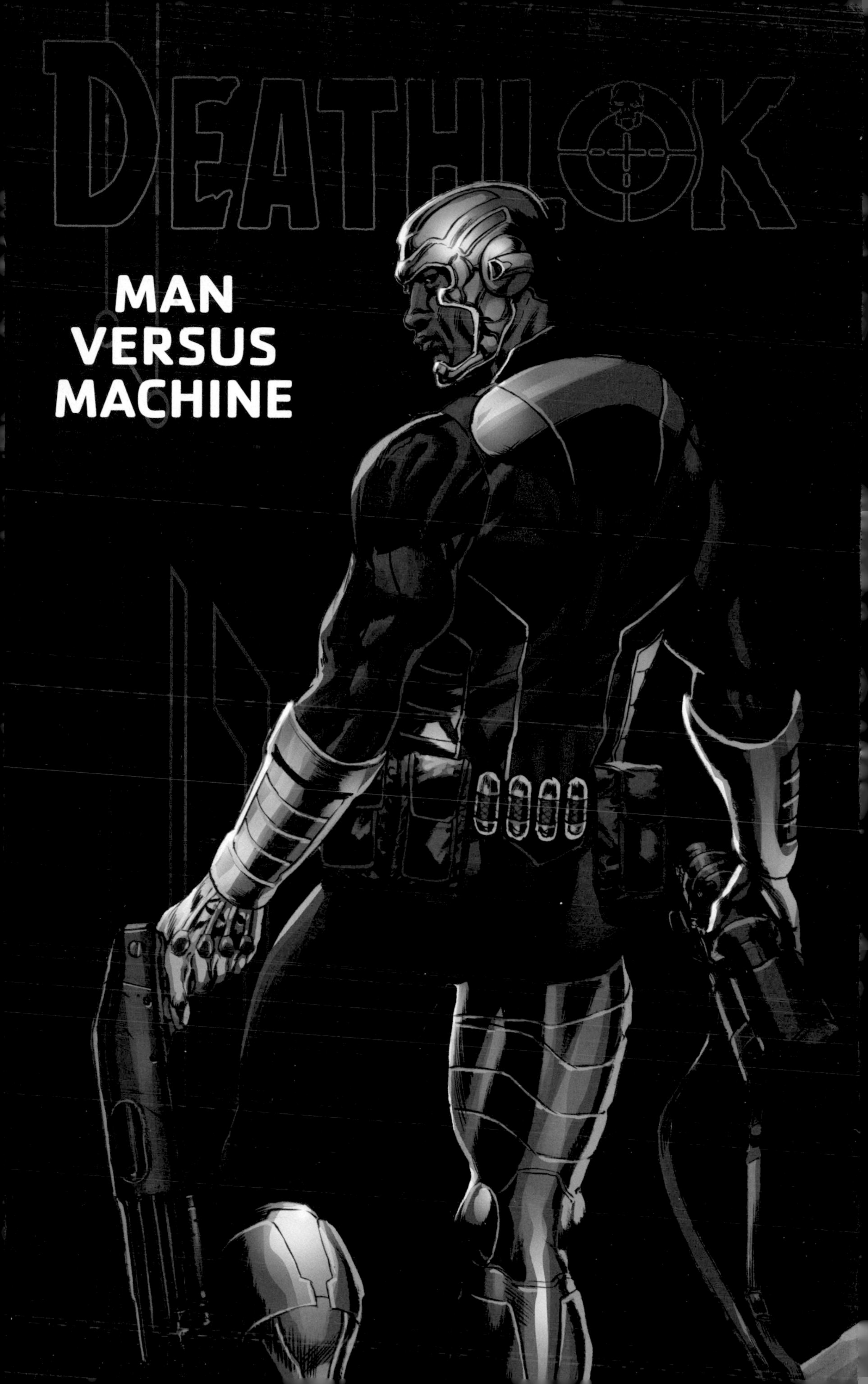
DEATHLOK
MAN VERSUS MACHINE

DEATHLOK

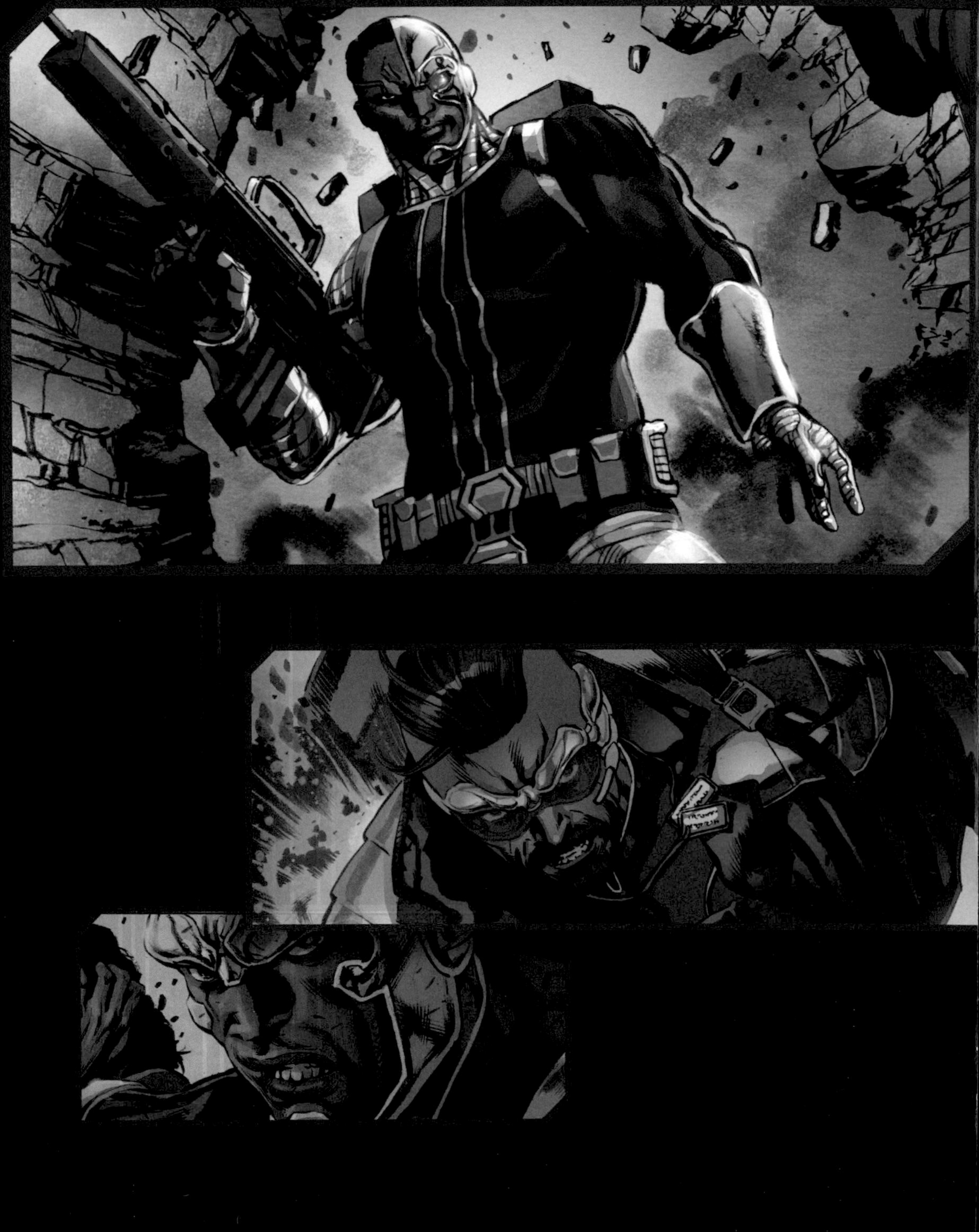

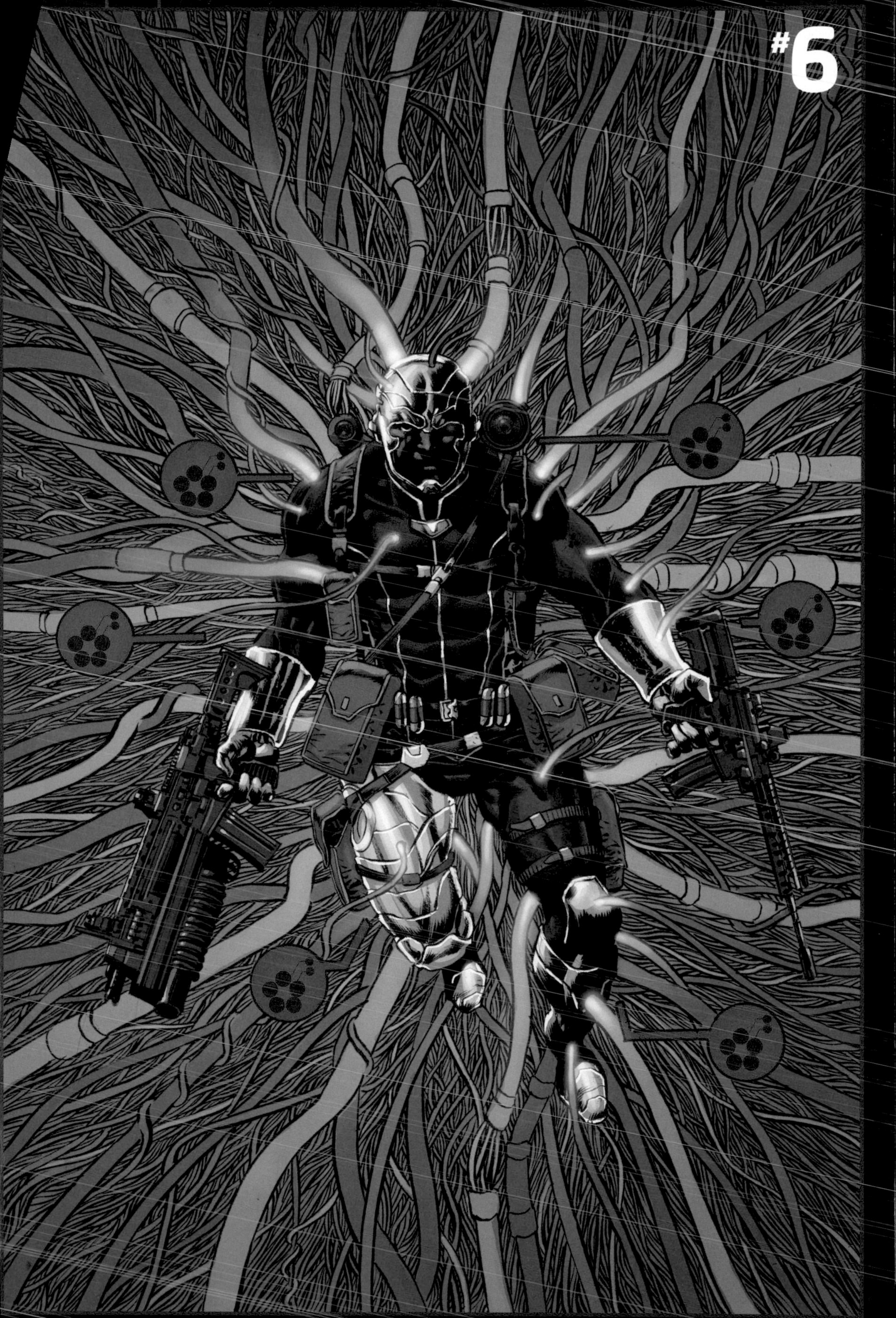
#6

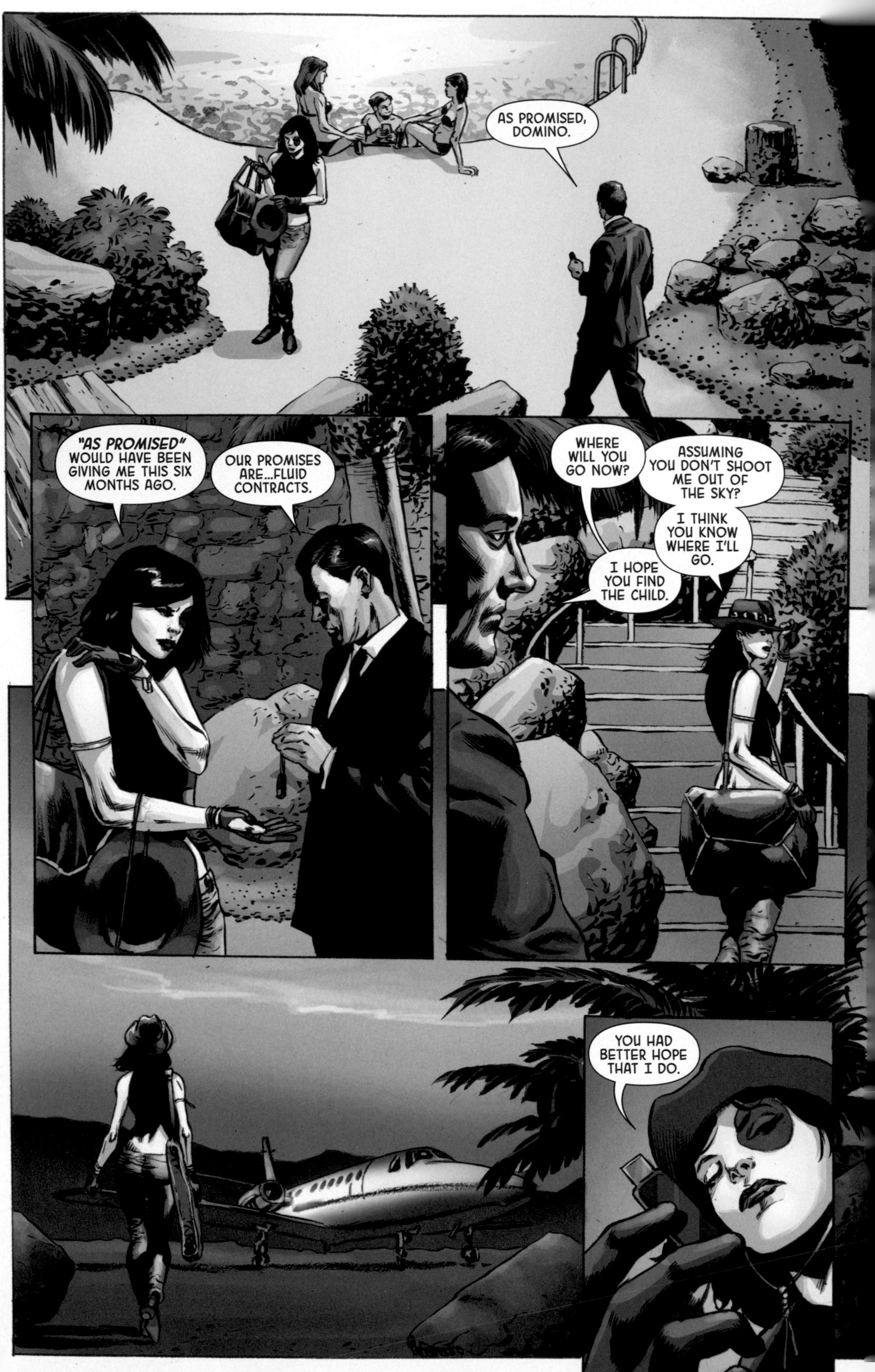
AS PROMISED, DOMINO.
"AS PROMISED" WOULD HAVE BEEN GIVING ME THIS SIX MONTHS AGO.
OUR PROMISES ARE...FLUID CONTRACTS.
WHERE WILL YOU GO NOW?
ASSUMING YOU DON'T SHOOT ME OUT OF THE SKY?
I THINK YOU KNOW WHERE I'LL GO.
I HOPE YOU FIND THE CHILD.
YOU HAD BETTER HOPE THAT I DO.

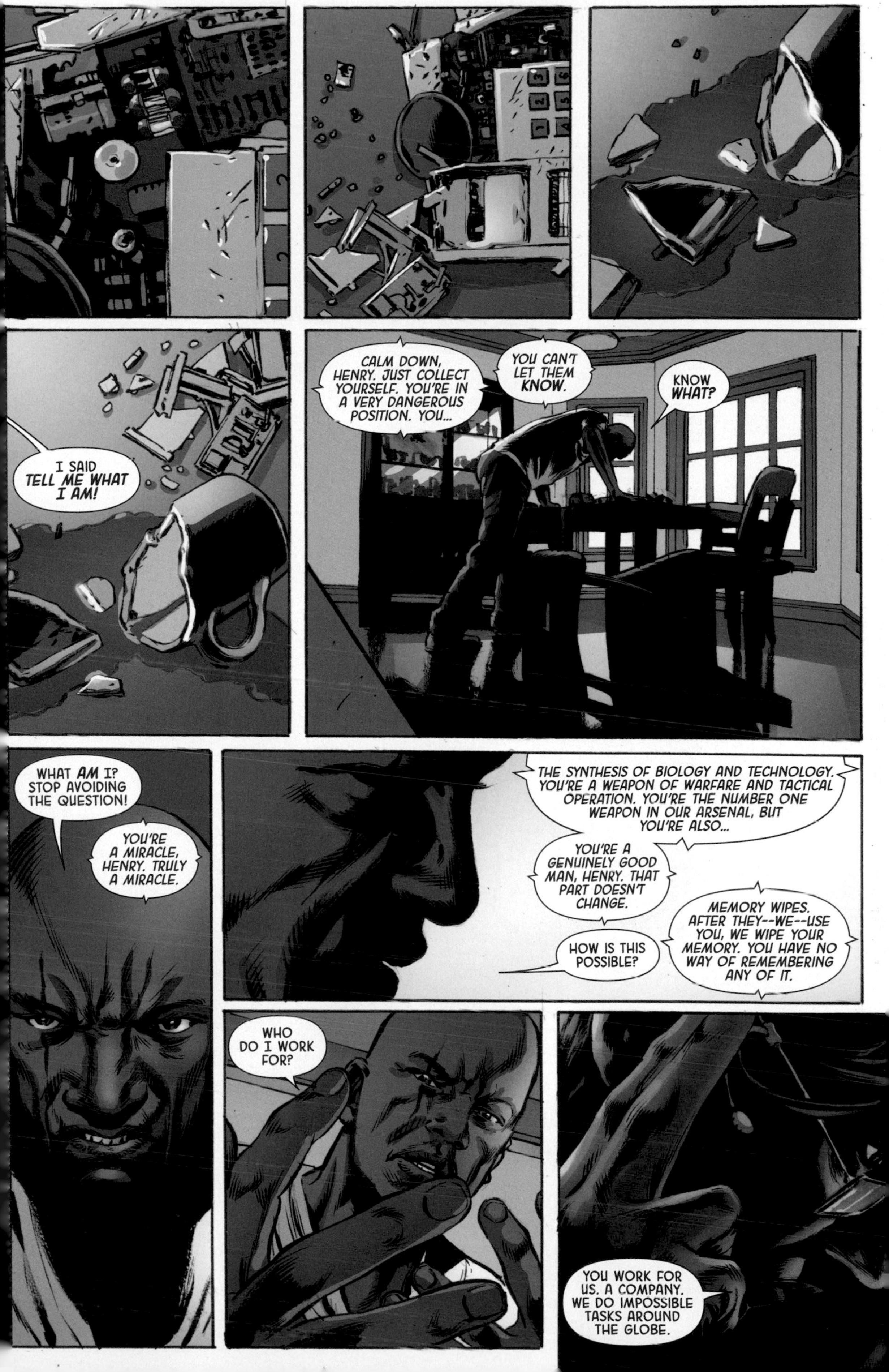
I SAID TELL ME WHAT I AM!
CALM DOWN, HENRY. JUST COLLECT YOURSELF. YOU'RE IN A VERY DANGEROUS POSITION. YOU...
YOU CAN'T LET THEM KNOW.
KNOW WHAT?
WHAT AM I? STOP AVOIDING THE QUESTION!
YOU'RE A MIRACLE, HENRY. TRULY A MIRACLE.
THE SYNTHESIS OF BIOLOGY AND TECHNOLOGY. YOU'RE A WEAPON OF WARFARE AND TACTICAL OPERATION. YOU'RE THE NUMBER ONE WEAPON IN OUR ARSENAL, BUT YOU'RE ALSO...
YOU'RE A GENUINELY GOOD MAN, HENRY. THAT PART DOESN'T CHANGE.
HOW IS THIS POSSIBLE?
MEMORY WIPES. AFTER THEY--WE--USE YOU, WE WIPE YOUR MEMORY. YOU HAVE NO WAY OF REMEMBERING ANY OF IT.
WHO DO I WORK FOR?
YOU WORK FOR US. A COMPANY. WE DO IMPOSSIBLE TASKS AROUND THE GLOBE.

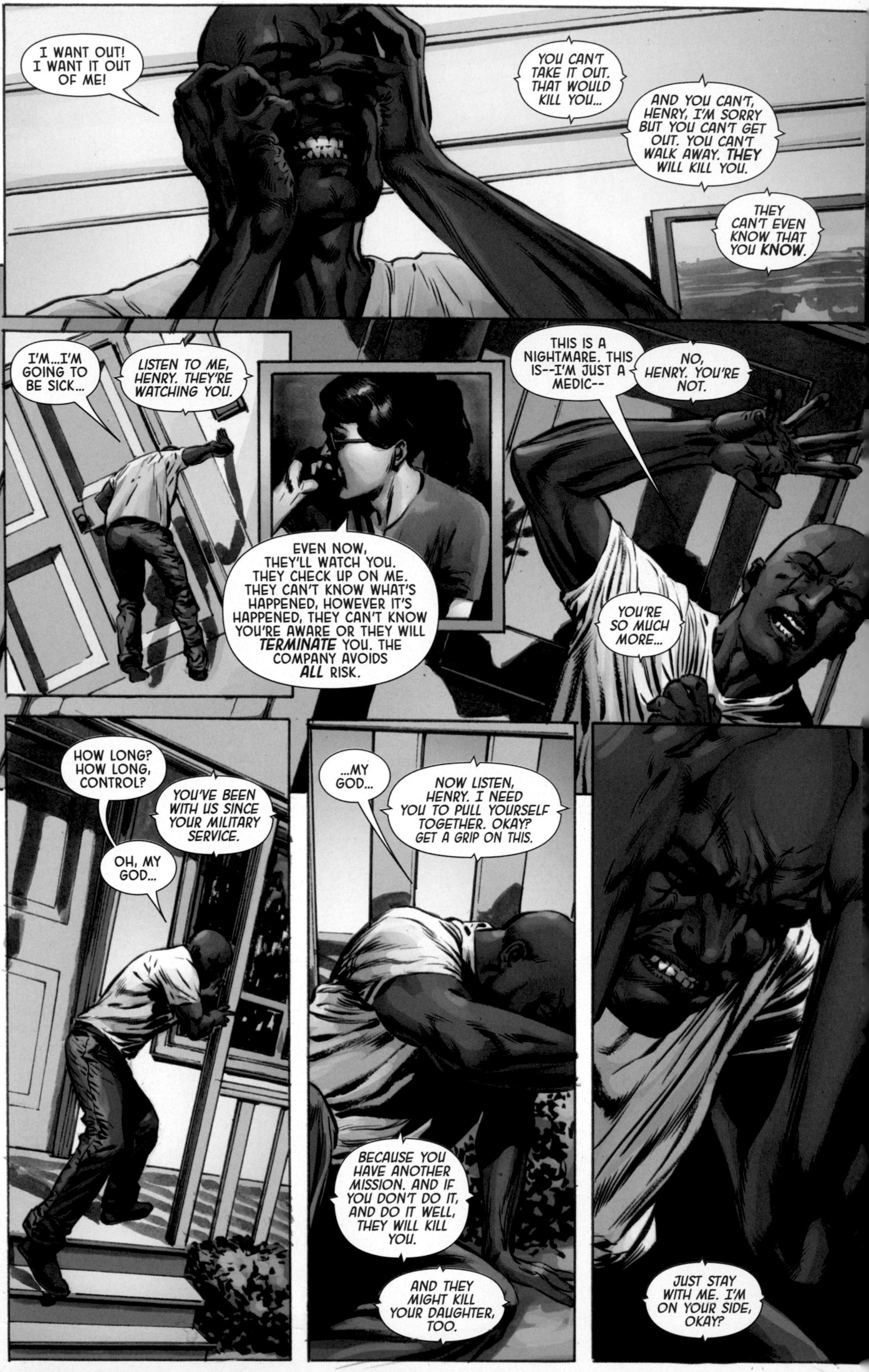

I WANT OUT! I WANT IT OUT OF ME!
YOU CAN'T TAKE IT OUT. THAT WOULD KILL YOU...
AND YOU CAN'T, HENRY, I'M SORRY BUT YOU CAN'T GET OUT. YOU CAN'T WALK AWAY. THEY WILL KILL YOU.
THEY CAN'T EVEN KNOW THAT YOU KNOW.
I'M...I'M GOING TO BE SICK...
LISTEN TO ME, HENRY. THEY'RE WATCHING YOU.
EVEN NOW, THEY'LL WATCH YOU. THEY CHECK UP ON ME. THEY CAN'T KNOW WHAT'S HAPPENED, HOWEVER IT'S HAPPENED, THEY CAN'T KNOW YOU'RE AWARE OR THEY WILL TERMINATE YOU. THE COMPANY AVOIDS ALL RISK.
THIS IS A NIGHTMARE. THIS IS--I'M JUST A MEDIC--
NO, HENRY. YOU'RE NOT.
YOU'RE SO MUCH MORE...
HOW LONG? HOW LONG, CONTROL?
YOU'VE BEEN WITH US SINCE YOUR MILITARY SERVICE.
OH, MY GOD...
...MY GOD...
NOW LISTEN, HENRY. I NEED YOU TO PULL YOURSELF TOGETHER. OKAY? GET A GRIP ON THIS.
BECAUSE YOU HAVE ANOTHER MISSION. AND IF YOU DON'T DO IT, AND DO IT WELL, THEY WILL KILL YOU.
AND THEY MIGHT KILL YOUR DAUGHTER, TOO.
JUST STAY WITH ME. I'M ON YOUR SIDE, OKAY?

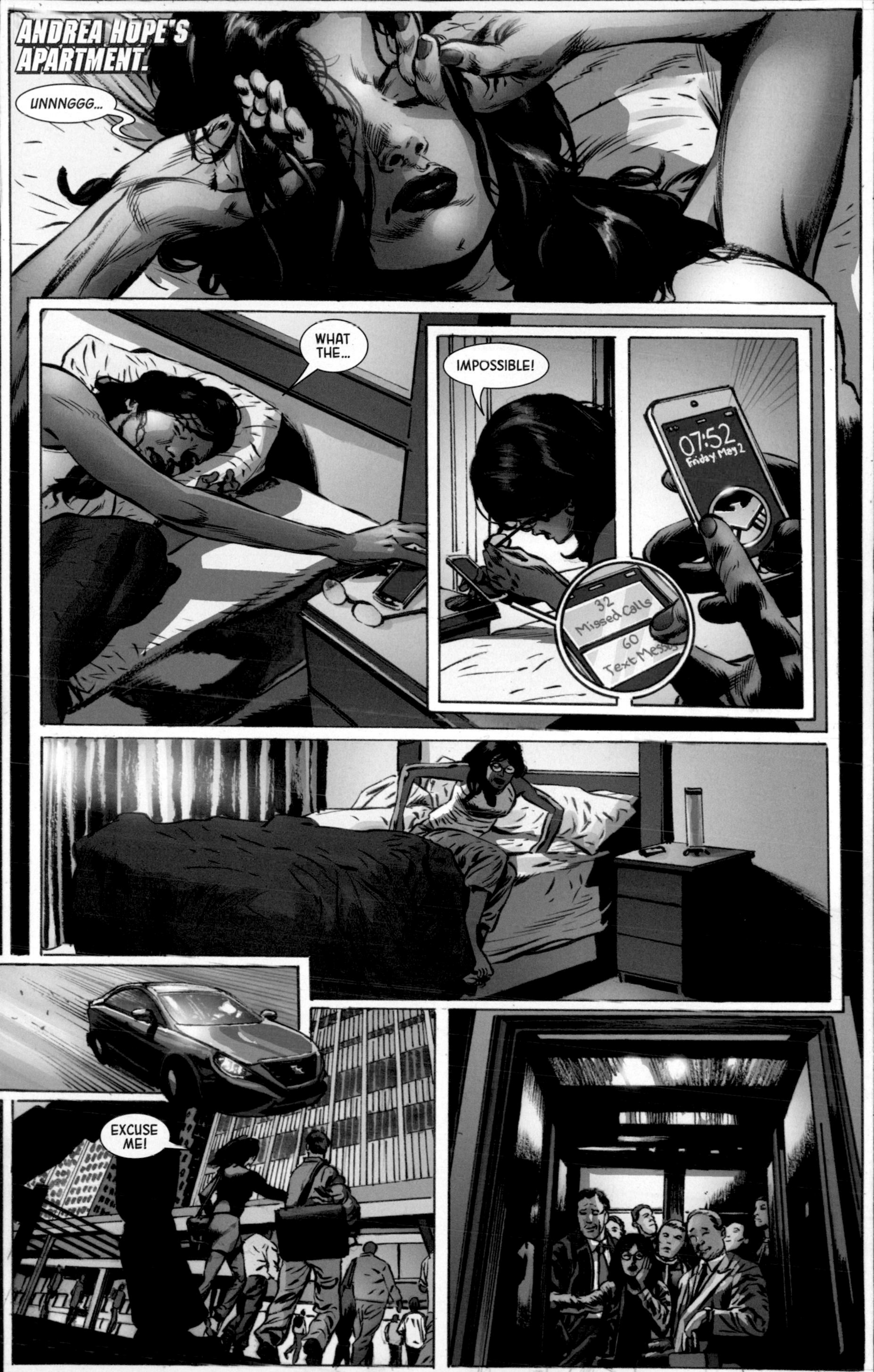
ANDREA HOPE'S APARTMENT.
UNNNGGG...
WHAT THE...
IMPOSSIBLE!
07:52
Friday May 2
32
Missed Calls
60
EXCUSE ME!

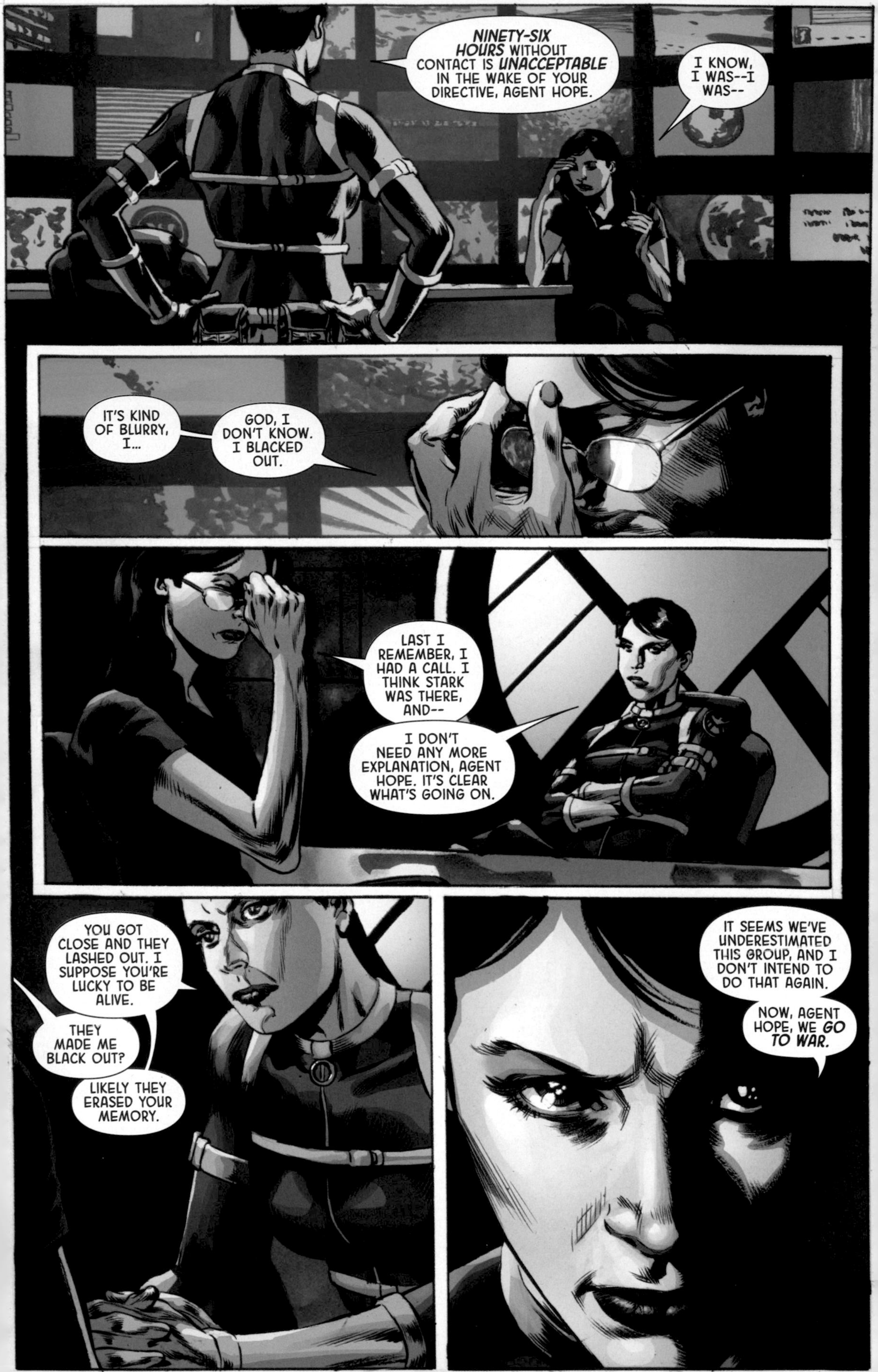
NINETY-SIX HOURS WITHOUT CONTACT IS UNACCEPTABLE IN THE WAKE OF YOUR DIRECTIVE, AGENT HOPE.
I KNOW, I WAS--I WAS--
IT'S KIND OF BLURRY, I...
GOD, I DON'T KNOW. I BLACKED OUT.
LAST I REMEMBER, I HAD A CALL. I THINK STARK WAS THERE, AND--
I DON'T NEED ANY MORE EXPLANATION, AGENT HOPE. IT'S CLEAR WHAT'S GOING ON.
YOU GOT CLOSE AND THEY LASHED OUT. I SUPPOSE YOU'RE LUCKY TO BE ALIVE.
THEY MADE ME BLACK OUT?
LIKELY THEY ERASED YOUR MEMORY.
IT SEEMS WE'VE UNDERESTIMATED THIS GROUP, AND I DON'T INTEND TO DO THAT AGAIN.
NOW, AGENT HOPE, WE GO TO WAR.

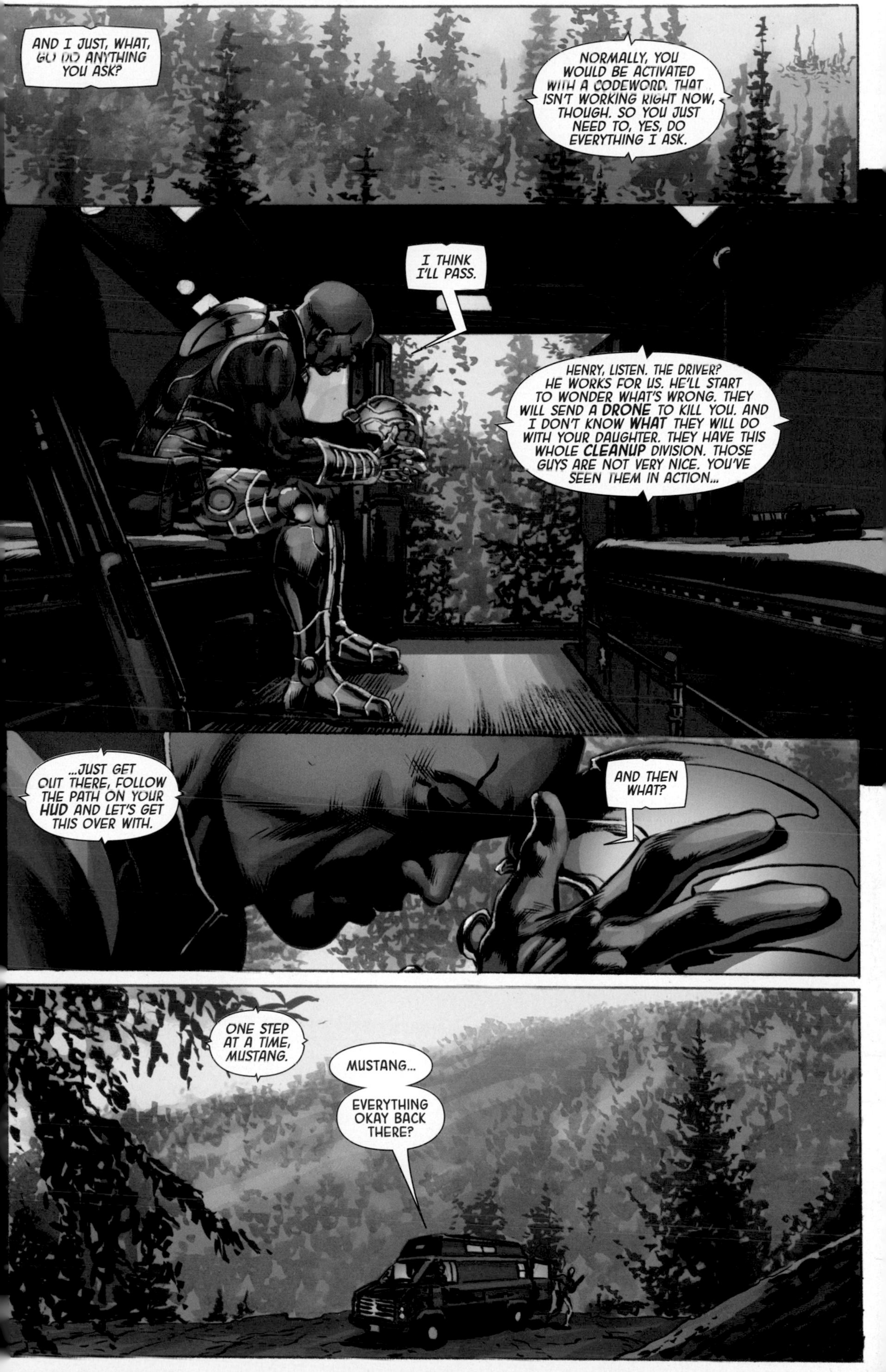
AND I JUST, WHAT, GO DO ANYTHING YOU ASK?
NORMALLY, YOU WOULD BE ACTIVATED WITH A CODEWORD. THAT ISN'T WORKING RIGHT NOW, THOUGH. SO YOU JUST NEED TO, YES, DO EVERYTHING I ASK.
I THINK I'LL PASS.
HENRY, LISTEN. THE DRIVER? HE WORKS FOR US. HE'LL START TO WONDER WHAT'S WRONG. THEY WILL SEND A DRONE TO KILL YOU. AND I DON'T KNOW WHAT THEY WILL DO WITH YOUR DAUGHTER. THEY HAVE THIS WHOLE CLEANUP DIVISION. THOSE GUYS ARE NOT VERY NICE. YOU'VE SEEN THEM IN ACTION...
...JUST GET OUT THERE, FOLLOW THE PATH ON YOUR HUD AND LET'S GET THIS OVER WITH.
AND THEN WHAT?
ONE STEP AT A TIME, MUSTANG.
MUSTANG...
EVERYTHING OKAY BACK THERE?

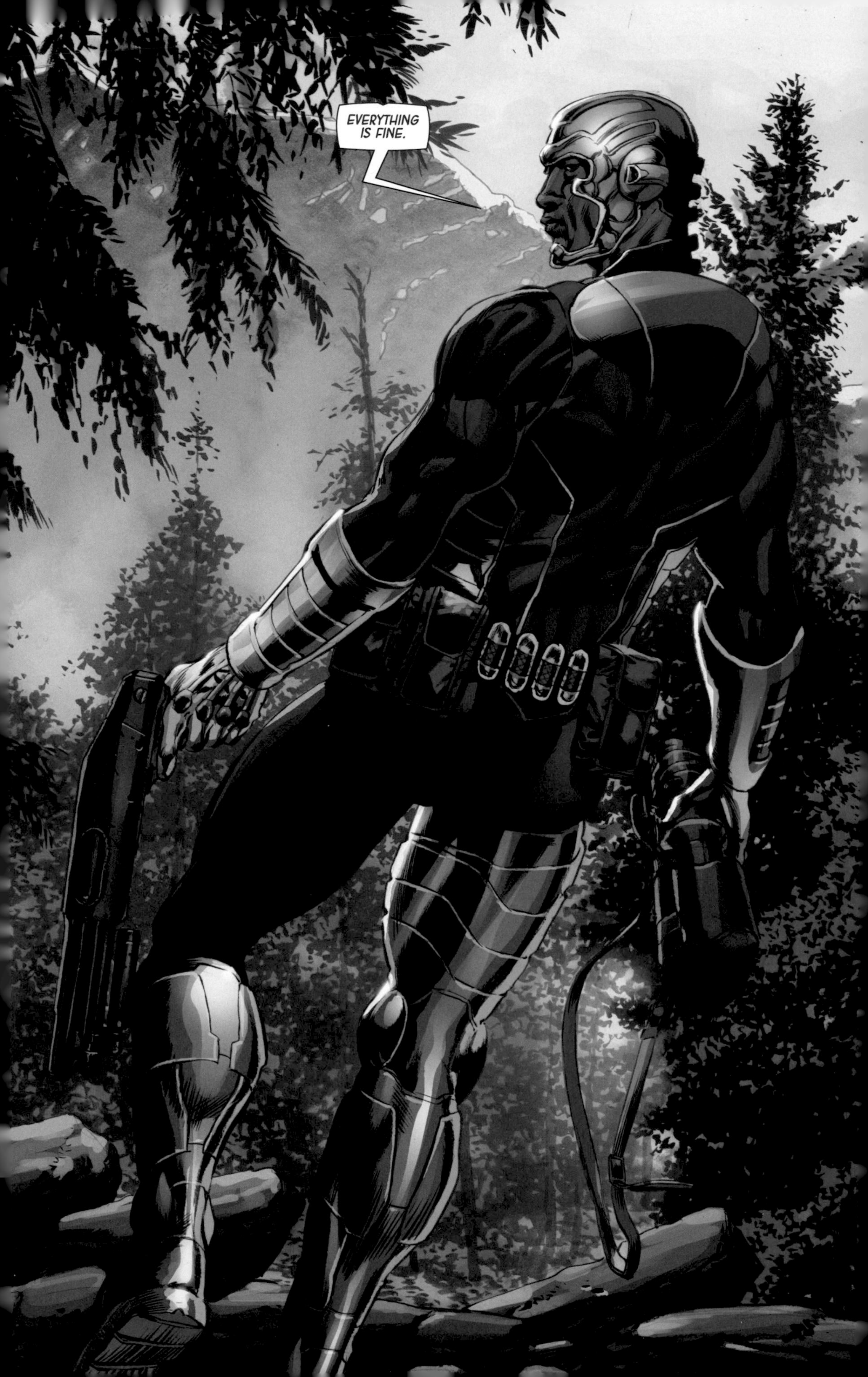
EVERYTHING IS FINE.

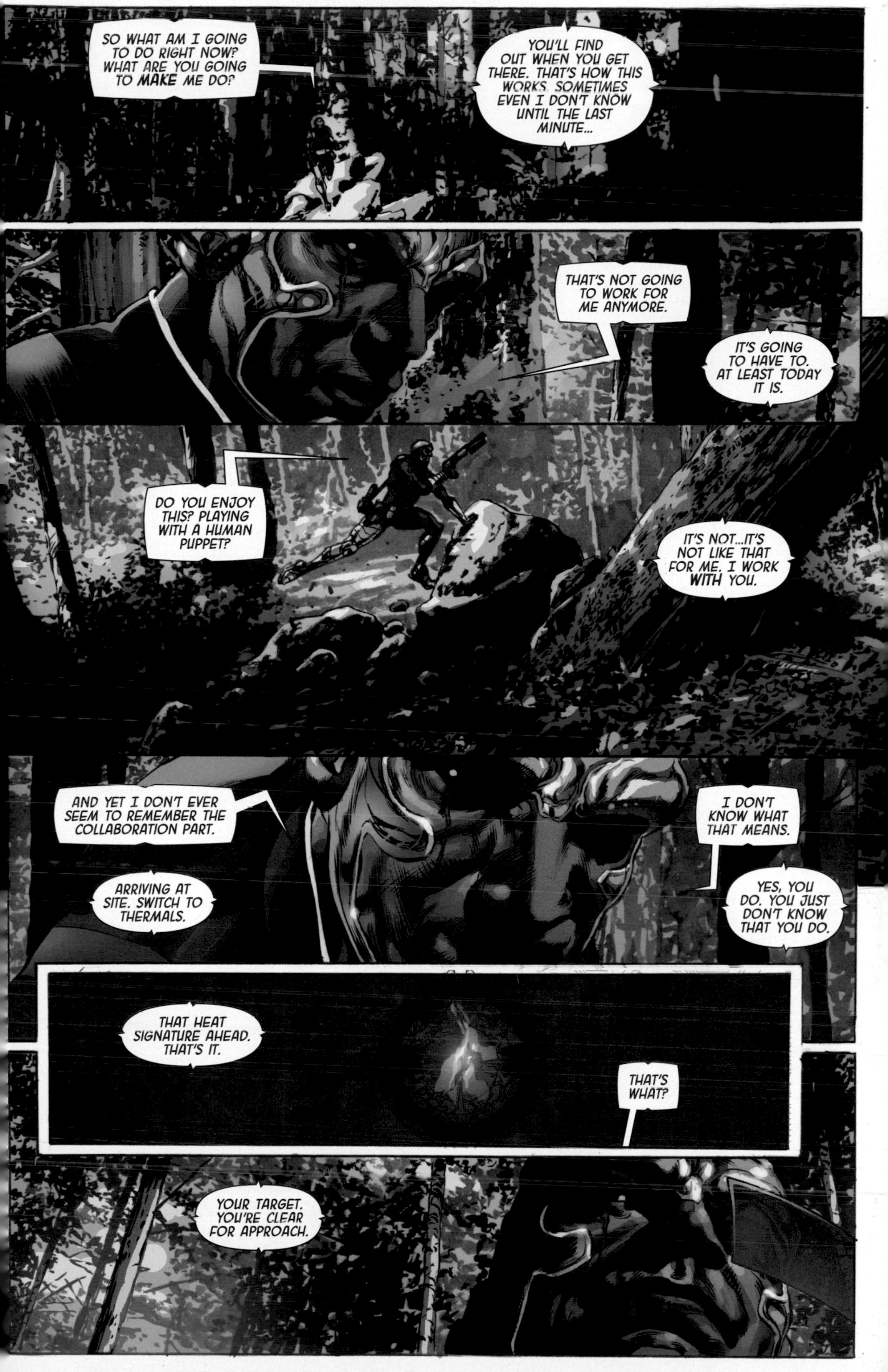
SO WHAT AM I GOING TO DO RIGHT NOW? WHAT ARE YOU GOING TO MAKE ME DO?
YOU'LL FIND OUT WHEN YOU GET THERE. THAT'S HOW THIS WORKS. SOMETIMES EVEN I DON'T KNOW UNTIL THE LAST MINUTE...
THAT'S NOT GOING TO WORK FOR ME ANYMORE.
IT'S GOING TO HAVE TO. AT LEAST TODAY IT IS.
DO YOU ENJOY THIS? PLAYING WITH A HUMAN PUPPET?
IT'S NOT...IT'S NOT LIKE THAT FOR ME. I WORK WITH YOU.
AND YET I DON'T EVER SEEM TO REMEMBER THE COLLABORATION PART.
I DON'T KNOW WHAT THAT MEANS.
ARRIVING AT SITE. SWITCH TO THERMALS.
YES, YOU DO. YOU JUST DON'T KNOW THAT YOU DO.
THAT HEAT SIGNATURE AHEAD. THAT'S IT.
THAT'S WHAT?
YOUR TARGET. YOU'RE CLEAR FOR APPROACH.

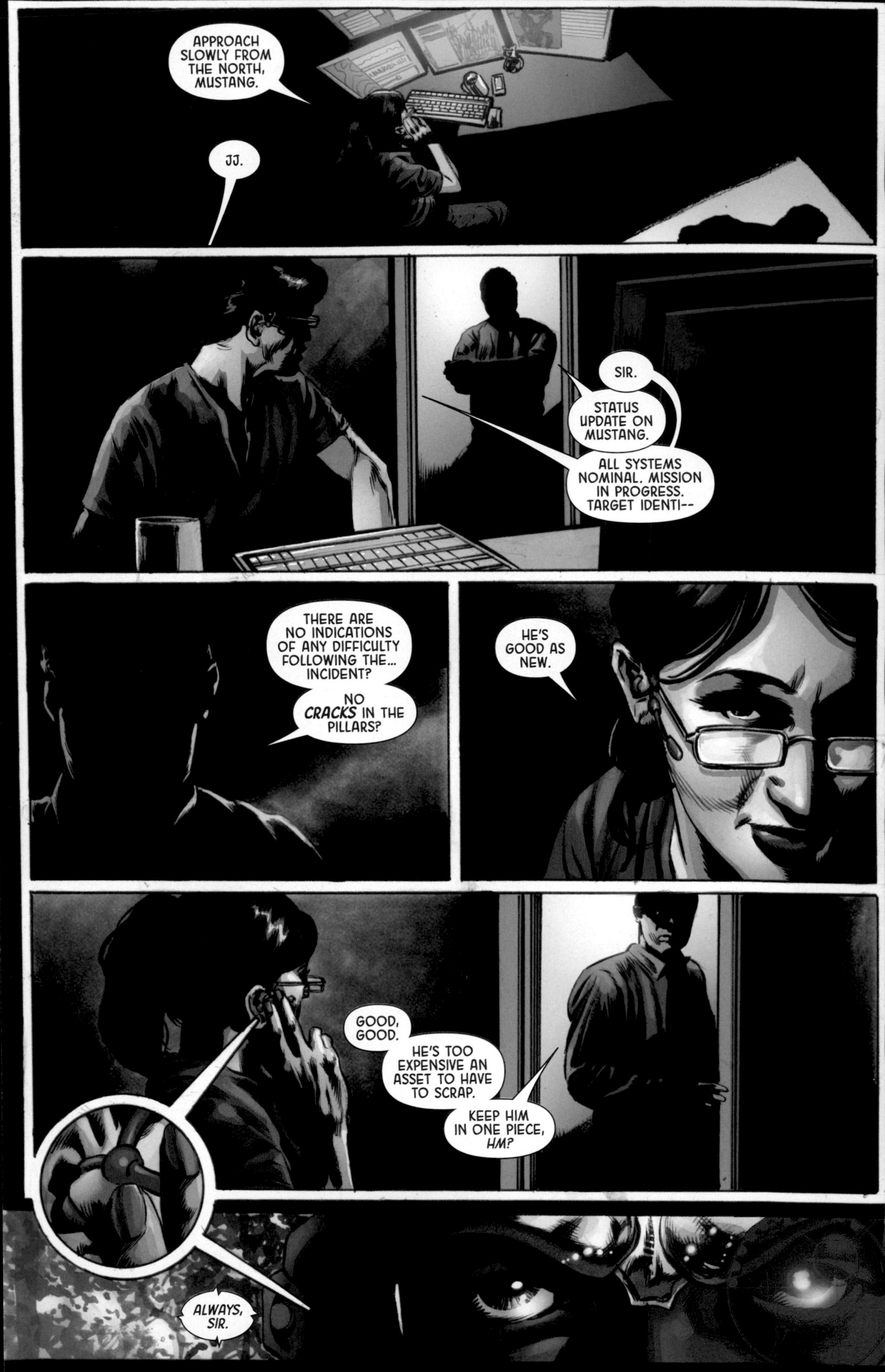
APPROACH SLOWLY FROM THE NORTH, MUSTANG.
JJ.
SIR.
STATUS UPDATE ON MUSTANG.
ALL SYSTEMS NOMINAL. MISSION IN PROGRESS. TARGET IDENTI--
THERE ARE NO INDICATIONS OF ANY DIFFICULTY FOLLOWING THE... INCIDENT?
NO CRACKS IN THE PILLARS?
HE'S GOOD AS NEW.
GOOD, GOOD.
HE'S TOO EXPENSIVE AN ASSET TO HAVE TO SCRAP.
KEEP HIM IN ONE PIECE, HM?
ALWAYS, SIR.

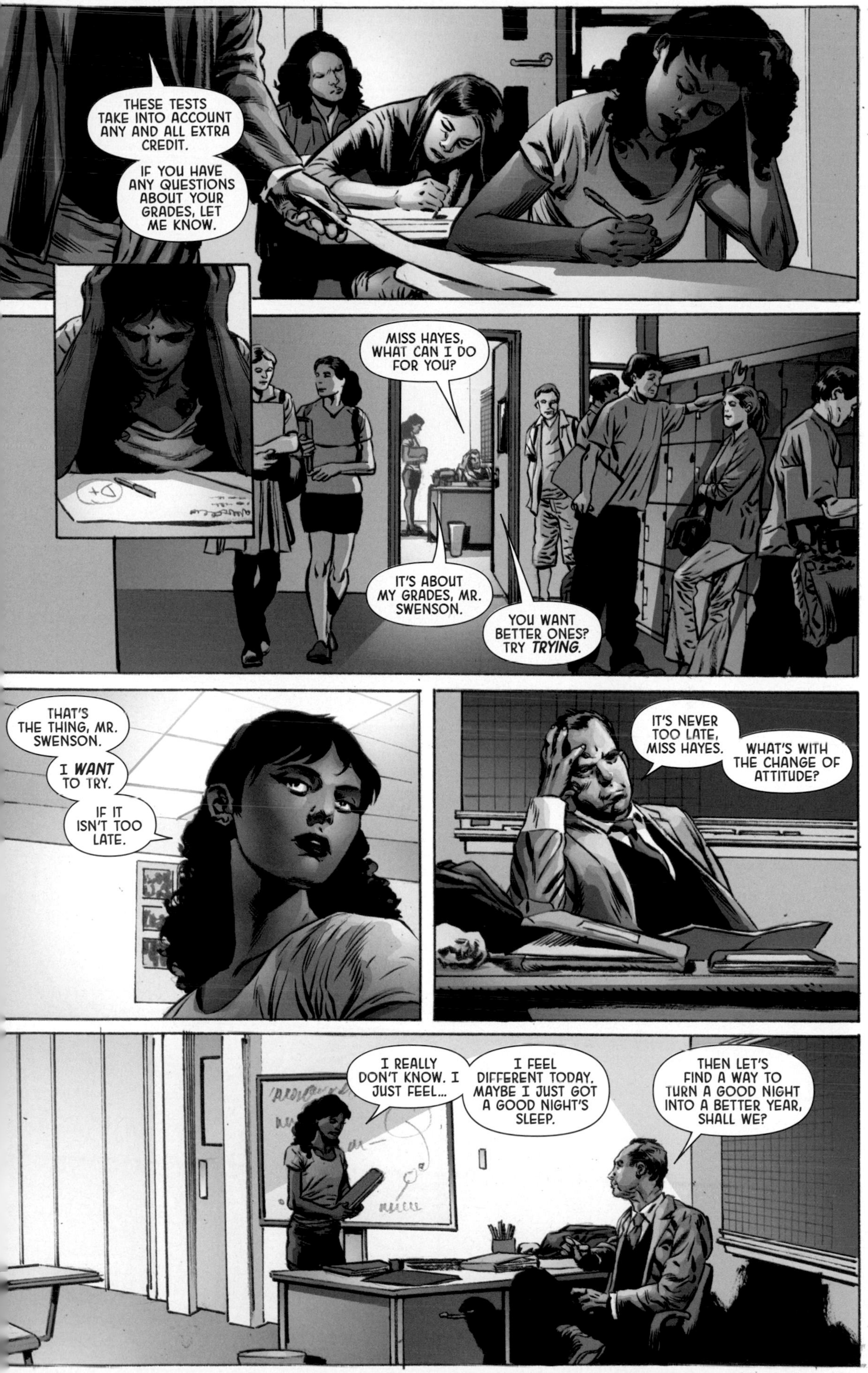
THESE TESTS TAKE INTO ACCOUNT ANY AND ALL EXTRA CREDIT.
IF YOU HAVE ANY QUESTIONS ABOUT YOUR GRADES, LET ME KNOW.
D+
MISS HAYES, WHAT CAN I DO FOR YOU?
IT'S ABOUT MY GRADES, MR. SWENSON.
YOU WANT BETTER ONES? TRY *TRYING*.
THAT'S THE THING, MR. SWENSON.
I *WANT* TO TRY.
IF IT ISN'T TOO LATE.
IT'S NEVER TOO LATE, MISS HAYES.
WHAT'S WITH THE CHANGE OF ATTITUDE?
I REALLY DON'T KNOW. I JUST FEEL...
I FEEL DIFFERENT TODAY. MAYBE I JUST GOT A GOOD NIGHT'S SLEEP.
THEN LET'S FIND A WAY TO TURN A GOOD NIGHT INTO A BETTER YEAR, SHALL WE?

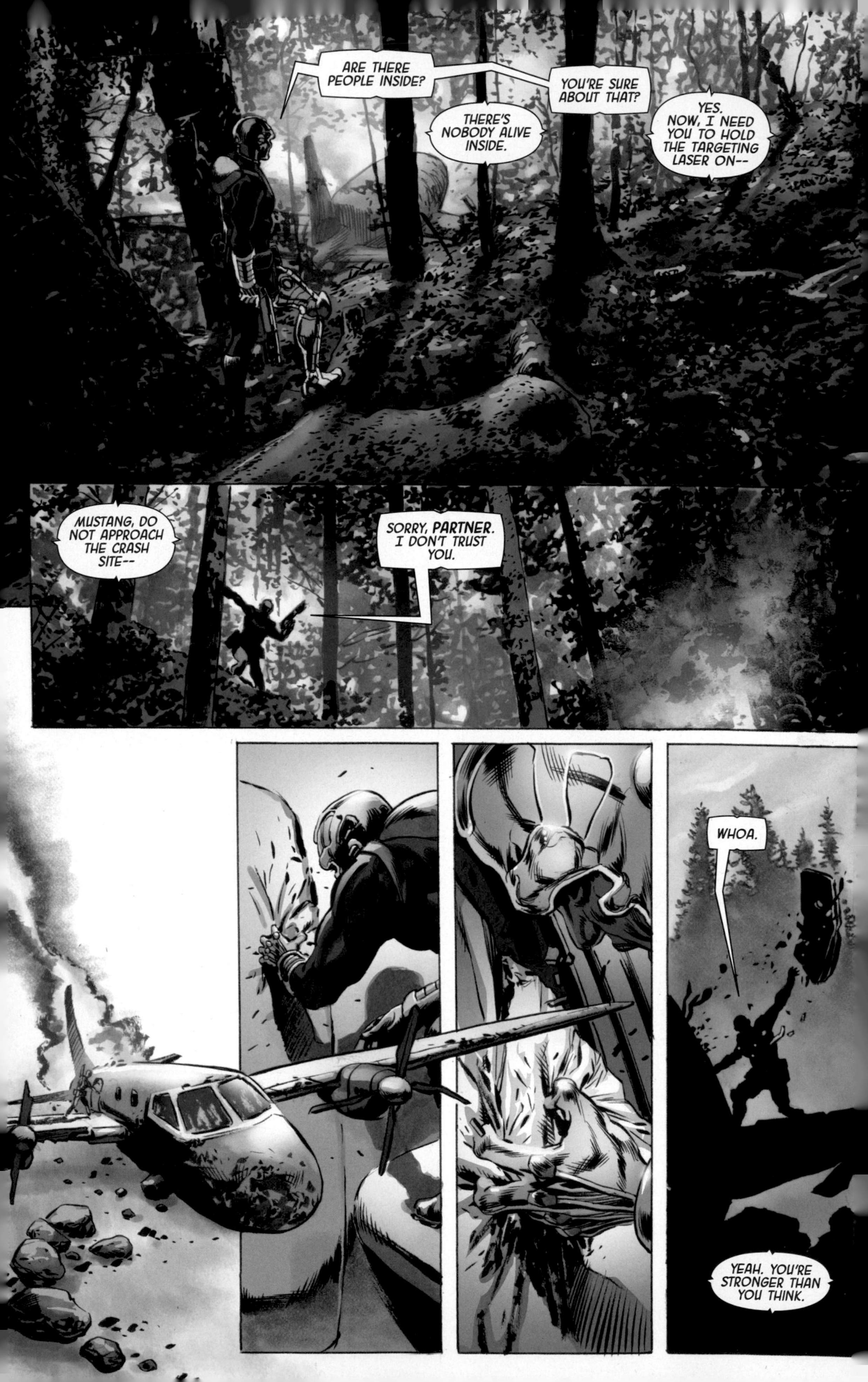
ARE THERE PEOPLE INSIDE?
THERE'S NOBODY ALIVE INSIDE.
YOU'RE SURE ABOUT THAT?
YES. NOW, I NEED YOU TO HOLD THE TARGETING LASER ON--
MUSTANG, DO NOT APPROACH THE CRASH SITE--
SORRY, PARTNER. I DON'T TRUST YOU.
WHOA.
YEAH. YOU'RE STRONGER THAN YOU THINK.

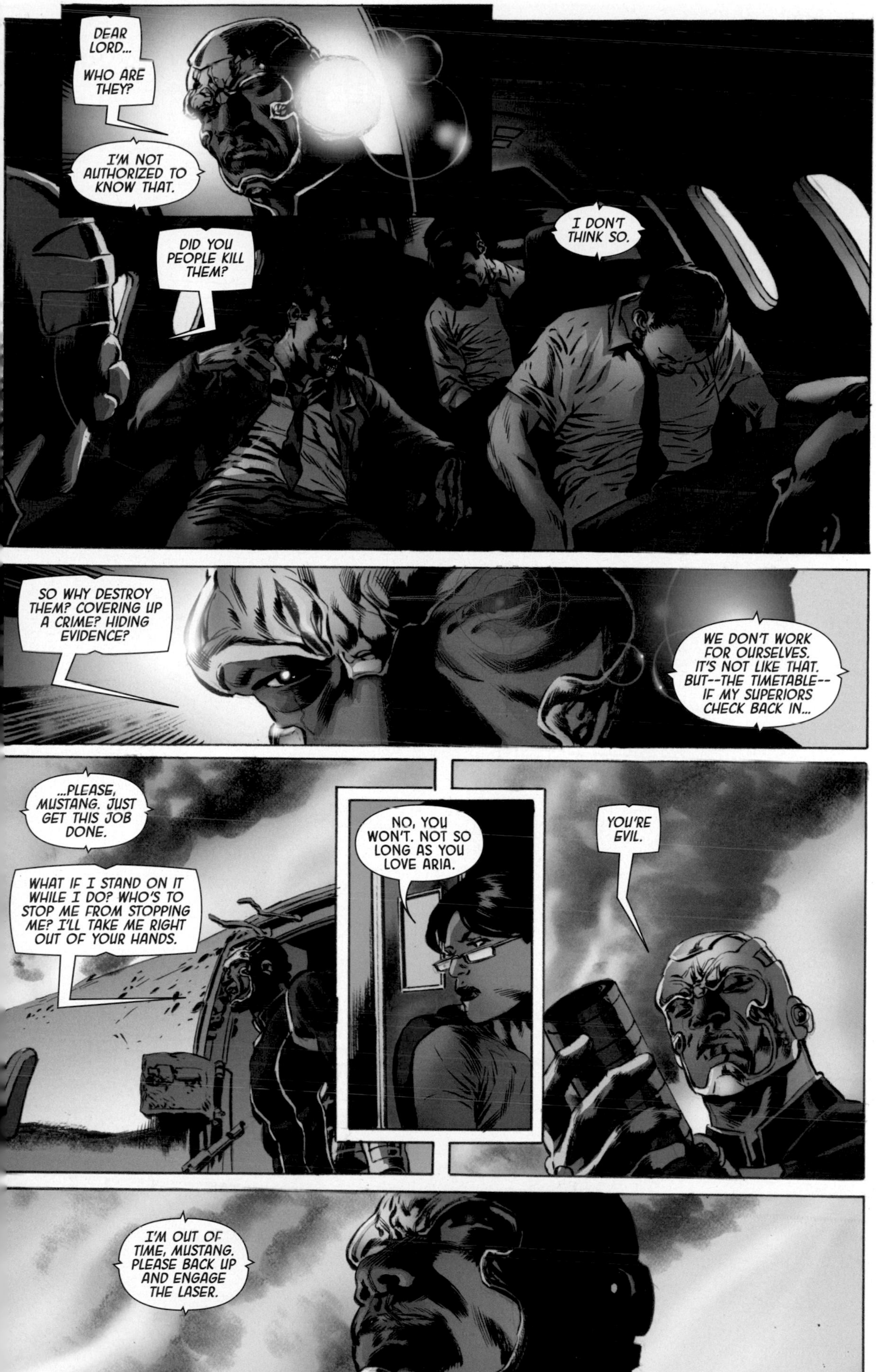
DEAR LORD...
WHO ARE THEY?
I'M NOT AUTHORIZED TO KNOW THAT.
DID YOU PEOPLE KILL THEM?
I DON'T THINK SO.
SO WHY DESTROY THEM? COVERING UP A CRIME? HIDING EVIDENCE?
WE DON'T WORK FOR OURSELVES. IT'S NOT LIKE THAT. BUT--THE TIMETABLE--IF MY SUPERIORS CHECK BACK IN...
...PLEASE, MUSTANG. JUST GET THIS JOB DONE.
WHAT IF I STAND ON IT WHILE I DO? WHO'S TO STOP ME FROM STOPPING ME? I'LL TAKE ME RIGHT OUT OF YOUR HANDS.
NO, YOU WON'T. NOT SO LONG AS YOU LOVE ARIA.
YOU'RE EVIL.
I'M OUT OF TIME, MUSTANG. PLEASE BACK UP AND ENGAGE THE LASER.

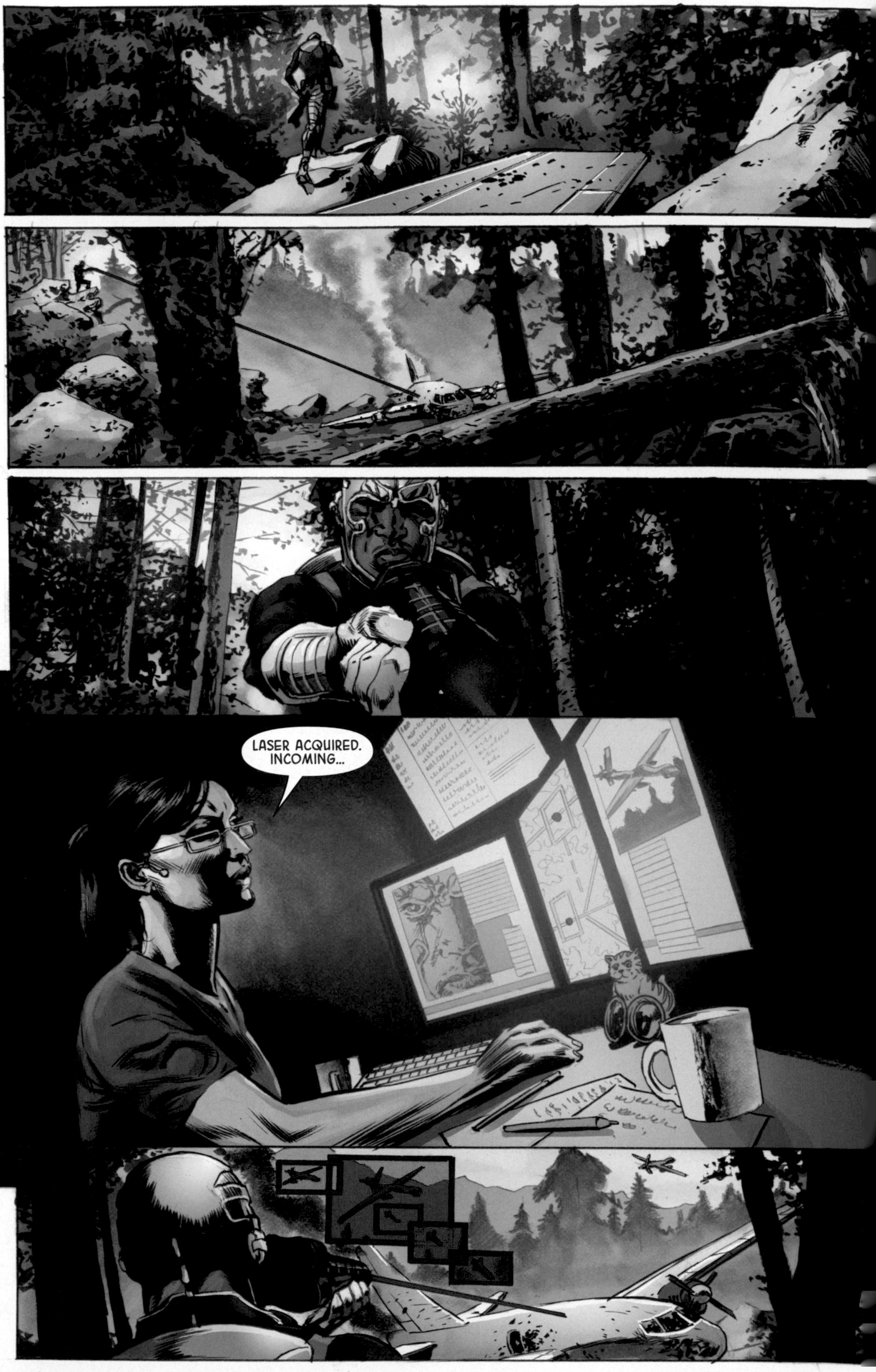
LASER ACQUIRED. INCOMING...

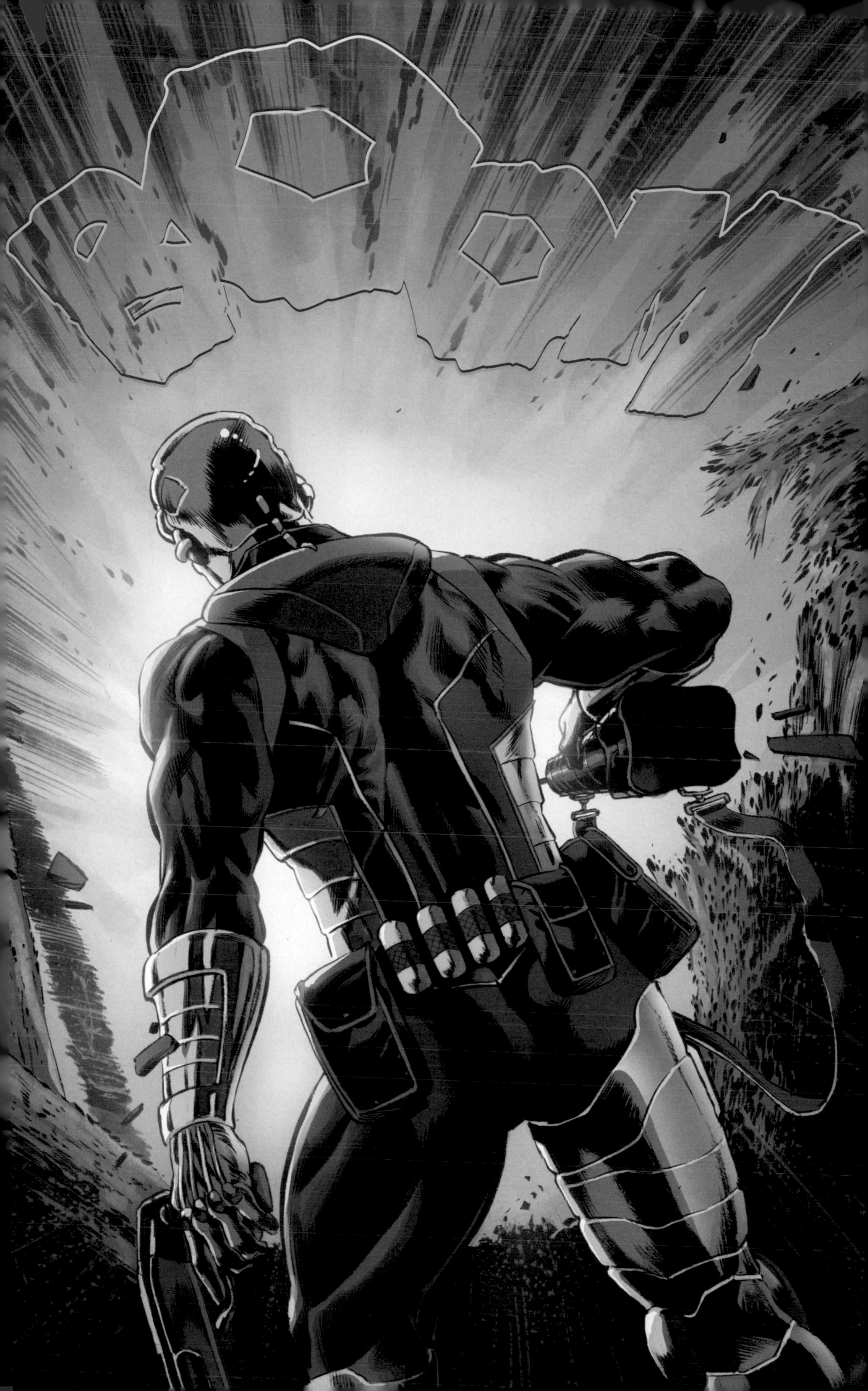
BADOOM

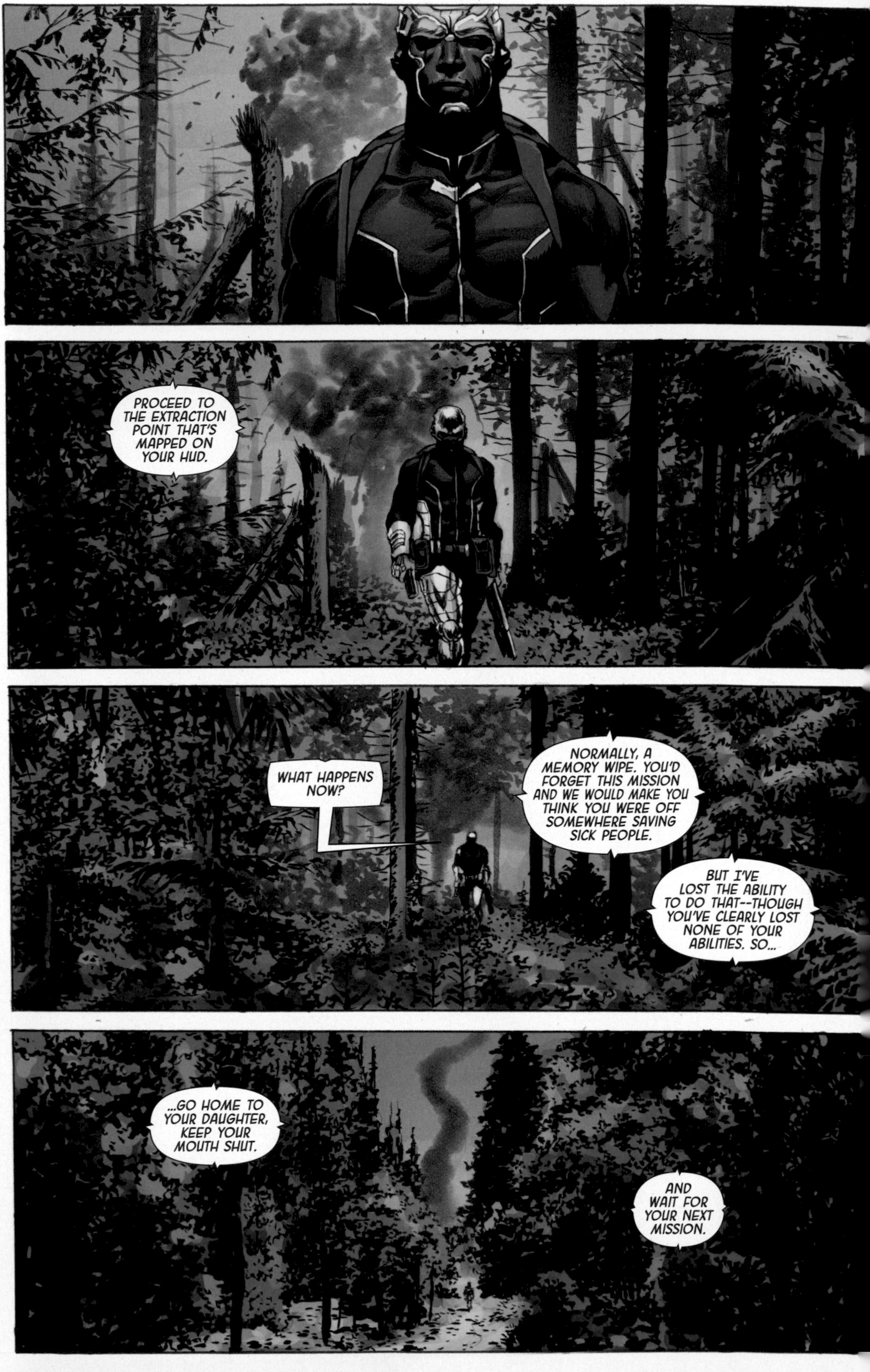
PROCEED TO THE EXTRACTION POINT THAT'S MAPPED ON YOUR HUD.
WHAT HAPPENS NOW?
NORMALLY, A MEMORY WIPE. YOU'D FORGET THIS MISSION AND WE WOULD MAKE YOU THINK YOU WERE OFF SOMEWHERE SAVING SICK PEOPLE.
BUT I'VE LOST THE ABILITY TO DO THAT--THOUGH YOU'VE CLEARLY LOST NONE OF YOUR ABILITIES. SO...
...GO HOME TO YOUR DAUGHTER, KEEP YOUR MOUTH SHUT.
AND WAIT FOR YOUR NEXT MISSION.

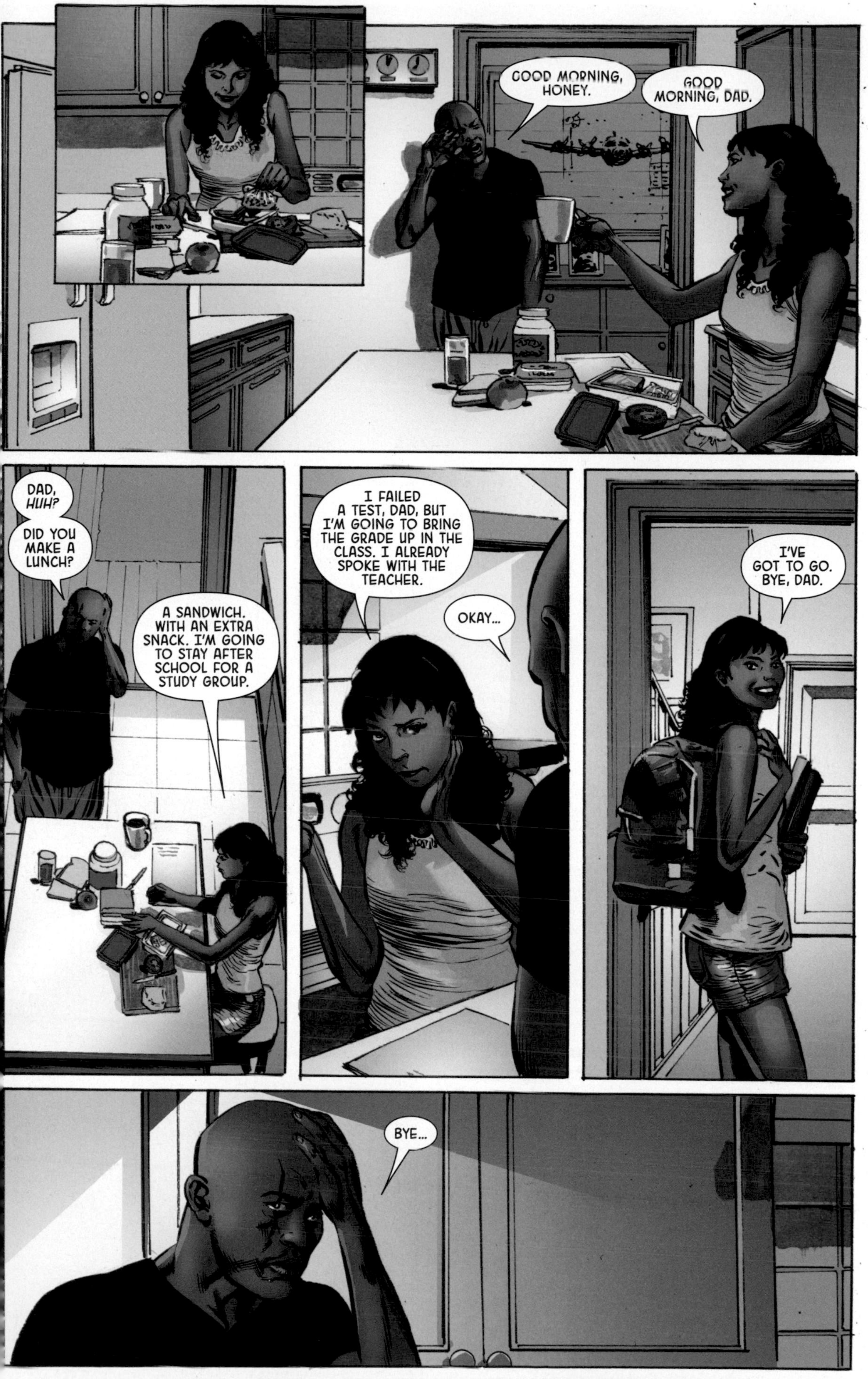
GOOD MORNING, HONEY.
GOOD MORNING, DAD.
DAD, HUH?
DID YOU MAKE A LUNCH?
A SANDWICH. WITH AN EXTRA SNACK. I'M GOING TO STAY AFTER SCHOOL FOR A STUDY GROUP.
I FAILED A TEST, DAD, BUT I'M GOING TO BRING THE GRADE UP IN THE CLASS. I ALREADY SPOKE WITH THE TEACHER.
OKAY...
I'VE GOT TO GO. BYE, DAD.
BYE...

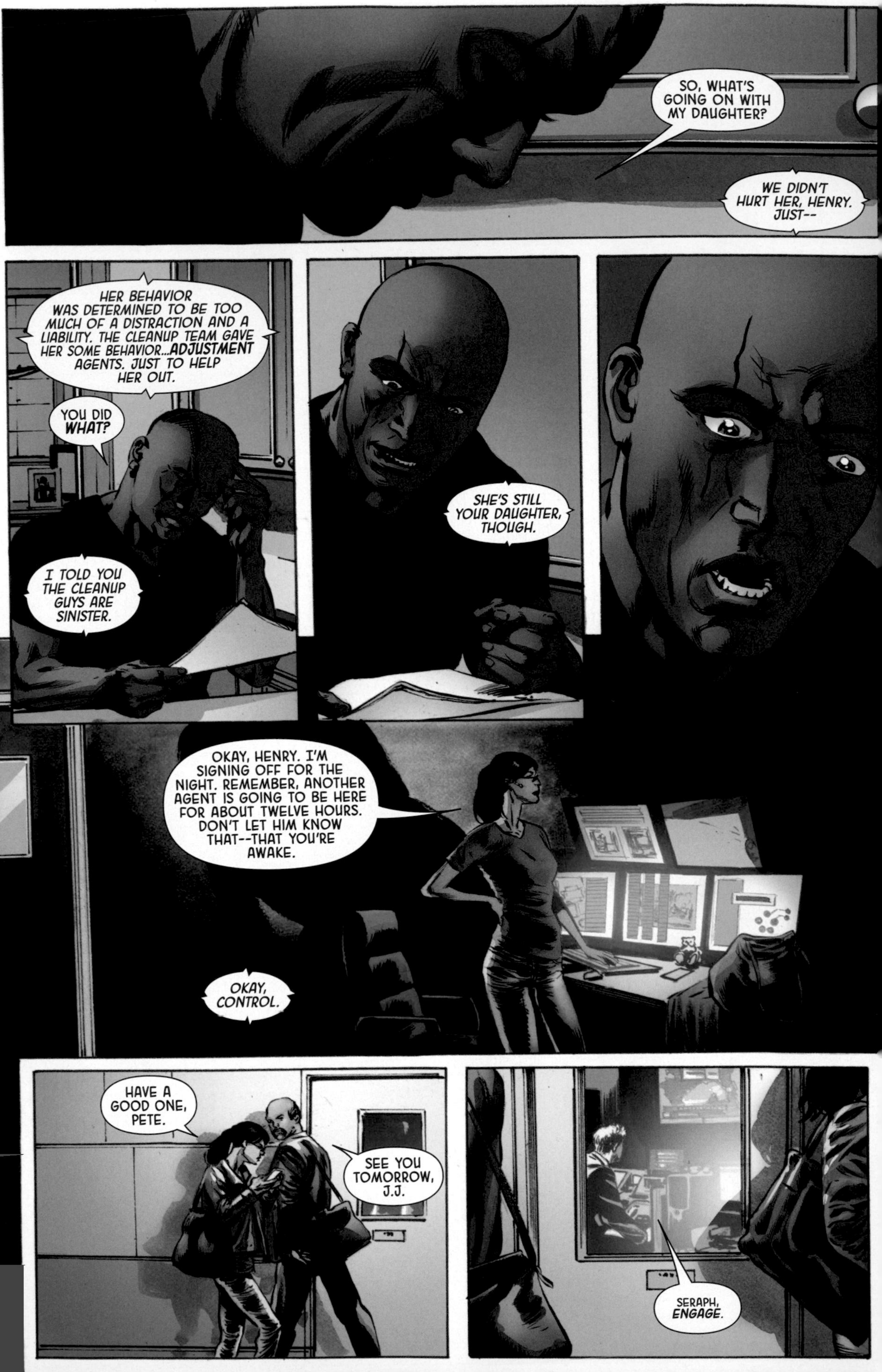
SO, WHAT'S GOING ON WITH MY DAUGHTER?
WE DIDN'T HURT HER, HENRY. JUST--
HER BEHAVIOR WAS DETERMINED TO BE TOO MUCH OF A DISTRACTION AND A LIABILITY. THE CLEANUP TEAM GAVE HER SOME BEHAVIOR...ADJUSTMENT AGENTS. JUST TO HELP HER OUT.
YOU DID WHAT?
I TOLD YOU THE CLEANUP GUYS ARE SINISTER.
SHE'S STILL YOUR DAUGHTER, THOUGH.
OKAY, HENRY. I'M SIGNING OFF FOR THE NIGHT. REMEMBER, ANOTHER AGENT IS GOING TO BE HERE FOR ABOUT TWELVE HOURS. DON'T LET HIM KNOW THAT--THAT YOU'RE AWAKE.
OKAY, CONTROL.
HAVE A GOOD ONE, PETE.
SEE YOU TOMORROW, J.J.
SERAPH, ENGAGE.

SERAPH
ENGAGING NOW.

SCANNING FOR
SURVIVORS.

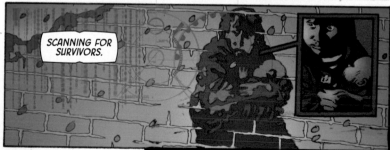

→CRUNCH←
COPY THAT, SERAPH.
ALL LOOKS →CRACK←
POSITIVE ON THIS END
WITH FLYOVER...

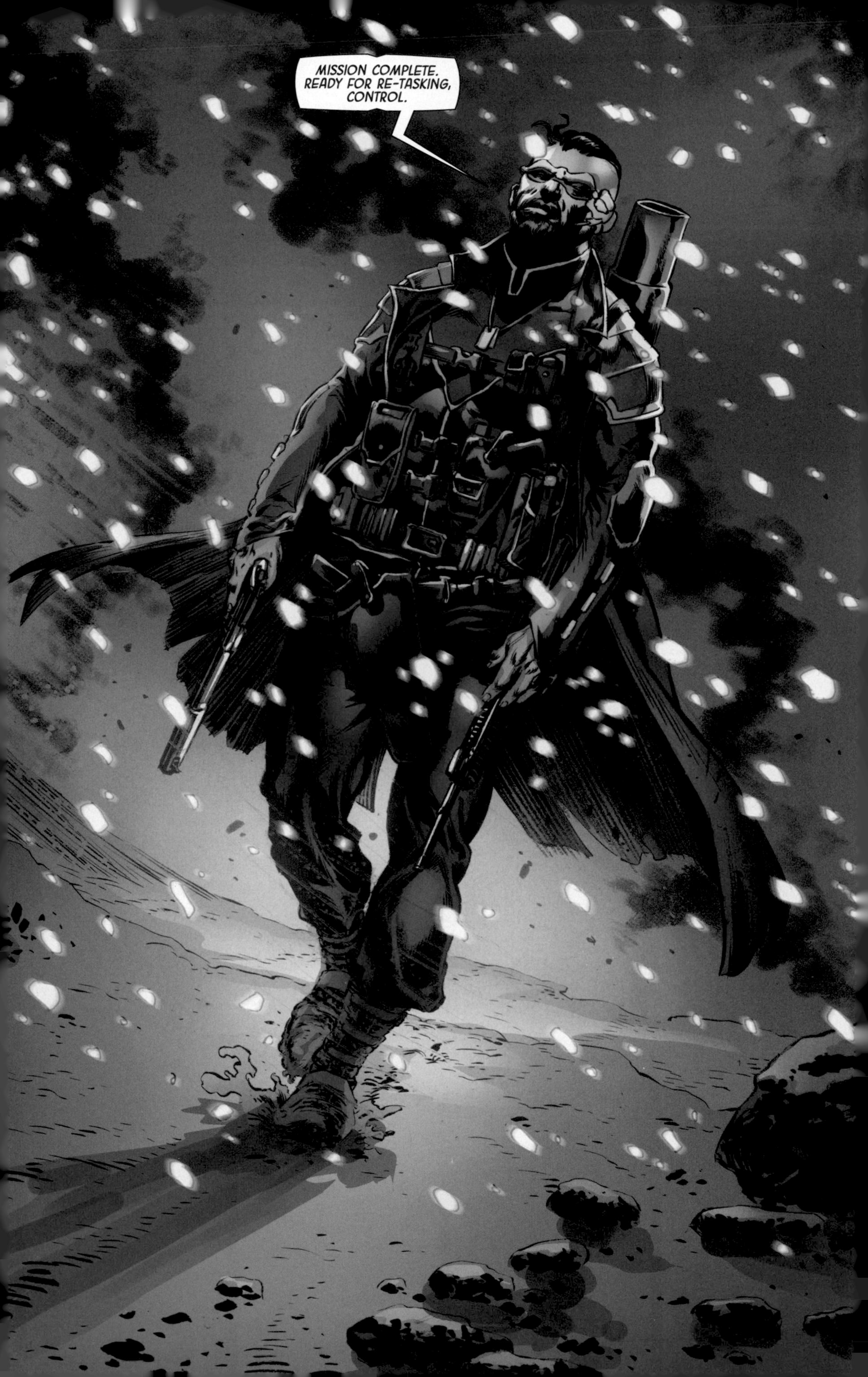
MISSION COMPLETE. READY FOR RE-TASKING, CONTROL.

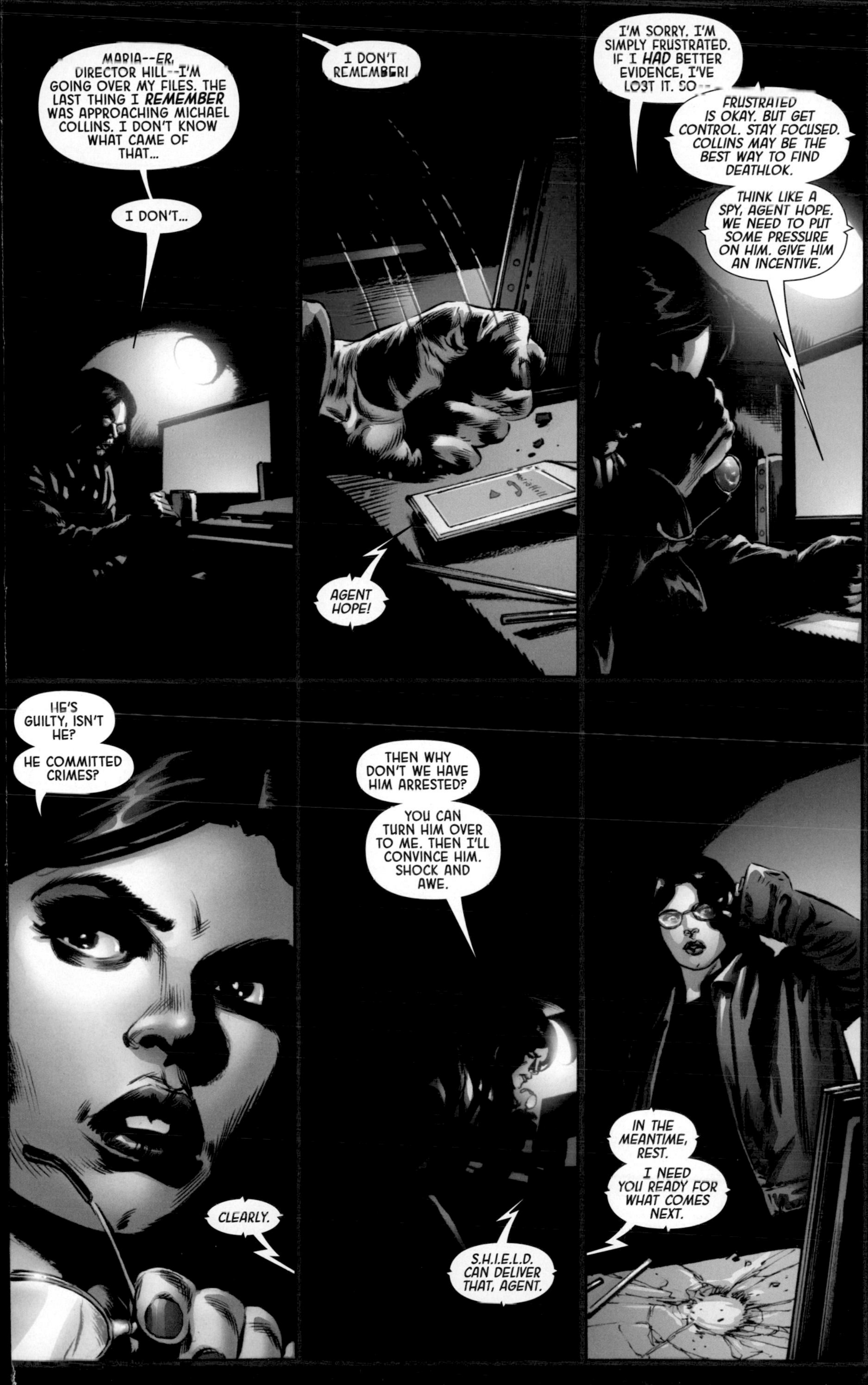
MARIA--ER, DIRECTOR HILL--I'M GOING OVER MY FILES. THE LAST THING I REMEMBER WAS APPROACHING MICHAEL COLLINS. I DON'T KNOW WHAT CAME OF THAT...
I DON'T...
I DON'T REMEMBER!
AGENT HOPE!
I'M SORRY. I'M SIMPLY FRUSTRATED. IF I HAD BETTER EVIDENCE, I'VE LOST IT. SO--
FRUSTRATED IS OKAY. BUT GET CONTROL. STAY FOCUSED. COLLINS MAY BE THE BEST WAY TO FIND DEATHLOK.
THINK LIKE A SPY, AGENT HOPE. WE NEED TO PUT SOME PRESSURE ON HIM. GIVE HIM AN INCENTIVE.
HE'S GUILTY, ISN'T HE?
HE COMMITTED CRIMES?
CLEARLY.
THEN WHY DON'T WE HAVE HIM ARRESTED?
YOU CAN TURN HIM OVER TO ME. THEN I'LL CONVINCE HIM. SHOCK AND AWE.
S.H.I.E.L.D. CAN DELIVER THAT, AGENT.
IN THE MEANTIME, REST.
I NEED YOU READY FOR WHAT COMES NEXT.

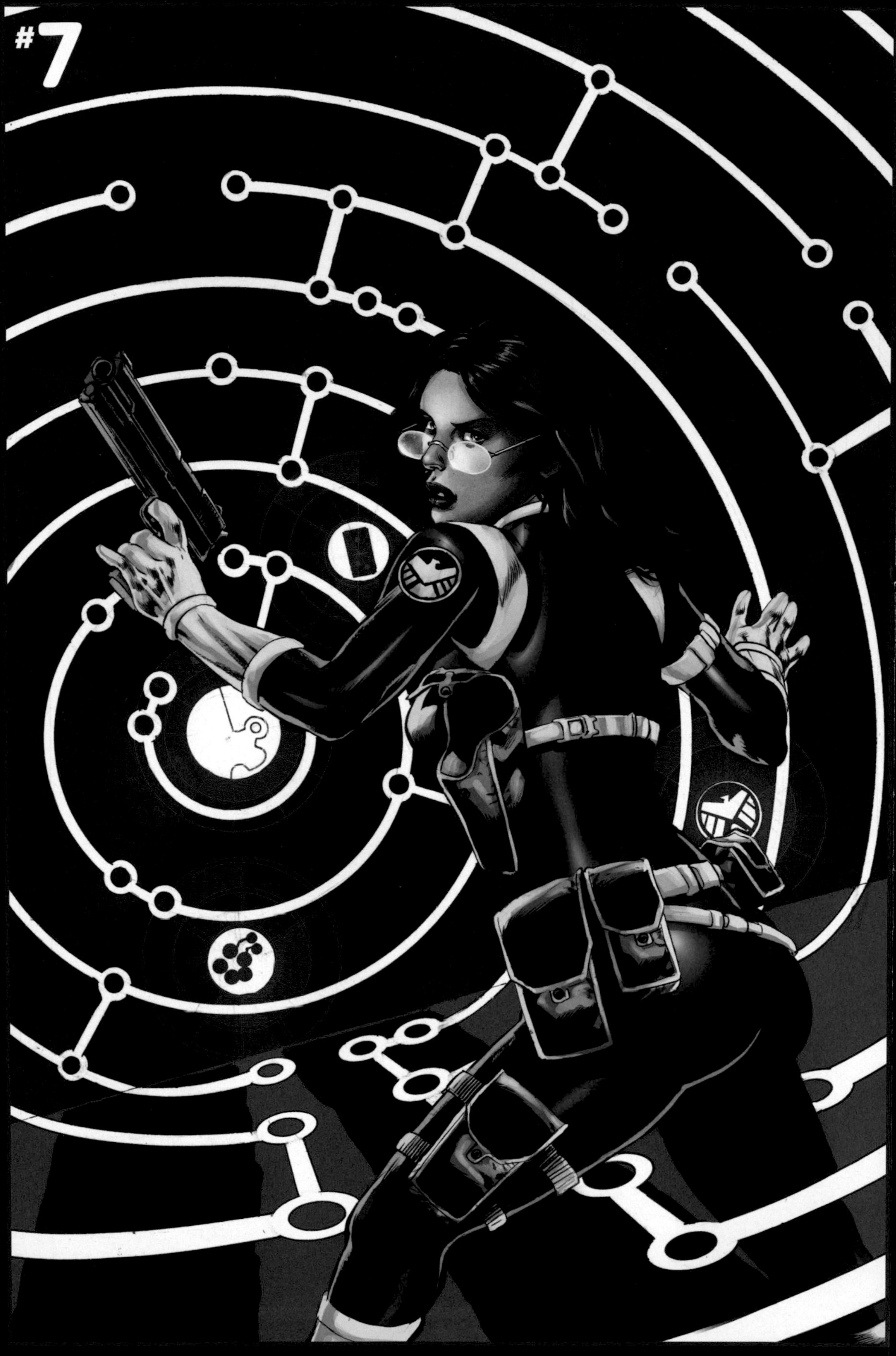
#7

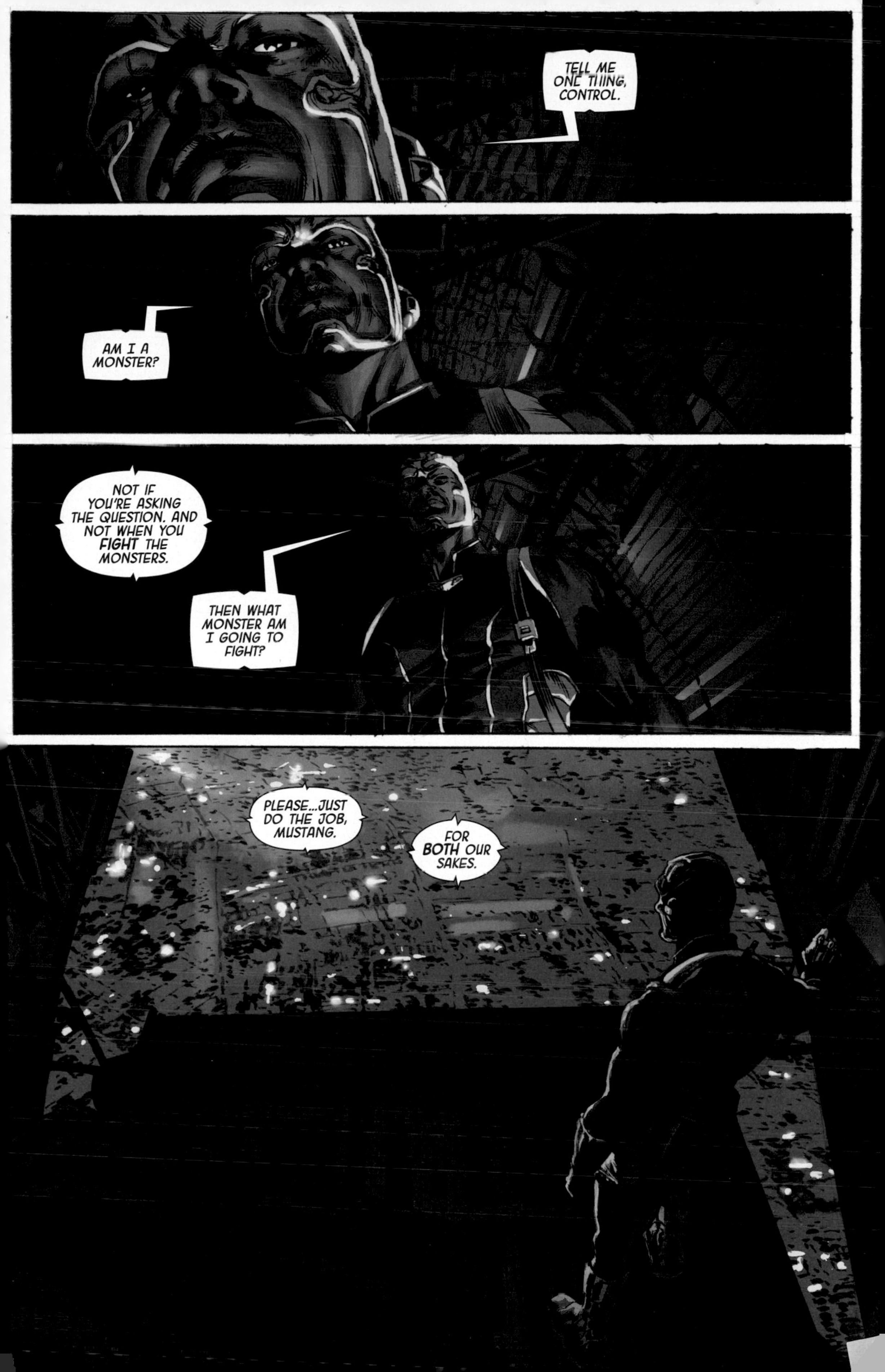
TELL ME ONE THING, CONTROL.
AM I A MONSTER?
NOT IF YOU'RE ASKING THE QUESTION. AND NOT WHEN YOU FIGHT THE MONSTERS.
THEN WHAT MONSTER AM I GOING TO FIGHT?
PLEASE...JUST DO THE JOB, MUSTANG.
FOR BOTH OUR SAKES.

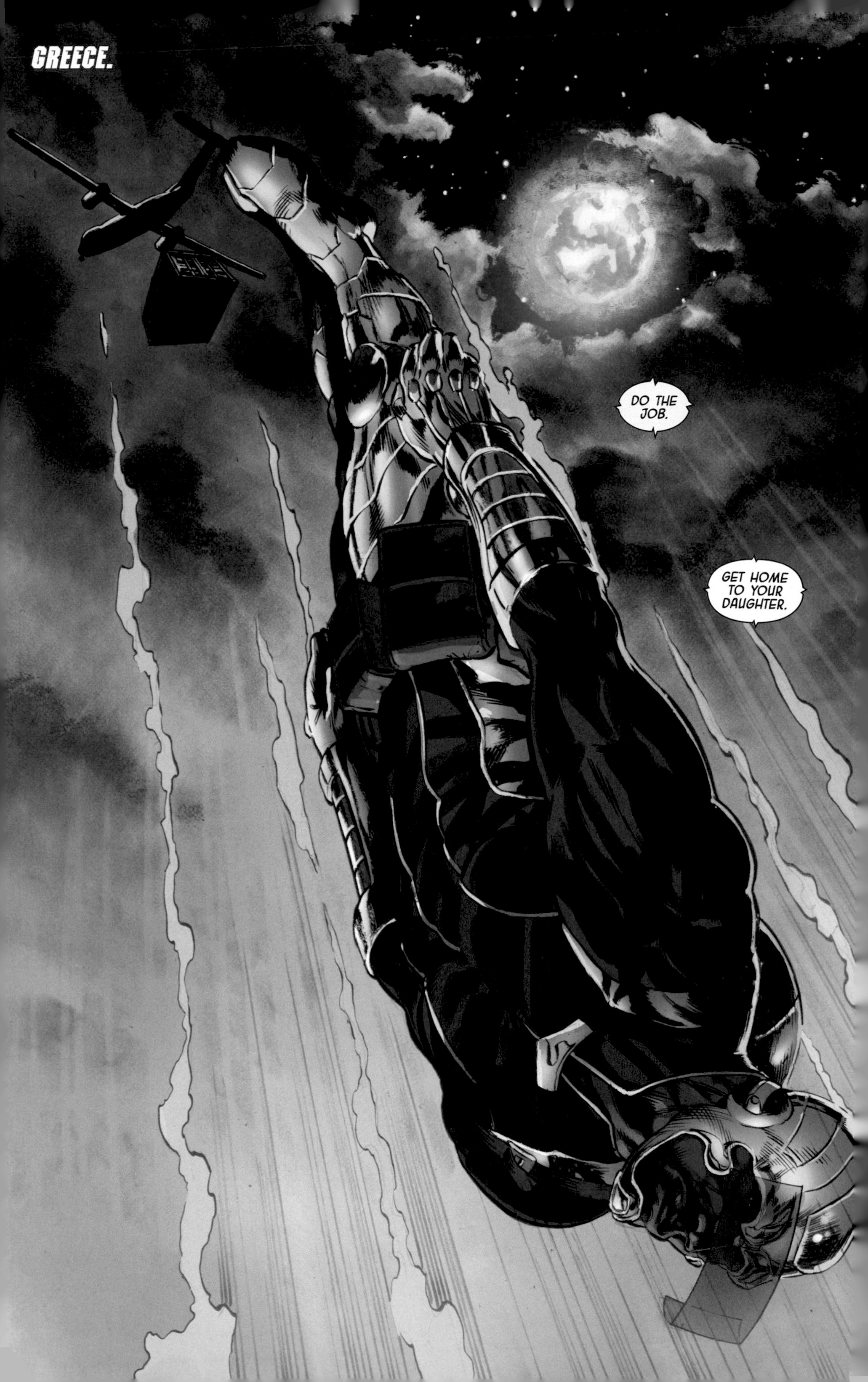
GREECE.
DO THE JOB.
GET HOME TO YOUR DAUGHTER.

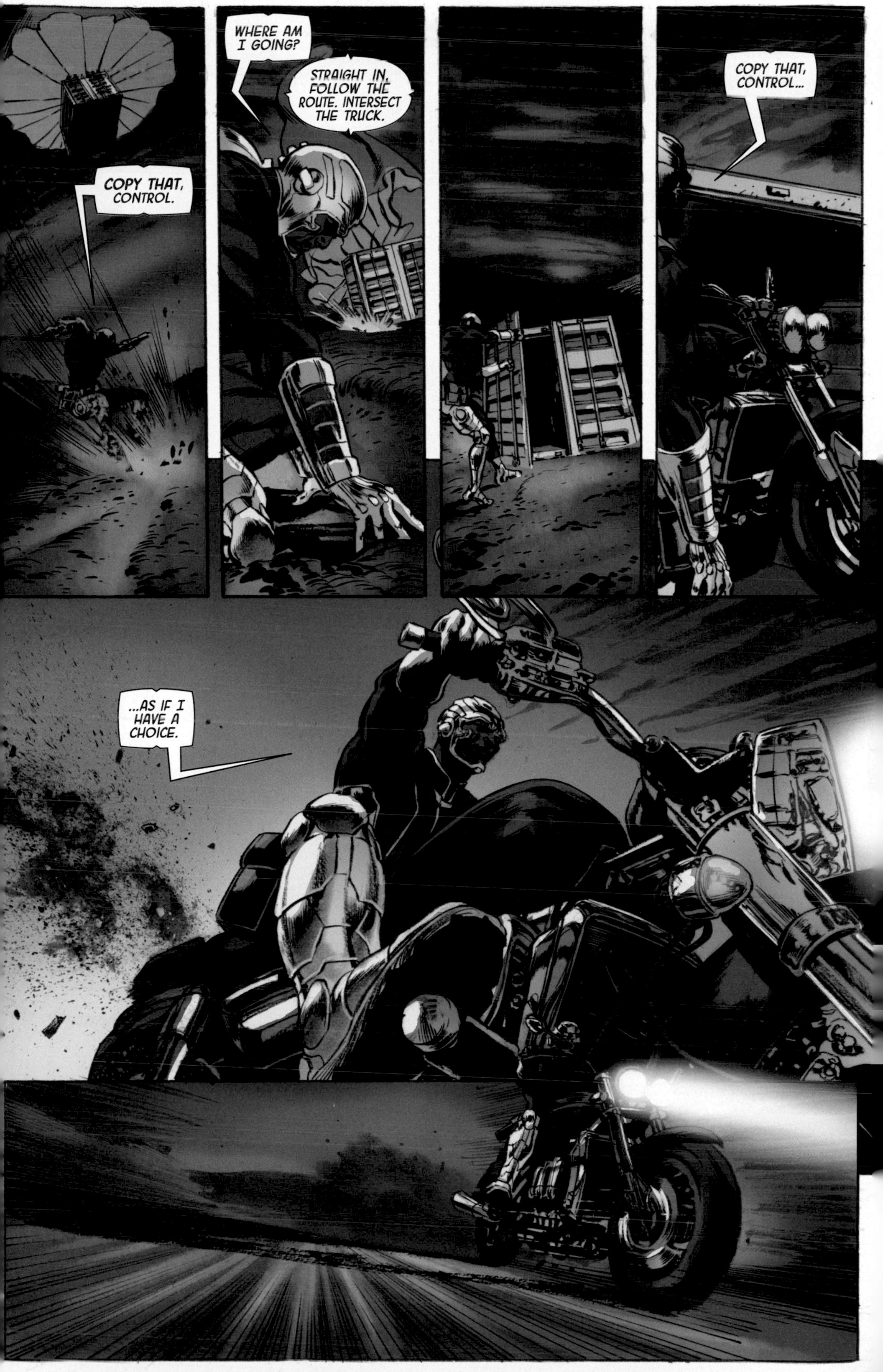
COPY THAT, CONTROL.
WHERE AM I GOING?
STRAIGHT IN. FOLLOW THE ROUTE. INTERSECT THE TRUCK.
COPY THAT, CONTROL...
...AS IF I HAVE A CHOICE.

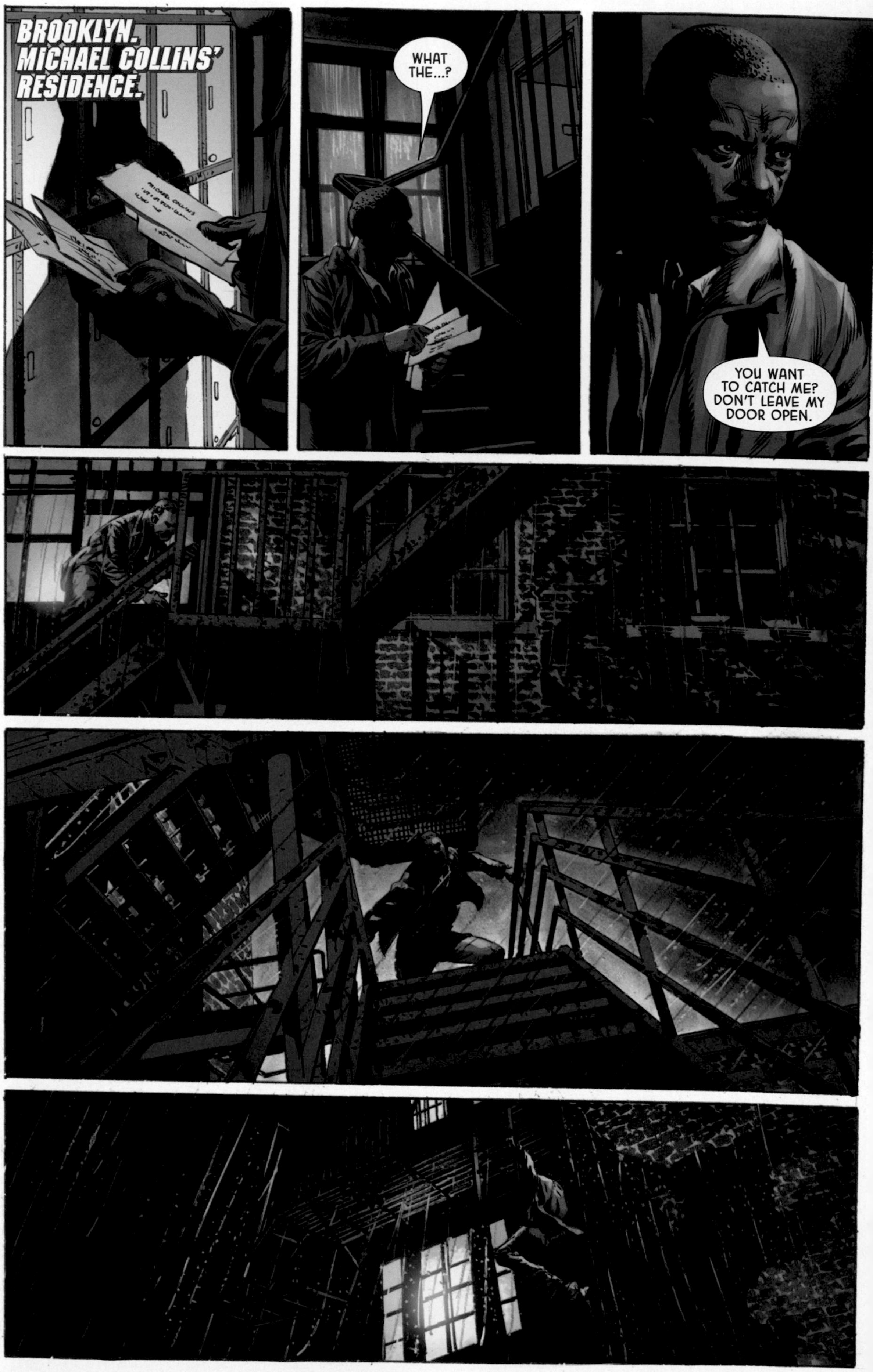
BROOKLYN. MICHAEL COLLINS' RESIDENCE.
WHAT THE...?
YOU WANT TO CATCH ME? DON'T LEAVE MY DOOR OPEN.

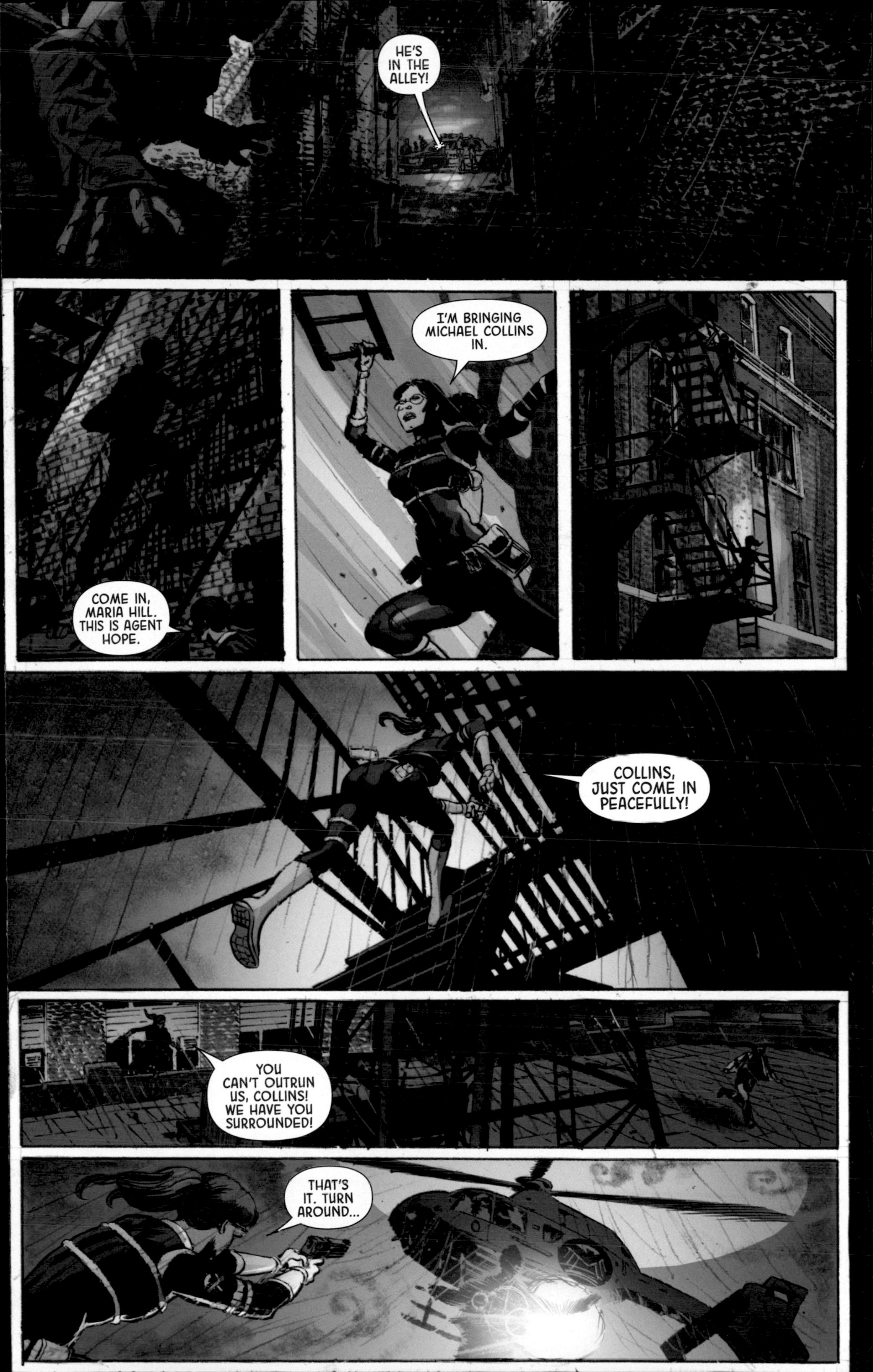
HE'S IN THE ALLEY!
COME IN, MARIA HILL. THIS IS AGENT HOPE.
I'M BRINGING MICHAEL COLLINS IN.
COLLINS, JUST COME IN PEACEFULLY!
YOU CAN'T OUTRUN US, COLLINS! WE HAVE YOU SURROUNDED!
THAT'S IT. TURN AROUND...

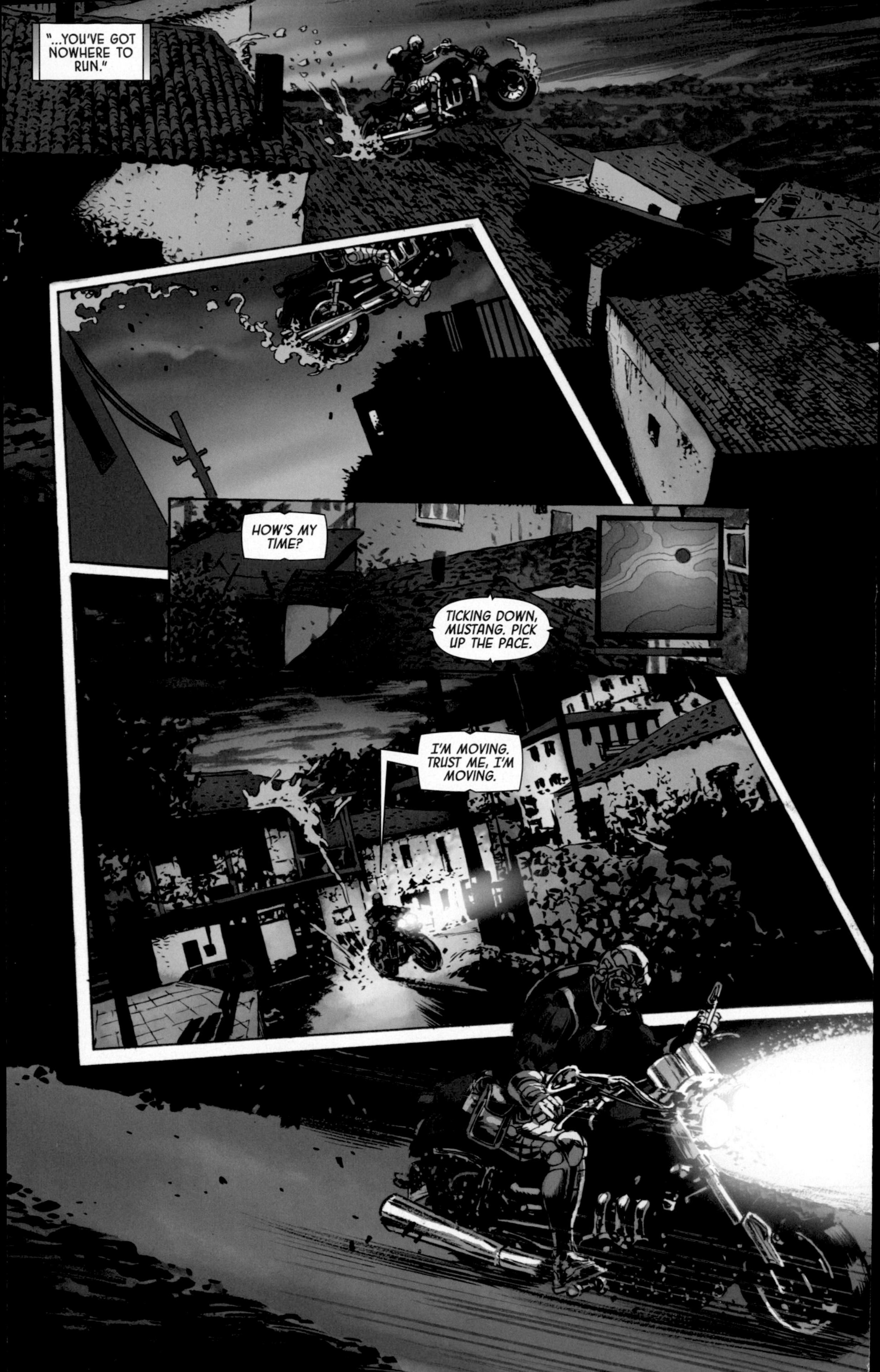
"...YOU'VE GOT NOWHERE TO RUN."
HOW'S MY TIME?
TICKING DOWN, MUSTANG. PICK UP THE PACE.
I'M MOVING. TRUST ME, I'M MOVING.

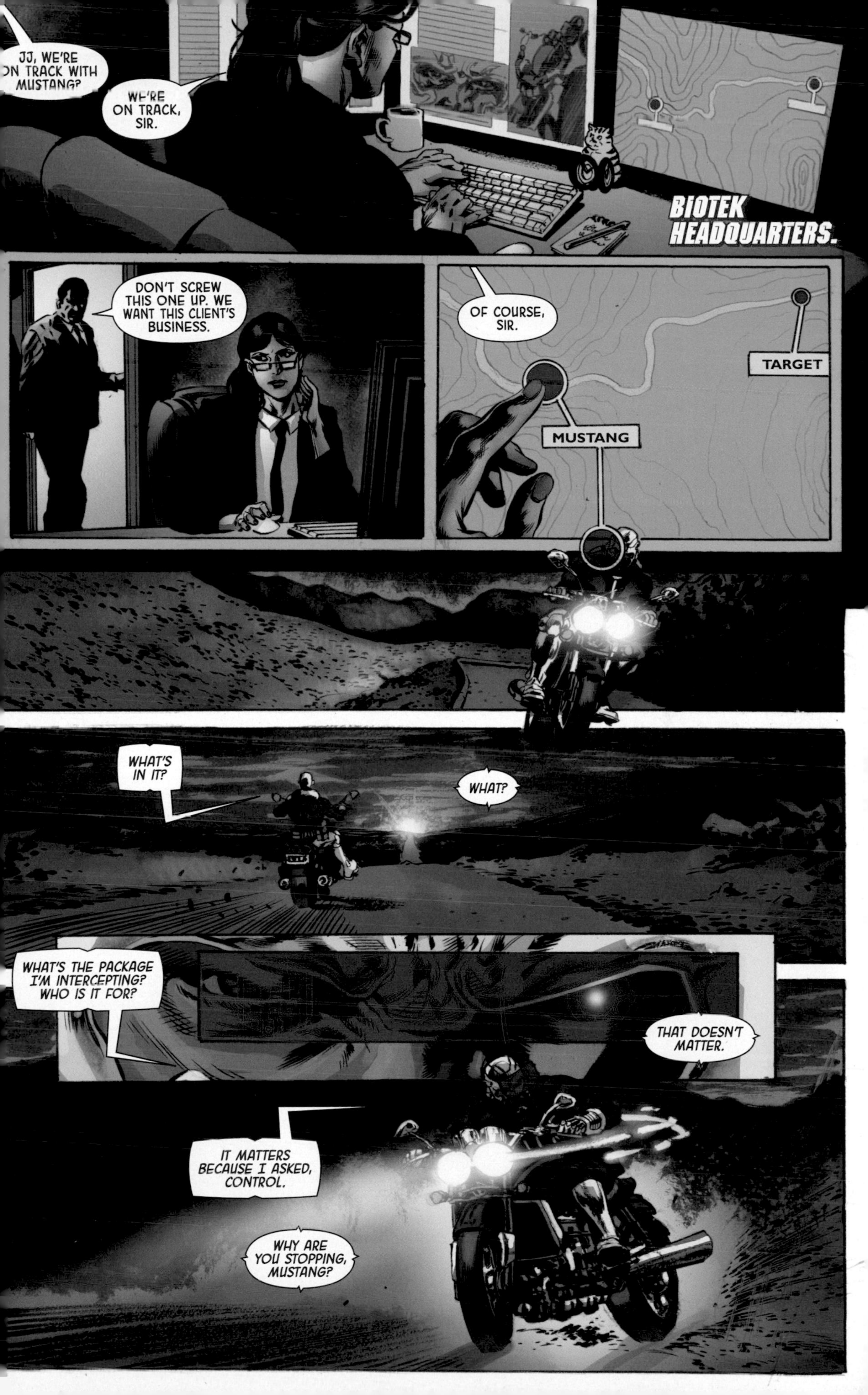
JJ, WE'RE ON TRACK WITH MUSTANG?
WE'RE ON TRACK, SIR.
BIOTEK HEADQUARTERS.
DON'T SCREW THIS ONE UP. WE WANT THIS CLIENT'S BUSINESS.
OF COURSE, SIR.
TARGET
MUSTANG
WHAT'S IN IT?
WHAT?
WHAT'S THE PACKAGE I'M INTERCEPTING? WHO IS IT FOR?
THAT DOESN'T MATTER.
IT MATTERS BECAUSE I ASKED, CONTROL.
WHY ARE YOU STOPPING, MUSTANG?

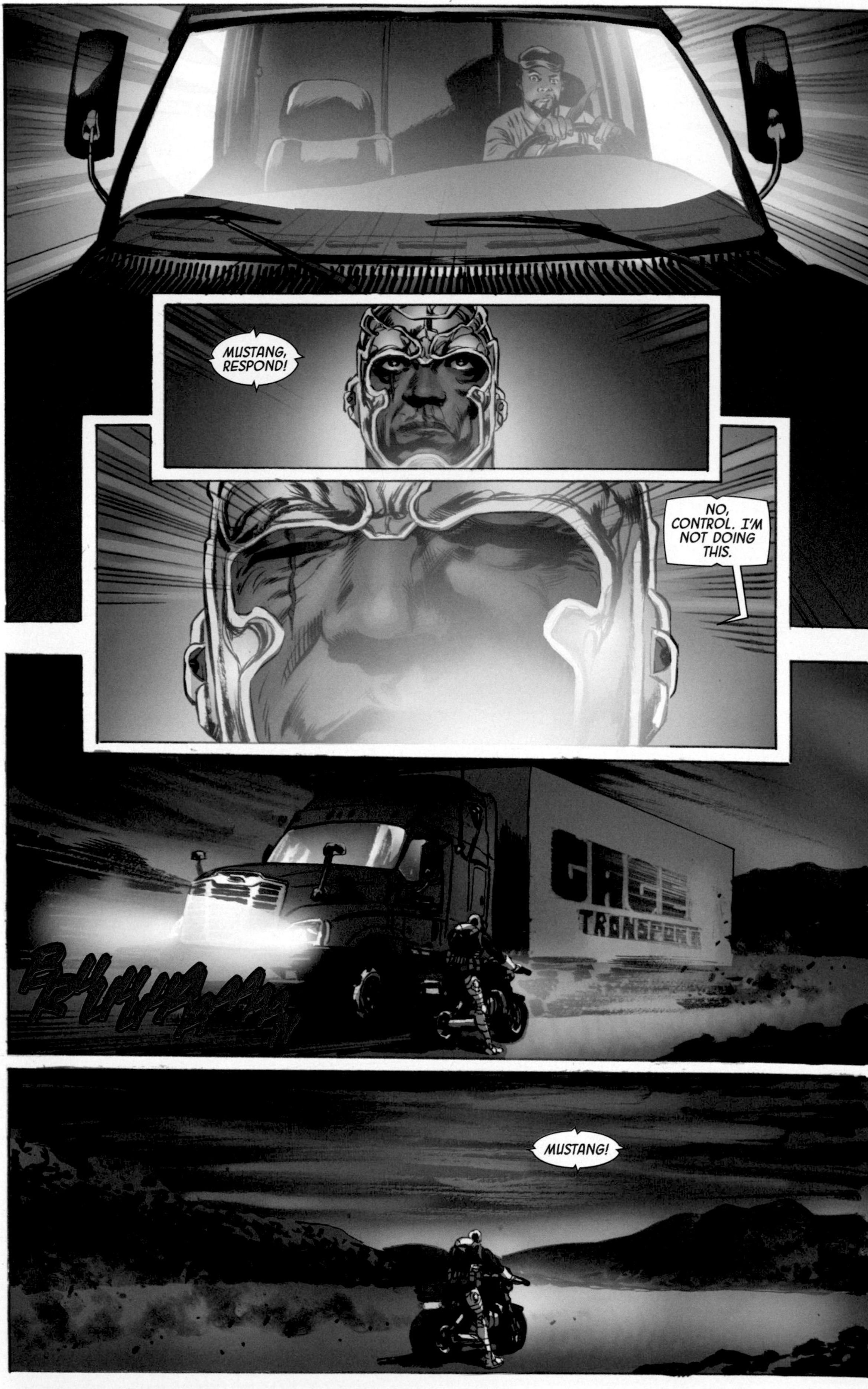
MUSTANG, RESPOND!
NO, CONTROL. I'M NOT DOING THIS.
MUSTANG!

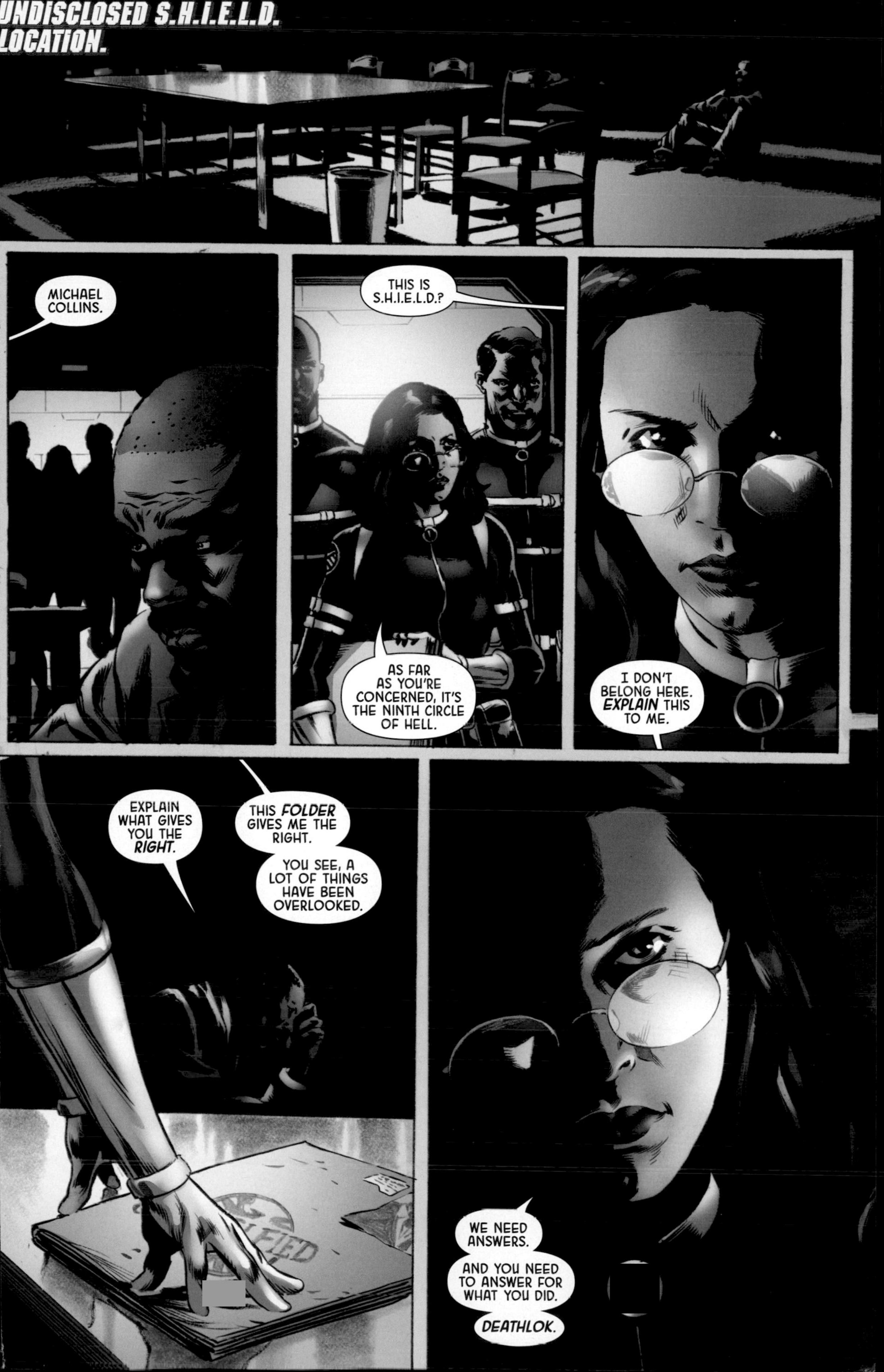
UNDISCLOSED S.H.I.E.L.D. LOCATION.
MICHAEL COLLINS.
THIS IS S.H.I.E.L.D.?
AS FAR AS YOU'RE CONCERNED, IT'S THE NINTH CIRCLE OF HELL.
I DON'T BELONG HERE. EXPLAIN THIS TO ME.
EXPLAIN WHAT GIVES YOU THE RIGHT.
THIS FOLDER GIVES ME THE RIGHT.
YOU SEE, A LOT OF THINGS HAVE BEEN OVERLOOKED.
WE NEED ANSWERS.
AND YOU NEED TO ANSWER FOR WHAT YOU DID.
DEATHLOK.

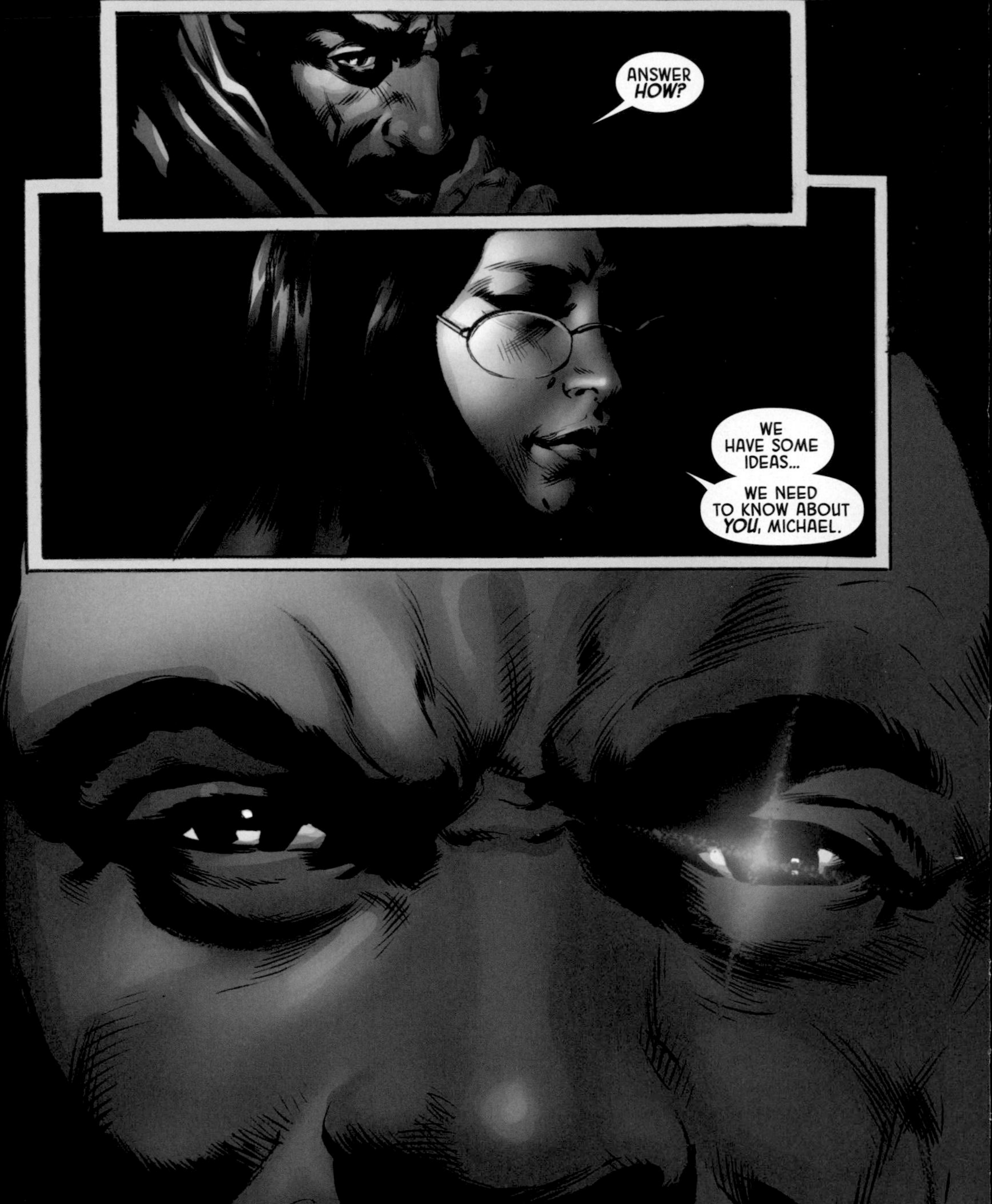
ANSWER HOW?
WE HAVE SOME IDEAS...
WE NEED TO KNOW ABOUT YOU, MICHAEL.

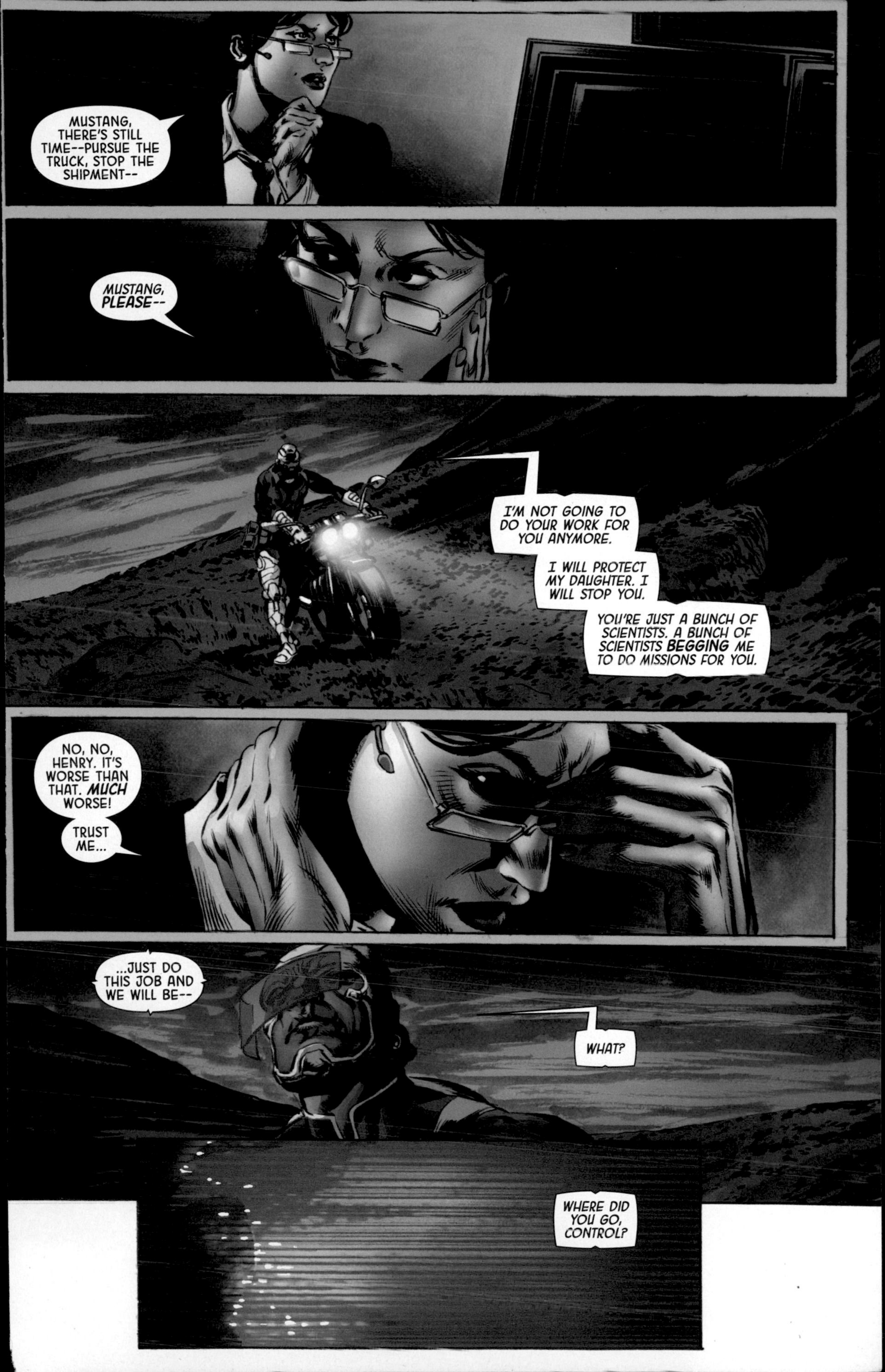
MUSTANG, THERE'S STILL TIME--PURSUE THE TRUCK, STOP THE SHIPMENT--
MUSTANG, PLEASE--
I'M NOT GOING TO DO YOUR WORK FOR YOU ANYMORE.
I WILL PROTECT MY DAUGHTER. I WILL STOP YOU.
YOU'RE JUST A BUNCH OF SCIENTISTS. A BUNCH OF SCIENTISTS BEGGING ME TO DO MISSIONS FOR YOU.
NO, NO, HENRY. IT'S WORSE THAN THAT. MUCH WORSE!
TRUST ME...
...JUST DO THIS JOB AND WE WILL BE--
WHAT?
WHERE DID YOU GO, CONTROL?

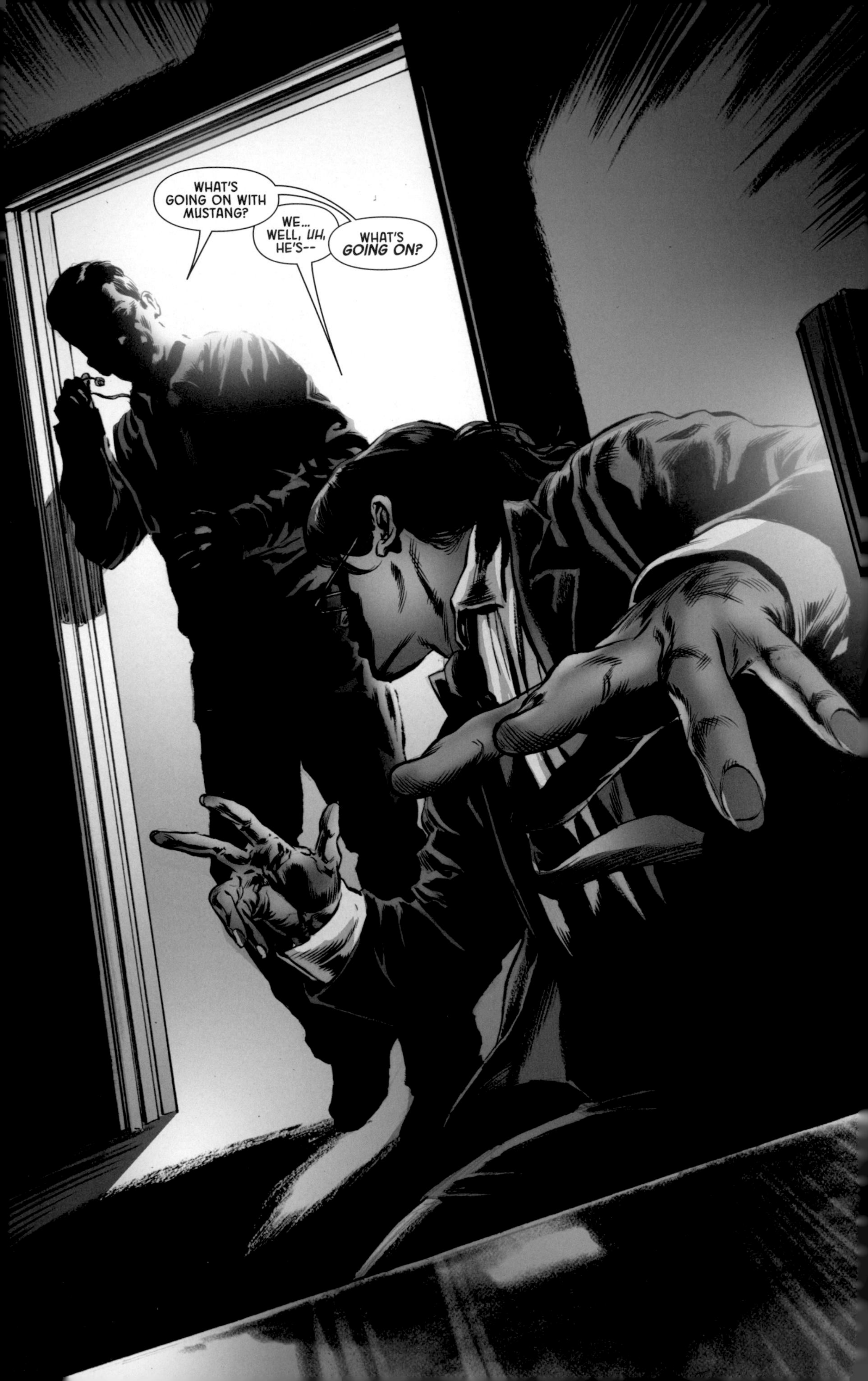
WHAT'S GOING ON WITH MUSTANG?
WE... WELL, UH, HE'S--
WHAT'S GOING ON?

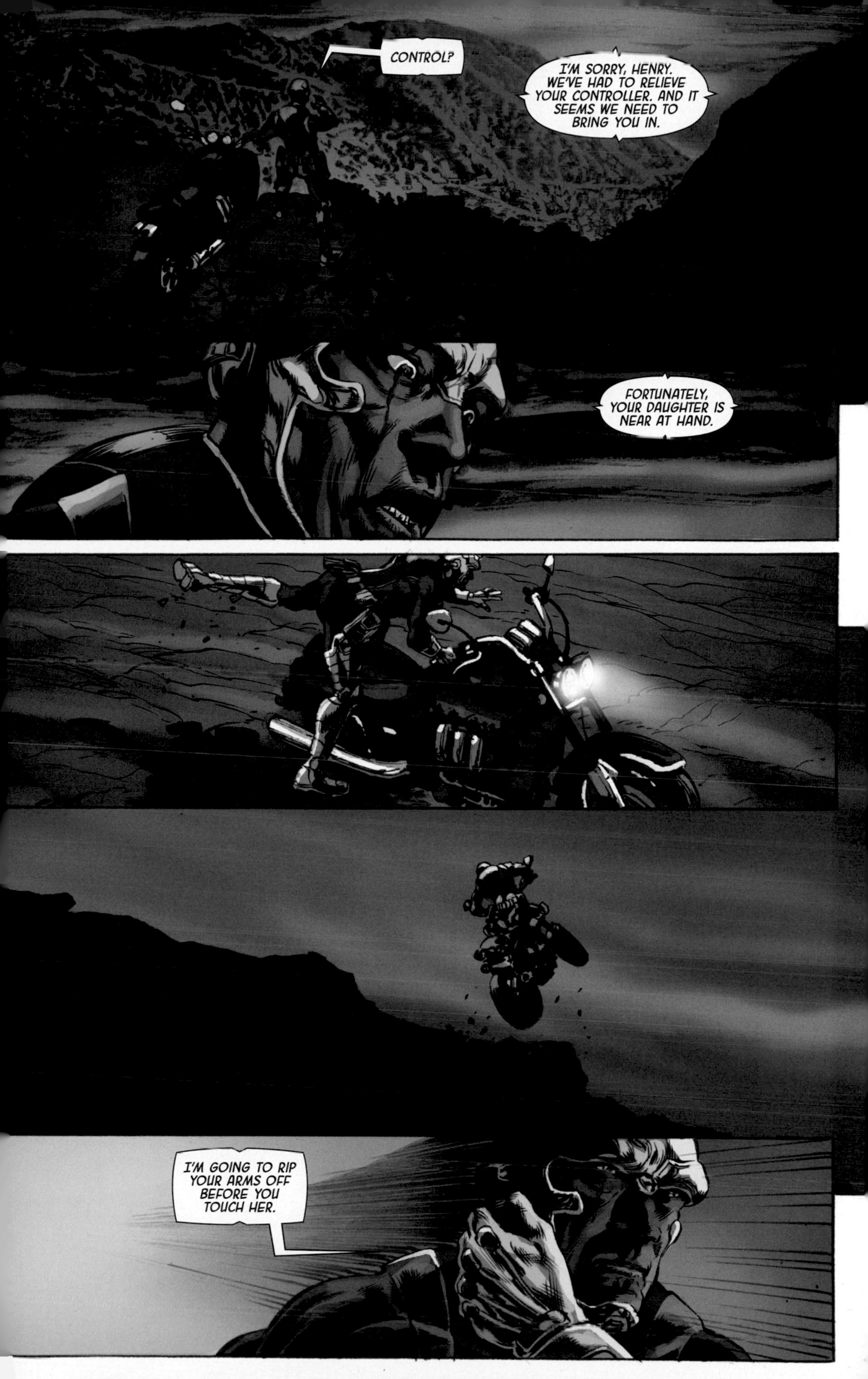
CONTROL?
I'M SORRY, HENRY. WE'VE HAD TO RELIEVE YOUR CONTROLLER. AND IT SEEMS WE NEED TO BRING YOU IN.
FORTUNATELY, YOUR DAUGHTER IS NEAR AT HAND.
I'M GOING TO RIP YOUR ARMS OFF BEFORE YOU TOUCH HER.

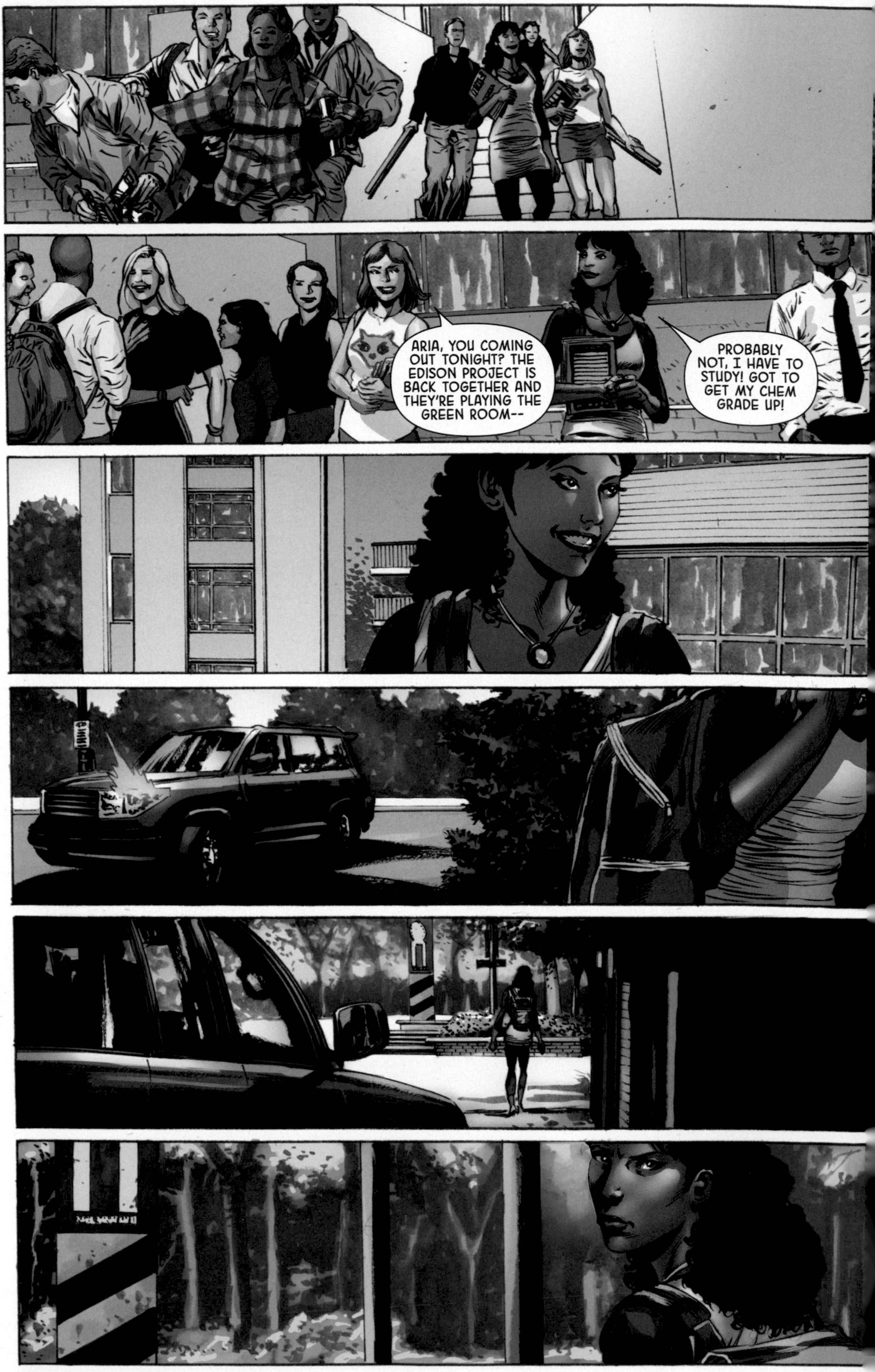
ARIA, YOU COMING OUT TONIGHT? THE EDISON PROJECT IS BACK TOGETHER AND THEY'RE PLAYING THE GREEN ROOM--
PROBABLY NOT, I HAVE TO STUDY! GOT TO GET MY CHEM GRADE UP!

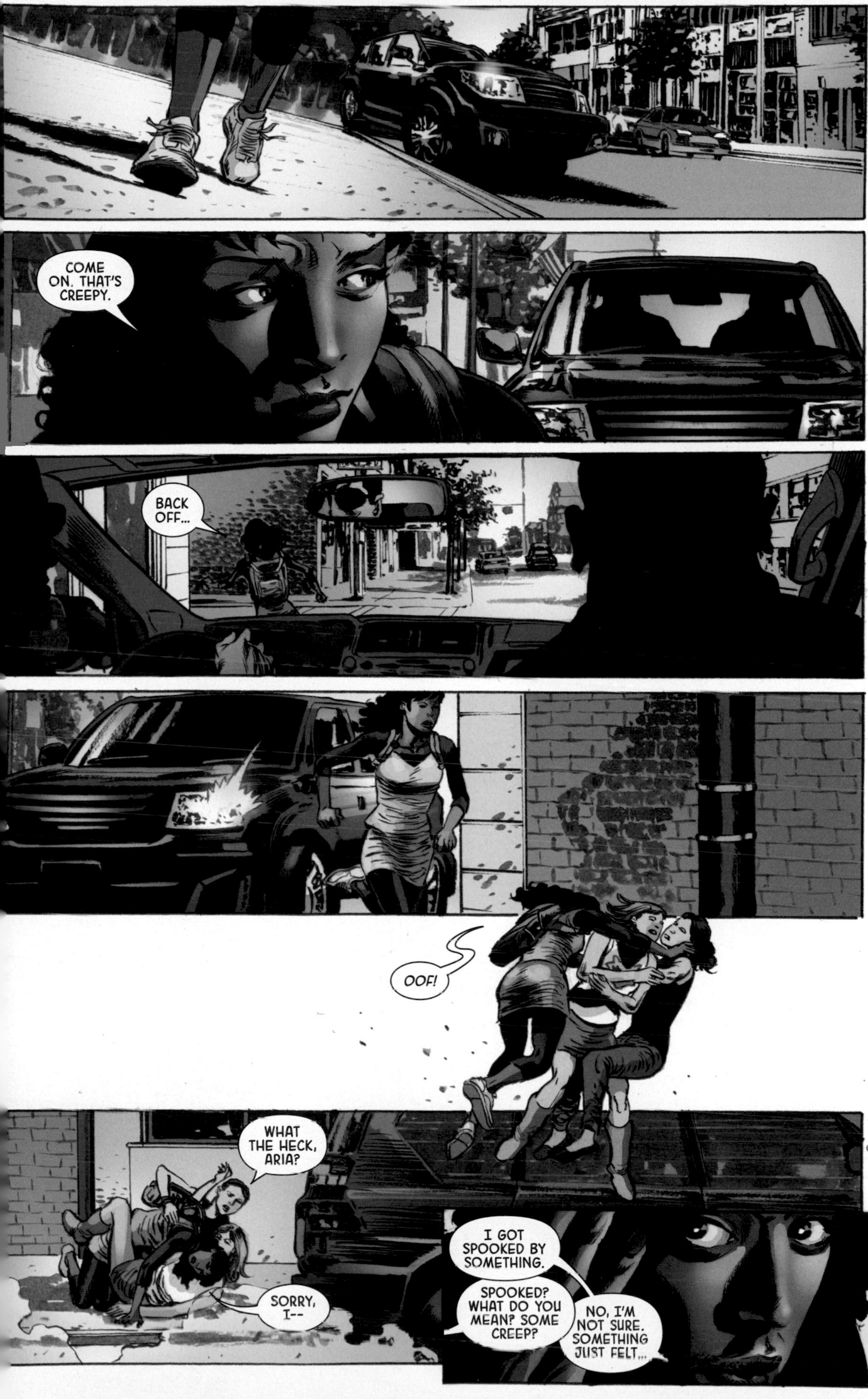
COME ON. THAT'S CREEPY.
BACK OFF...
OOF!
WHAT THE HECK, ARIA?
SORRY, I--
I GOT SPOOKED BY SOMETHING.
SPOOKED? WHAT DO YOU MEAN? SOME CREEP?
NO, I'M NOT SURE. SOMETHING JUST FELT...

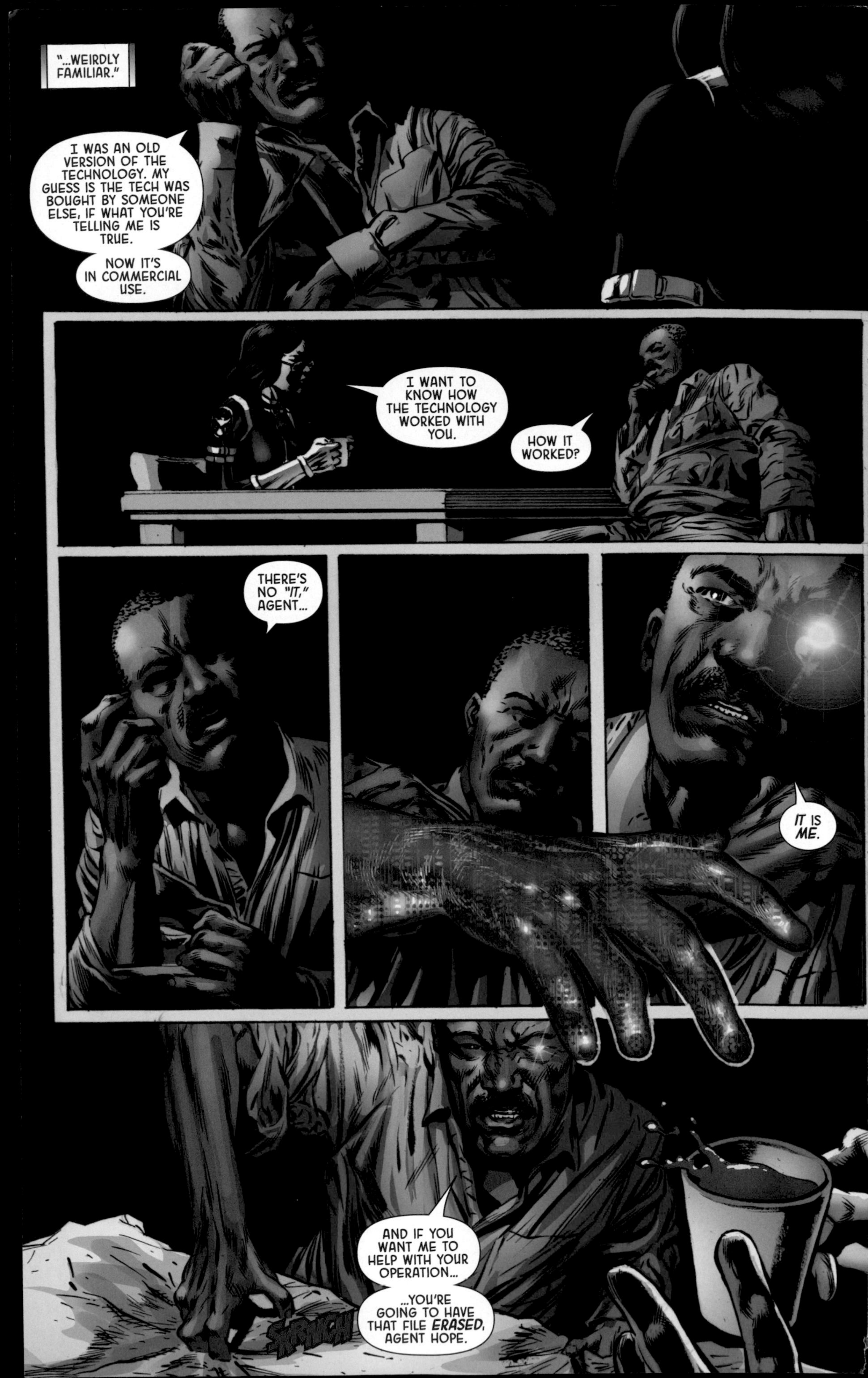
"...WEIRDLY FAMILIAR."
I WAS AN OLD VERSION OF THE TECHNOLOGY. MY GUESS IS THE TECH WAS BOUGHT BY SOMEONE ELSE, IF WHAT YOU'RE TELLING ME IS TRUE.
NOW IT'S IN COMMERCIAL USE.
I WANT TO KNOW HOW THE TECHNOLOGY WORKED WITH YOU.
HOW IT WORKED?
THERE'S NO "IT," AGENT...
IT IS ME.
AND IF YOU WANT ME TO HELP WITH YOUR OPERATION...
...YOU'RE GOING TO HAVE THAT FILE ERASED, AGENT HOPE.
SKRNCH

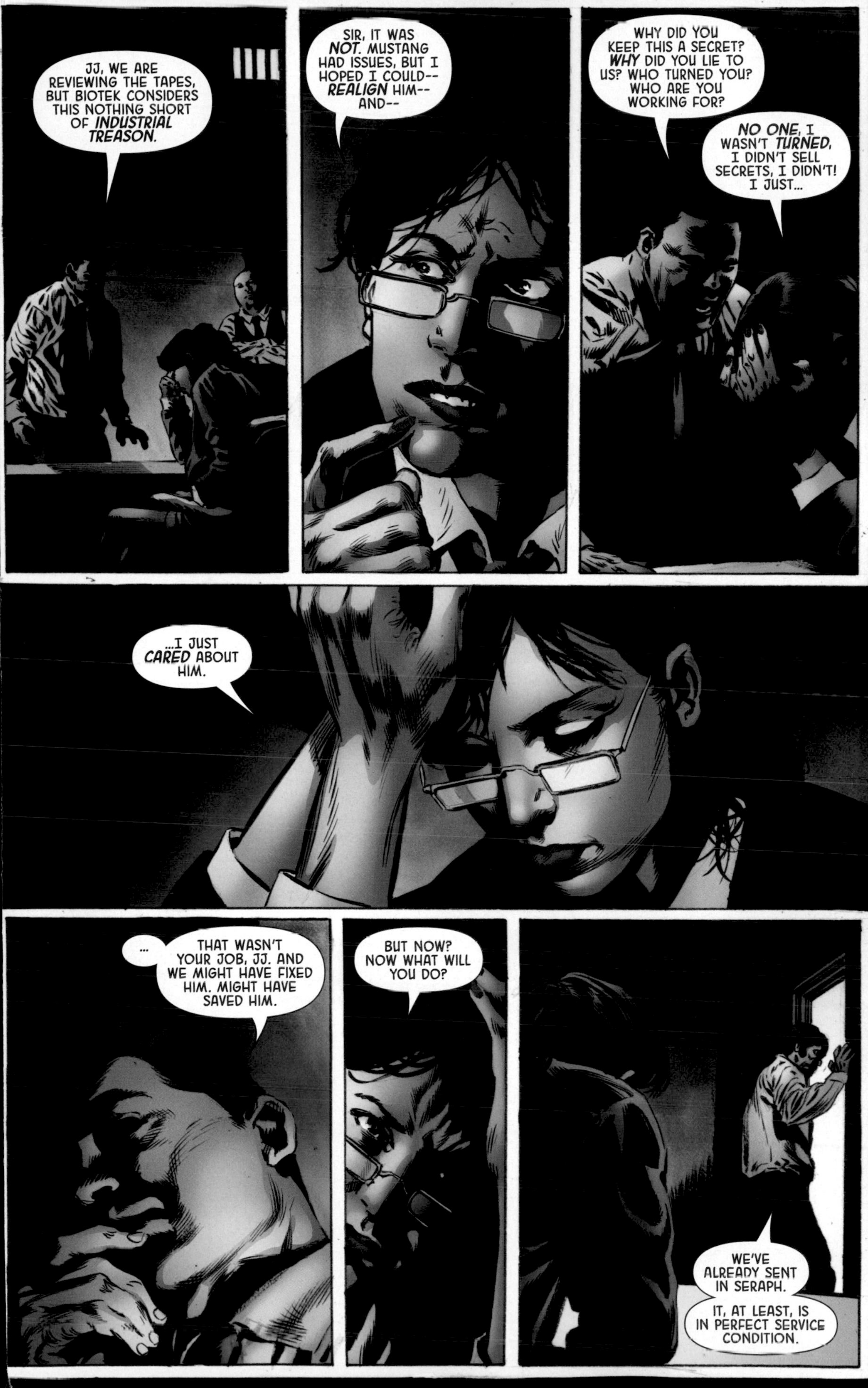
JJ, WE ARE REVIEWING THE TAPES, BUT BIOTEK CONSIDERS THIS NOTHING SHORT OF INDUSTRIAL TREASON.
SIR, IT WAS NOT. MUSTANG HAD ISSUES, BUT I HOPED I COULD-- REALIGN HIM-- AND--
WHY DID YOU KEEP THIS A SECRET? WHY DID YOU LIE TO US? WHO TURNED YOU? WHO ARE YOU WORKING FOR?
NO ONE, I WASN'T TURNED, I DIDN'T SELL SECRETS, I DIDN'T! I JUST...
...I JUST CARED ABOUT HIM.
...
THAT WASN'T YOUR JOB, JJ. AND WE MIGHT HAVE FIXED HIM. MIGHT HAVE SAVED HIM.
BUT NOW? NOW WHAT WILL YOU DO?
WE'VE ALREADY SENT IN SERAPH.
IT, AT LEAST, IS IN PERFECT SERVICE CONDITION.

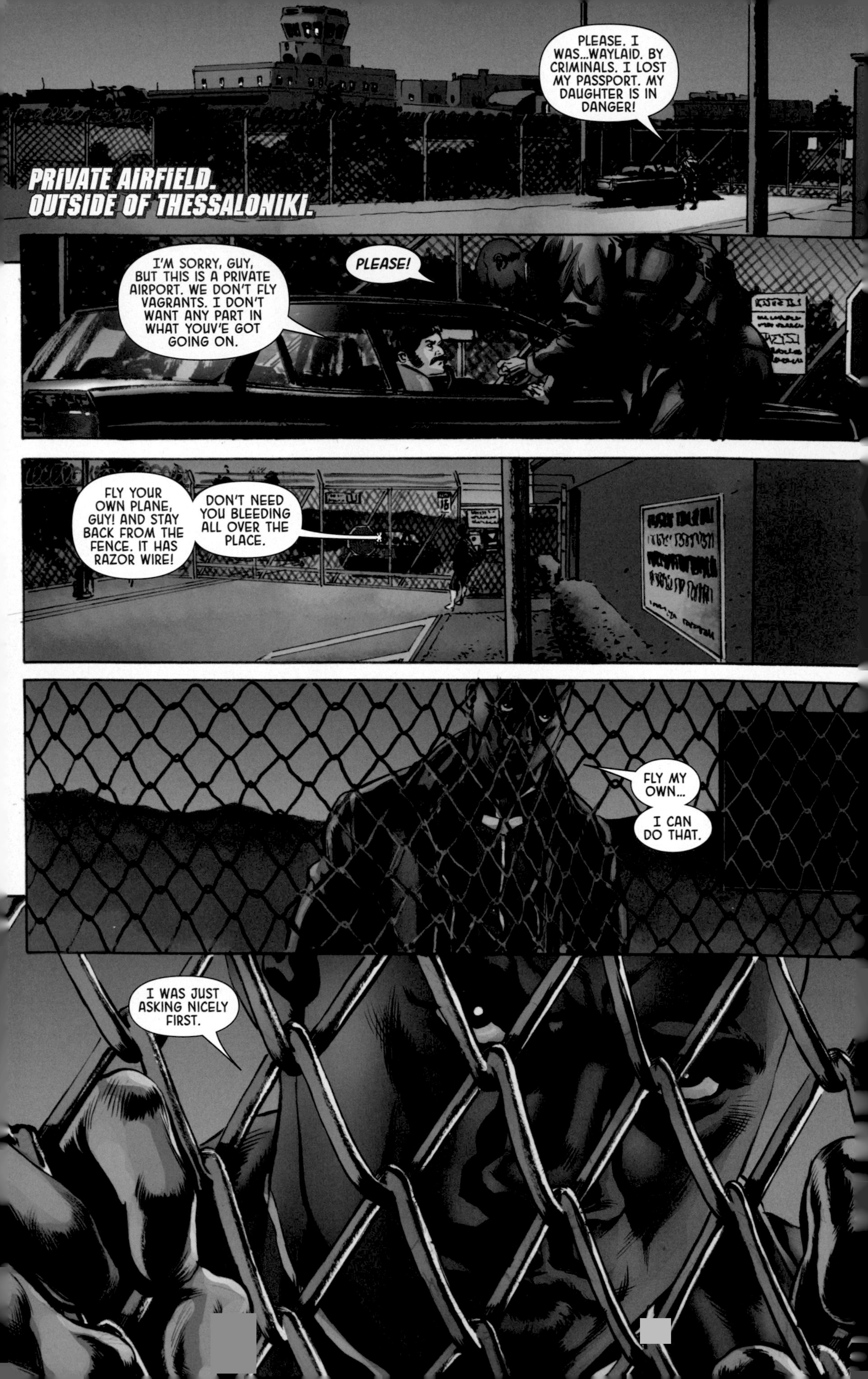
PRIVATE AIRFIELD. OUTSIDE OF THESSALONIKI.
PLEASE. I WAS...WAYLAID. BY CRIMINALS. I LOST MY PASSPORT. MY DAUGHTER IS IN DANGER!
I'M SORRY, GUY, BUT THIS IS A PRIVATE AIRPORT. WE DON'T FLY VAGRANTS. I DON'T WANT ANY PART IN WHAT YOUV'E GOT GOING ON.
PLEASE!
FLY YOUR OWN PLANE, GUY! AND STAY BACK FROM THE FENCE. IT HAS RAZOR WIRE!
DON'T NEED YOU BLEEDING ALL OVER THE PLACE.
FLY MY OWN...
I CAN DO THAT.
I WAS JUST ASKING NICELY FIRST.

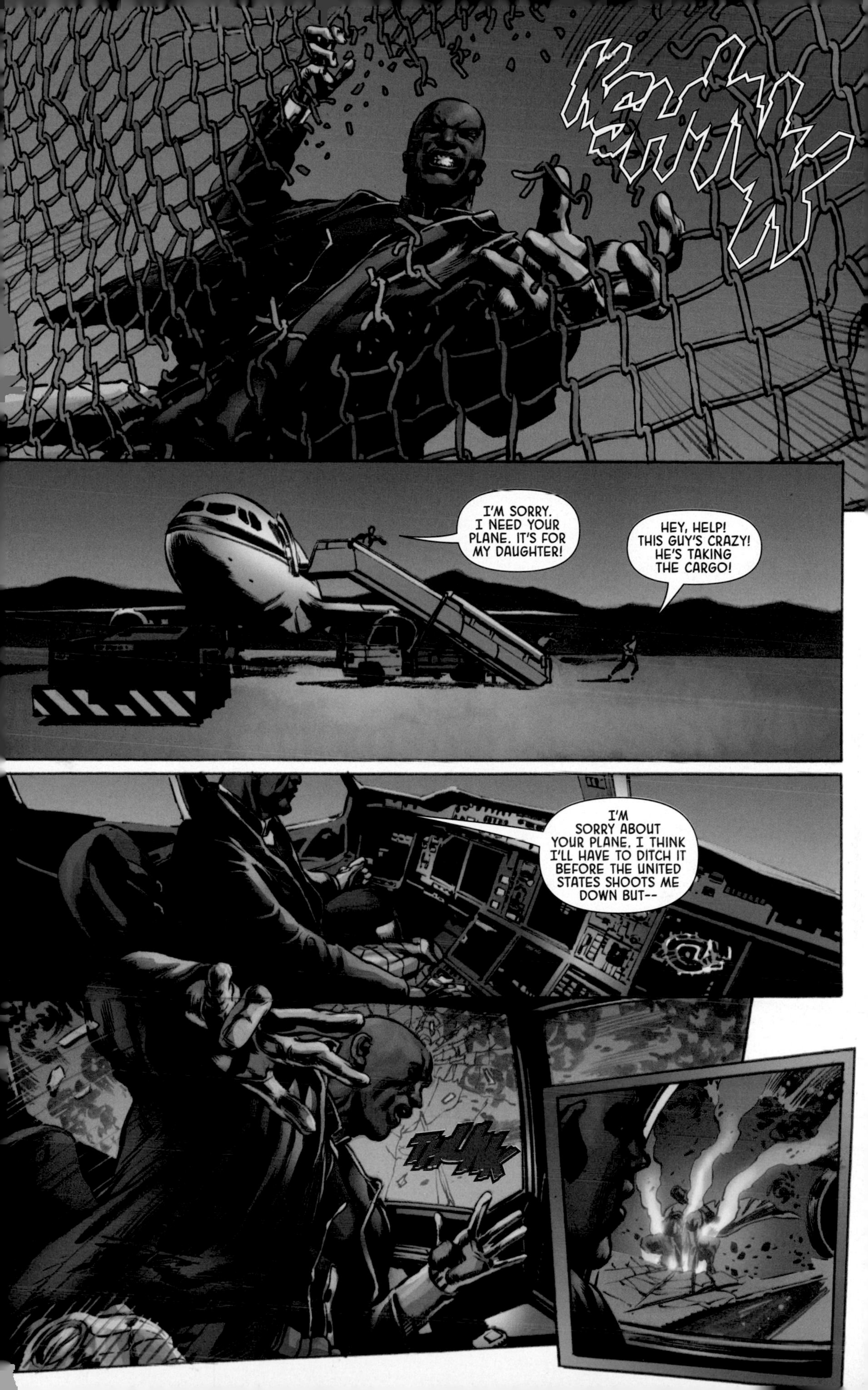
I'M SORRY. I NEED YOUR PLANE. IT'S FOR MY DAUGHTER!
HEY, HELP! THIS GUY'S CRAZY! HE'S TAKING THE CARGO!
I'M SORRY ABOUT YOUR PLANE. I THINK I'LL HAVE TO DITCH IT BEFORE THE UNITED STATES SHOOTS ME DOWN BUT--
THUNK

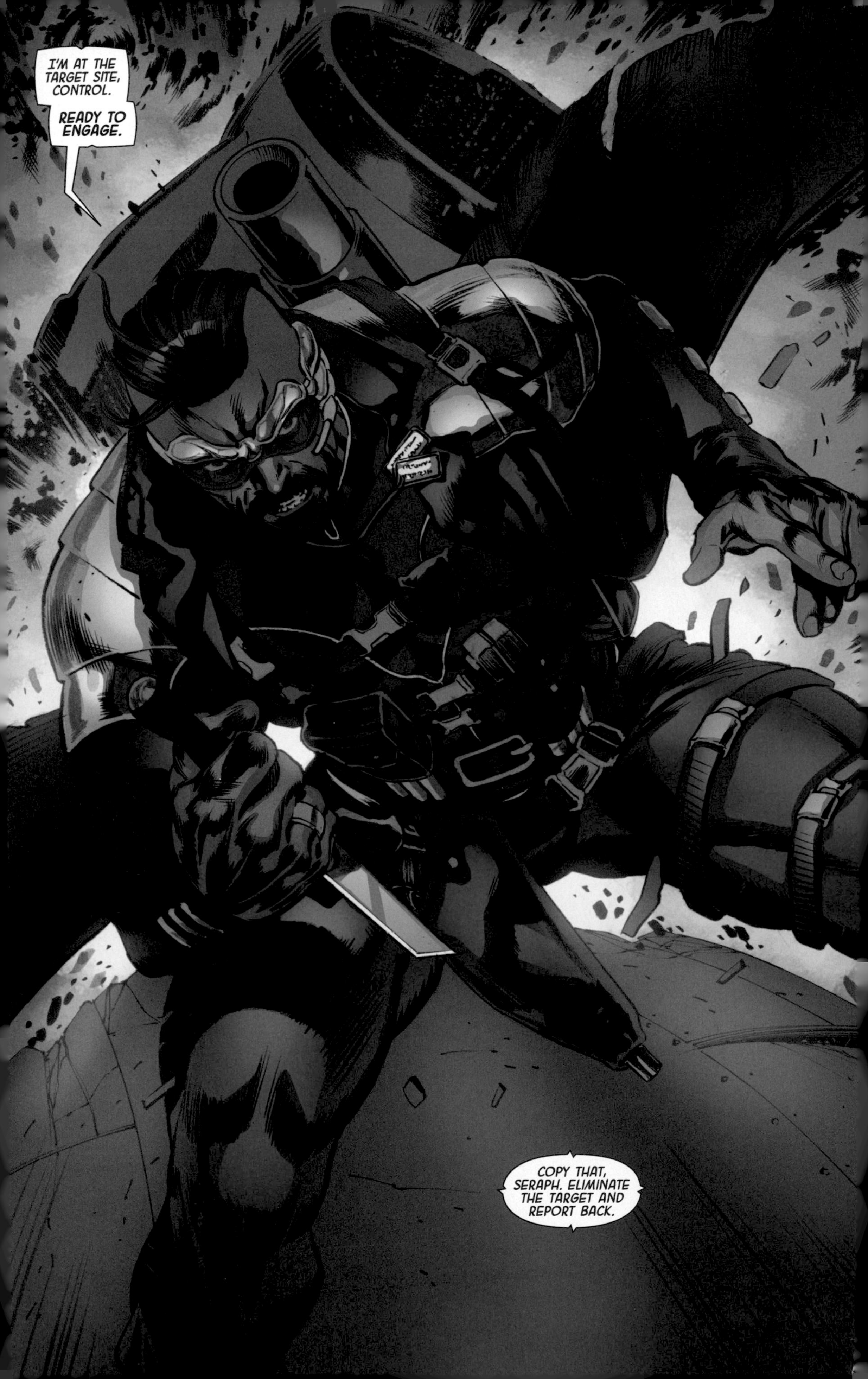
I'M AT THE TARGET SITE, CONTROL.
READY TO ENGAGE.
COPY THAT, SERAPH. ELIMINATE THE TARGET AND REPORT BACK.

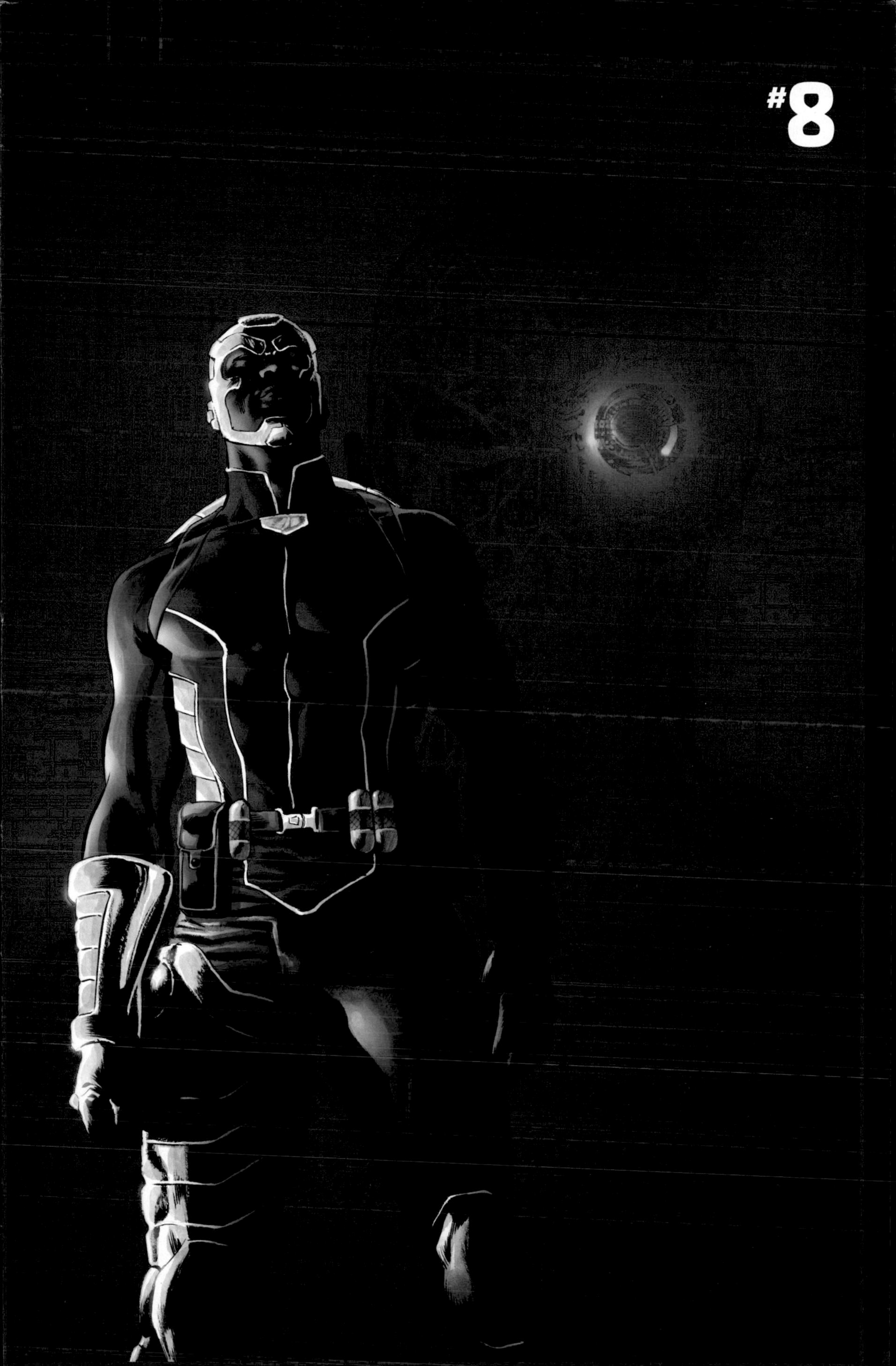
#8

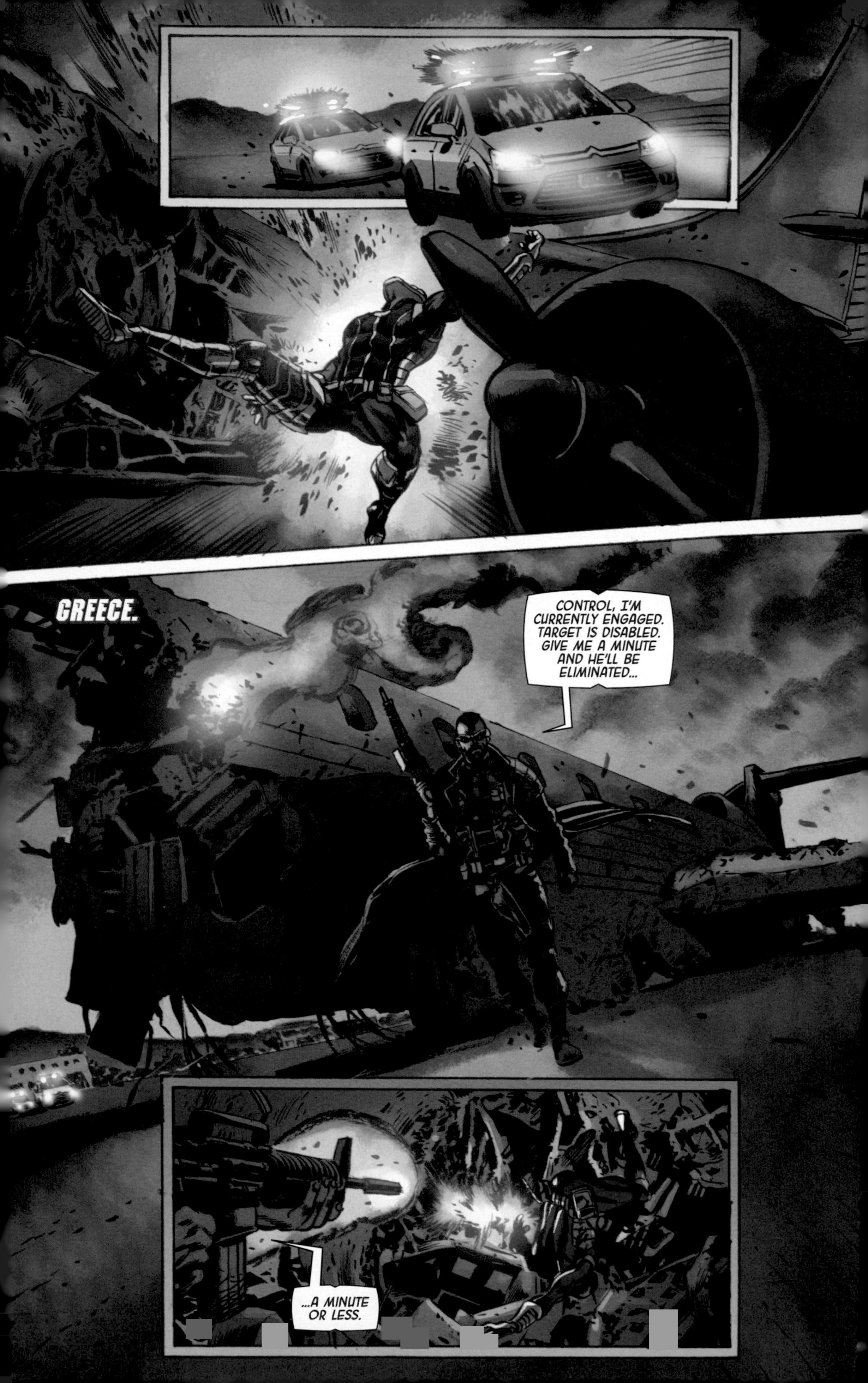
GREECE.
CONTROL, I'M CURRENTLY ENGAGED. TARGET IS DISABLED. GIVE ME A MINUTE AND HE'LL BE ELIMINATED...
...A MINUTE OR LESS.

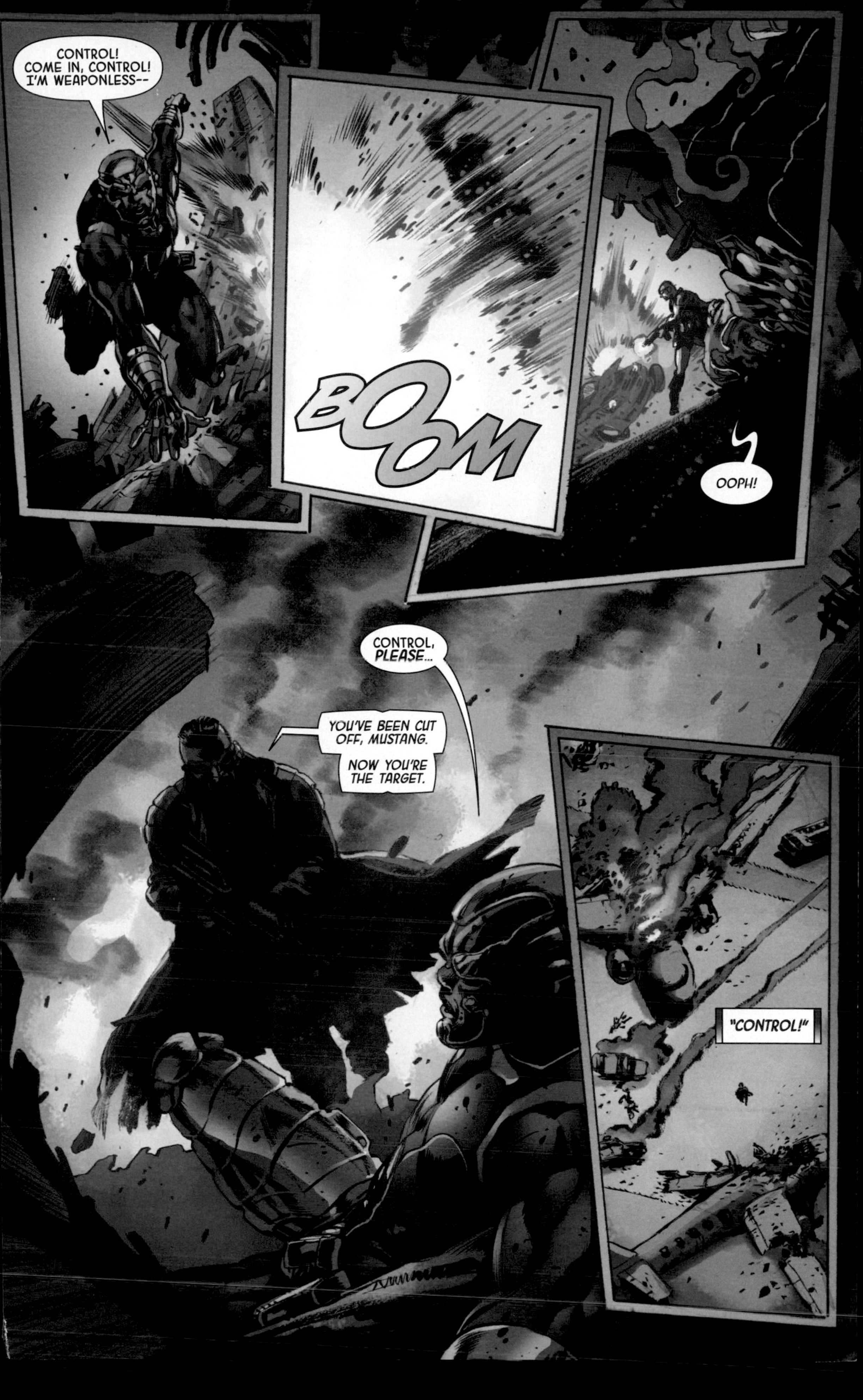
CONTROL! COME IN, CONTROL! I'M WEAPONLESS--
BOOOM
OOPH!
CONTROL, PLEASE...
YOU'VE BEEN CUT OFF, MUSTANG.
NOW YOU'RE THE TARGET.
"CONTROL!"

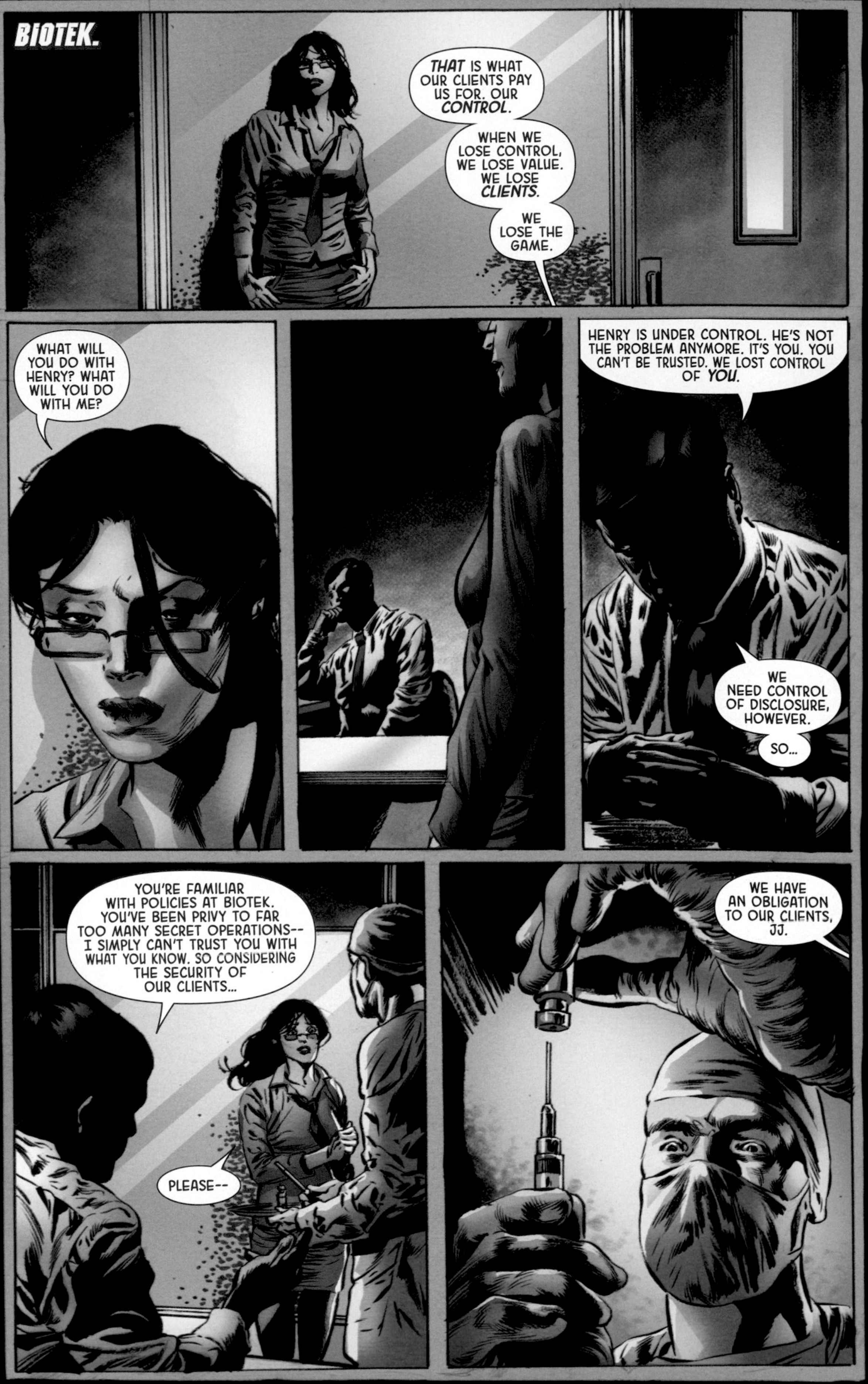
BIOTEK.
THAT IS WHAT OUR CLIENTS PAY US FOR. OUR CONTROL.
WHEN WE LOSE CONTROL, WE LOSE VALUE. WE LOSE CLIENTS.
WE LOSE THE GAME.
WHAT WILL YOU DO WITH HENRY? WHAT WILL YOU DO WITH ME?
HENRY IS UNDER CONTROL. HE'S NOT THE PROBLEM ANYMORE. IT'S YOU. YOU CAN'T BE TRUSTED. WE LOST CONTROL OF YOU.
WE NEED CONTROL OF DISCLOSURE, HOWEVER.
SO...
YOU'RE FAMILIAR WITH POLICIES AT BIOTEK. YOU'VE BEEN PRIVY TO FAR TOO MANY SECRET OPERATIONS-- I SIMPLY CAN'T TRUST YOU WITH WHAT YOU KNOW. SO CONSIDERING THE SECURITY OF OUR CLIENTS...
PLEASE--
WE HAVE AN OBLIGATION TO OUR CLIENTS, JJ.

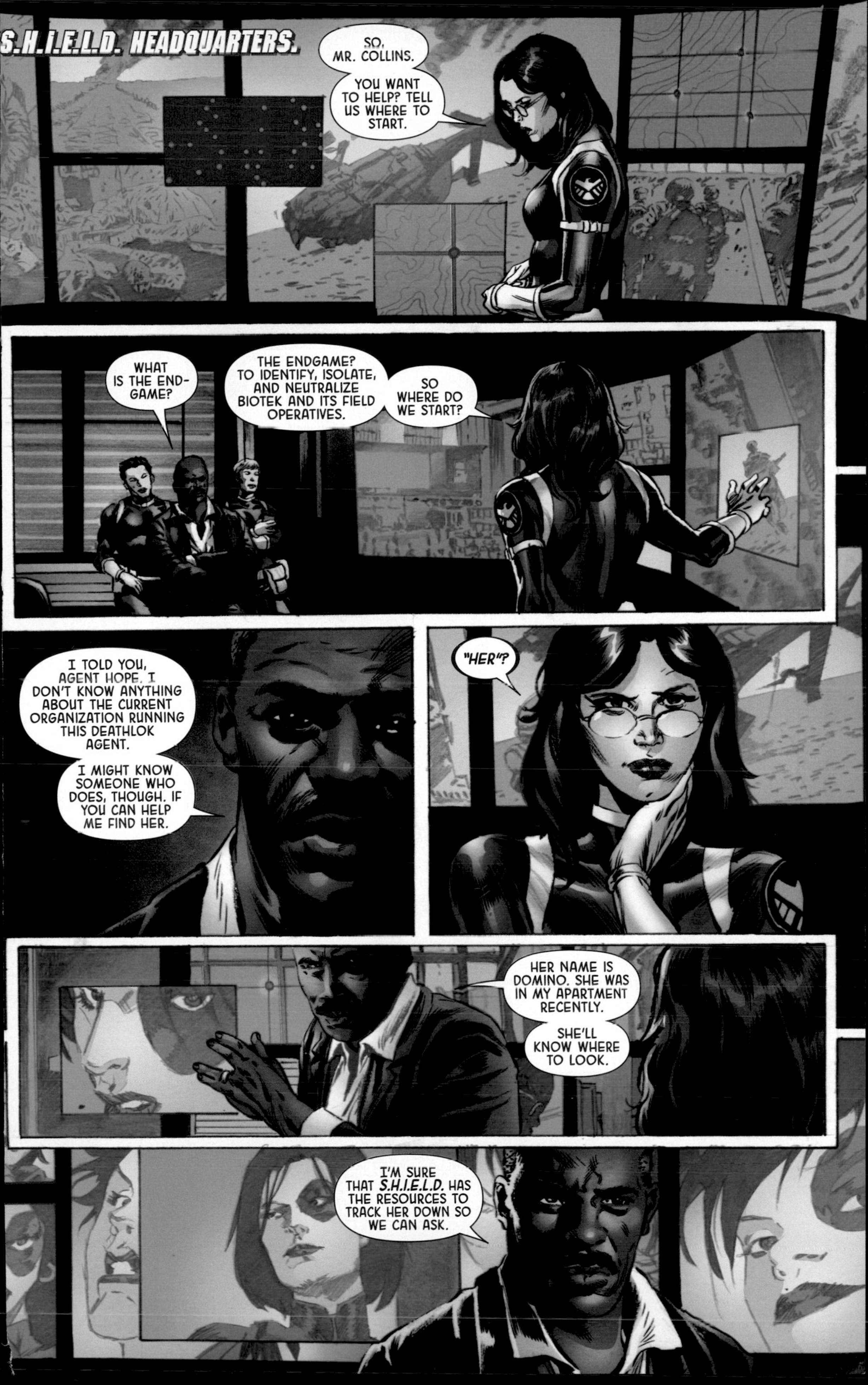
S.H.I.E.L.D. HEADQUARTERS.
SO, MR. COLLINS.
YOU WANT TO HELP? TELL US WHERE TO START.
WHAT IS THE END-GAME?
THE ENDGAME? TO IDENTIFY, ISOLATE, AND NEUTRALIZE BIOTEK AND ITS FIELD OPERATIVES.
SO WHERE DO WE START?
I TOLD YOU, AGENT HOPE. I DON'T KNOW ANYTHING ABOUT THE CURRENT ORGANIZATION RUNNING THIS DEATHLOK AGENT.
I MIGHT KNOW SOMEONE WHO DOES, THOUGH. IF YOU CAN HELP ME FIND HER.
"HER"?
HER NAME IS DOMINO. SHE WAS IN MY APARTMENT RECENTLY.
SHE'LL KNOW WHERE TO LOOK.
I'M SURE THAT S.H.I.E.L.D. HAS THE RESOURCES TO TRACK HER DOWN SO WE CAN ASK.

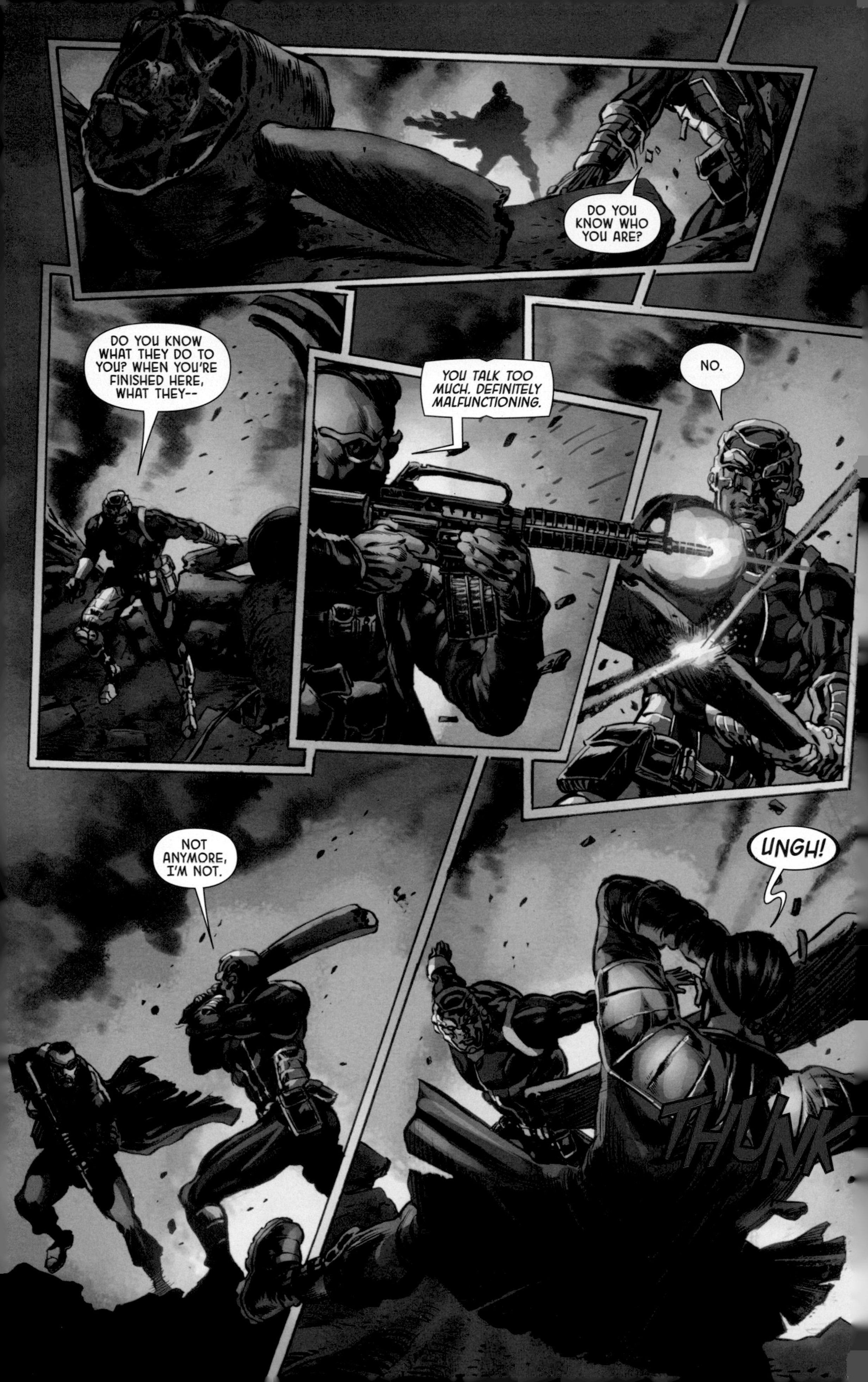
DO YOU KNOW WHO YOU ARE?
DO YOU KNOW WHAT THEY DO TO YOU? WHEN YOU'RE FINISHED HERE, WHAT THEY--
YOU TALK TOO MUCH. DEFINITELY MALFUNCTIONING.
NO.
NOT ANYMORE, I'M NOT.
UNGH!
THUNK

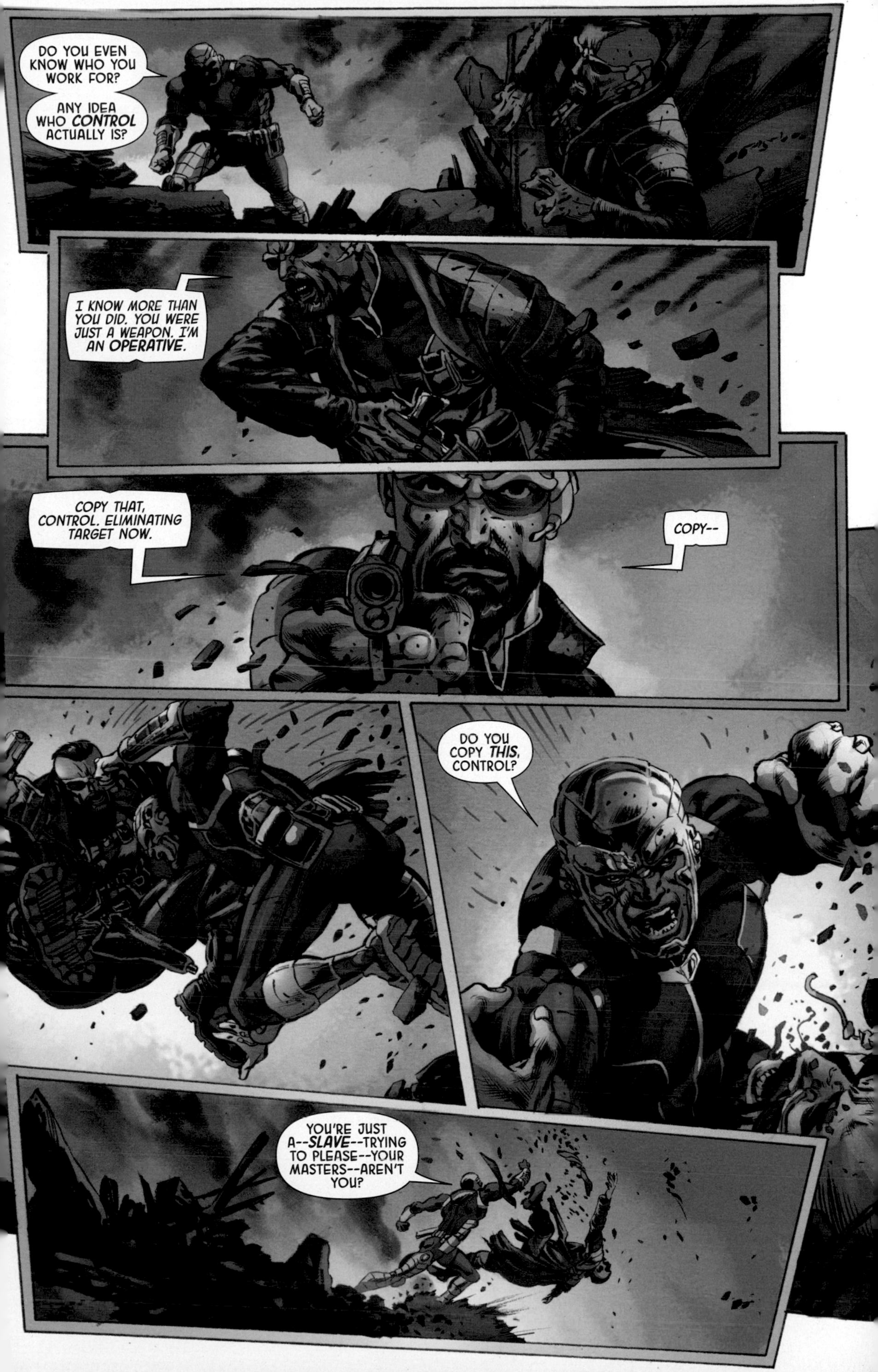
DO YOU EVEN KNOW WHO YOU WORK FOR?
ANY IDEA WHO CONTROL ACTUALLY IS?
I KNOW MORE THAN YOU DID. YOU WERE JUST A WEAPON. I'M AN OPERATIVE.
COPY THAT, CONTROL. ELIMINATING TARGET NOW.
COPY--
DO YOU COPY THIS, CONTROL?
YOU'RE JUST A--SLAVE--TRYING TO PLEASE--YOUR MASTERS--AREN'T YOU?

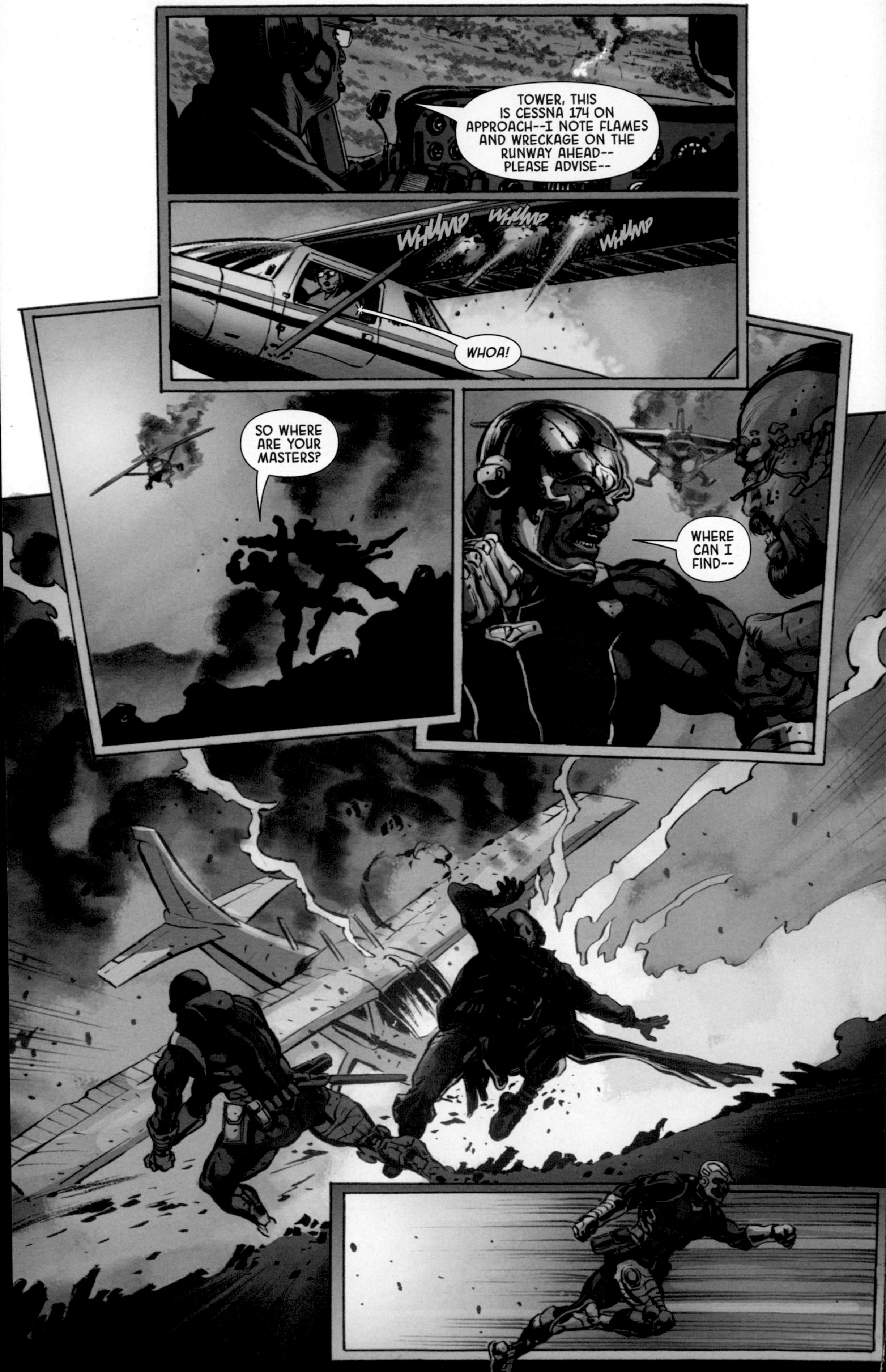
TOWER, THIS IS CESSNA 174 ON APPROACH--I NOTE FLAMES AND WRECKAGE ON THE RUNWAY AHEAD--PLEASE ADVISE--
WHUMP
WHUMP
WHUMP
WHOA!
SO WHERE ARE YOUR MASTERS?
WHERE CAN I FIND--

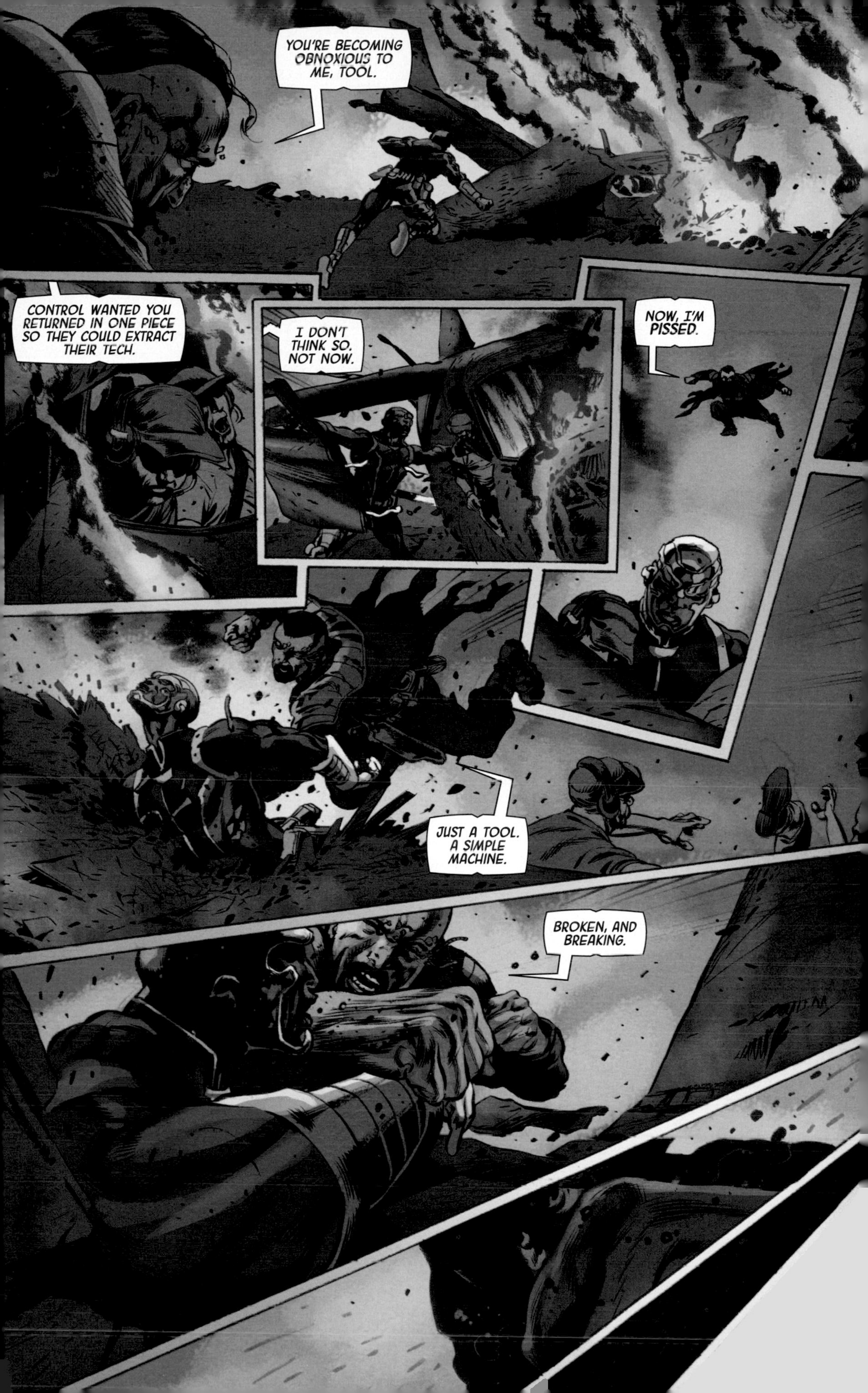
YOU'RE BECOMING OBNOXIOUS TO ME, TOOL.
CONTROL WANTED YOU RETURNED IN ONE PIECE SO THEY COULD EXTRACT THEIR TECH.
I DON'T THINK SO. NOT NOW.
NOW, I'M PISSED.
JUST A TOOL. A SIMPLE MACHINE.
BROKEN, AND BREAKING.

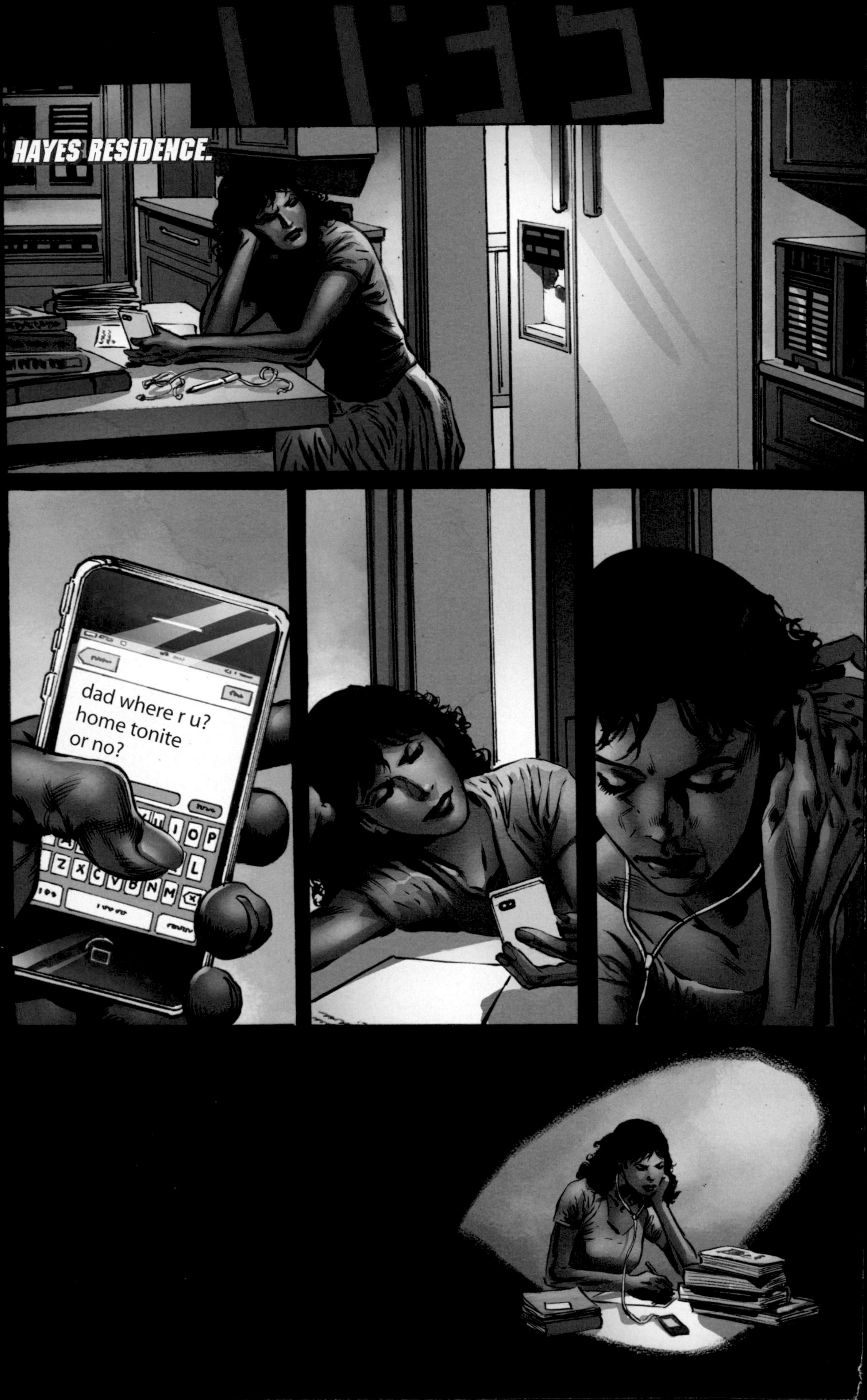
11:35
HAYES RESIDENCE.
dad where r u?
home tonite
or no?

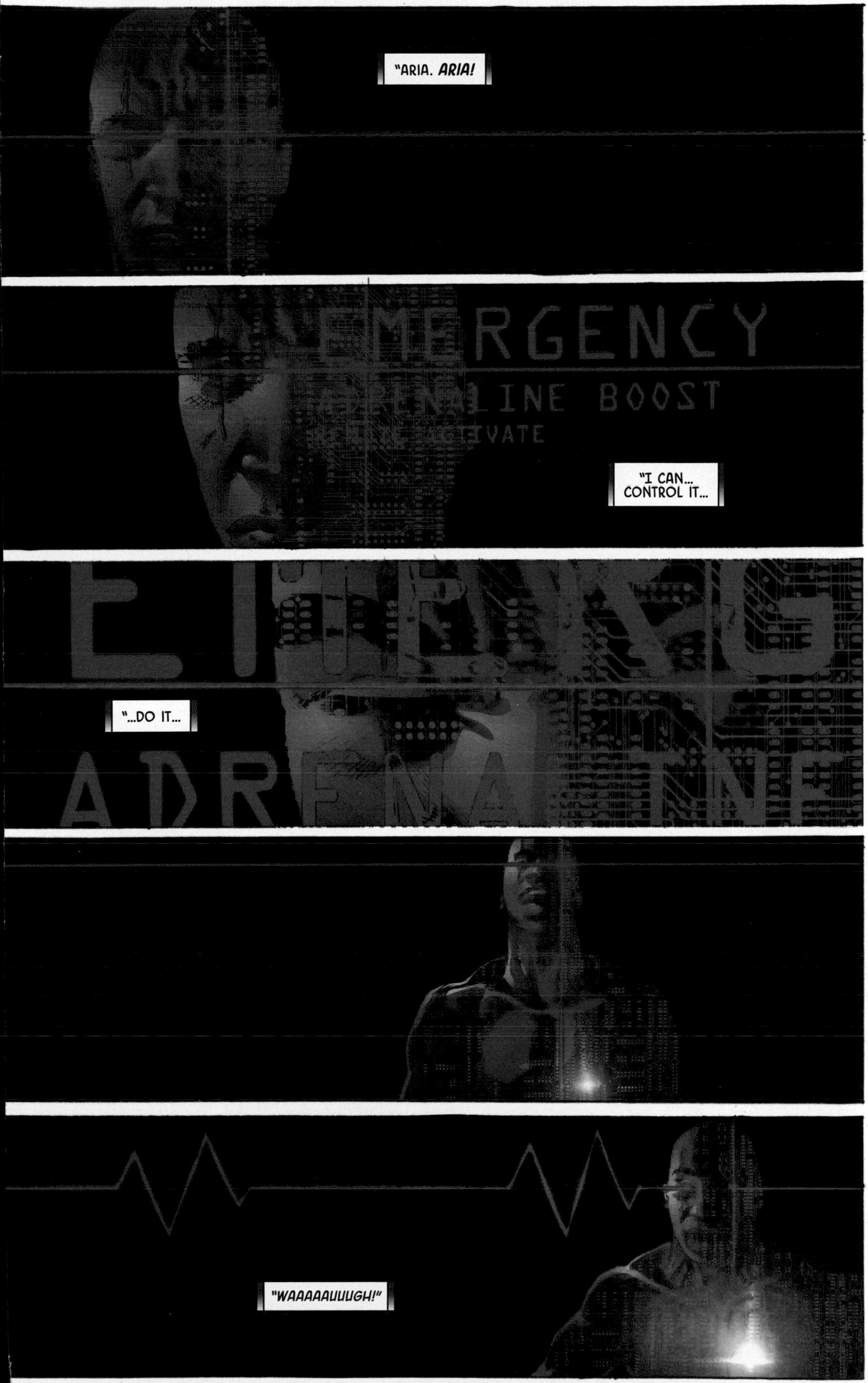

"ARIA. *ARIA!*"

EMERGENCY
ADRENALINE BOOST
ACTIVATE

"I CAN...
CONTROL IT..."

"...DO IT..."

"WAAAAAUUUGH!"

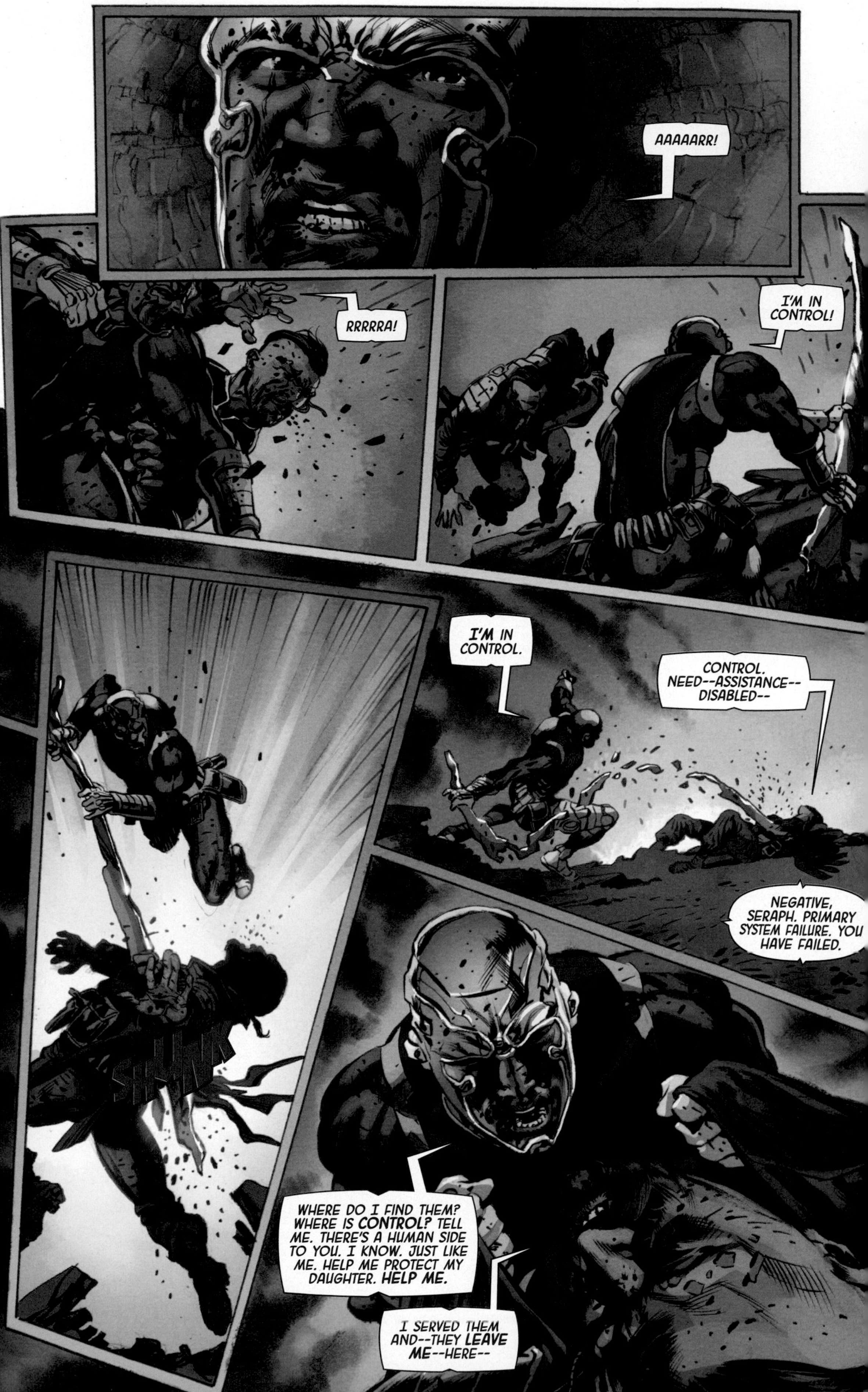
AAAAARR!
RRRRRA!
I'M IN CONTROL!
I'M IN CONTROL.
CONTROL. NEED--ASSISTANCE--DISABLED--
NEGATIVE, SERAPH. PRIMARY SYSTEM FAILURE. YOU HAVE FAILED.
WHERE DO I FIND THEM? WHERE IS CONTROL? TELL ME. THERE'S A HUMAN SIDE TO YOU. I KNOW. JUST LIKE ME. HELP ME PROTECT MY DAUGHTER. HELP ME.
I SERVED THEM AND--THEY LEAVE ME--HERE--

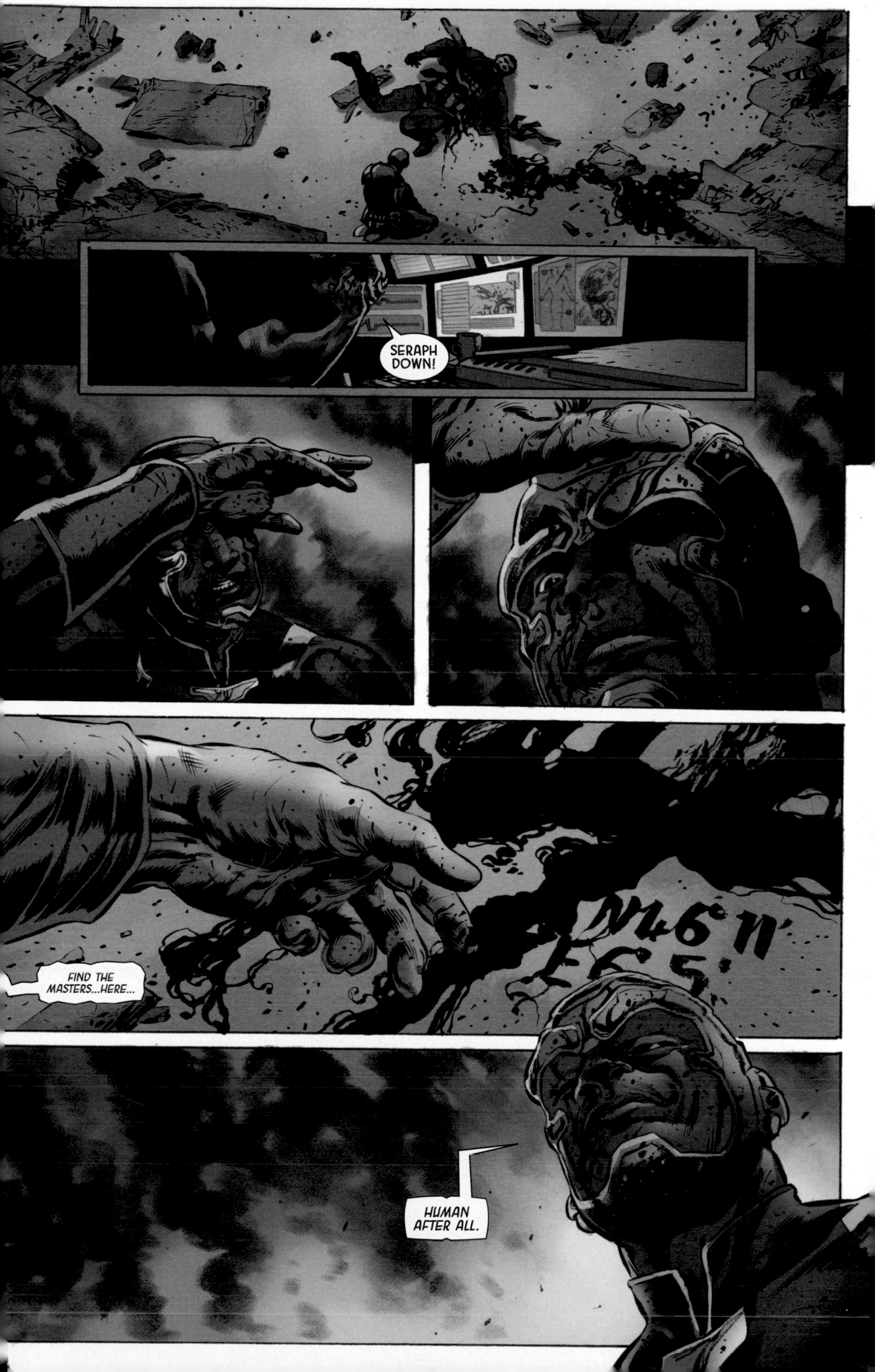
SERAPH DOWN!
FIND THE MASTERS...HERE...
HUMAN AFTER ALL.

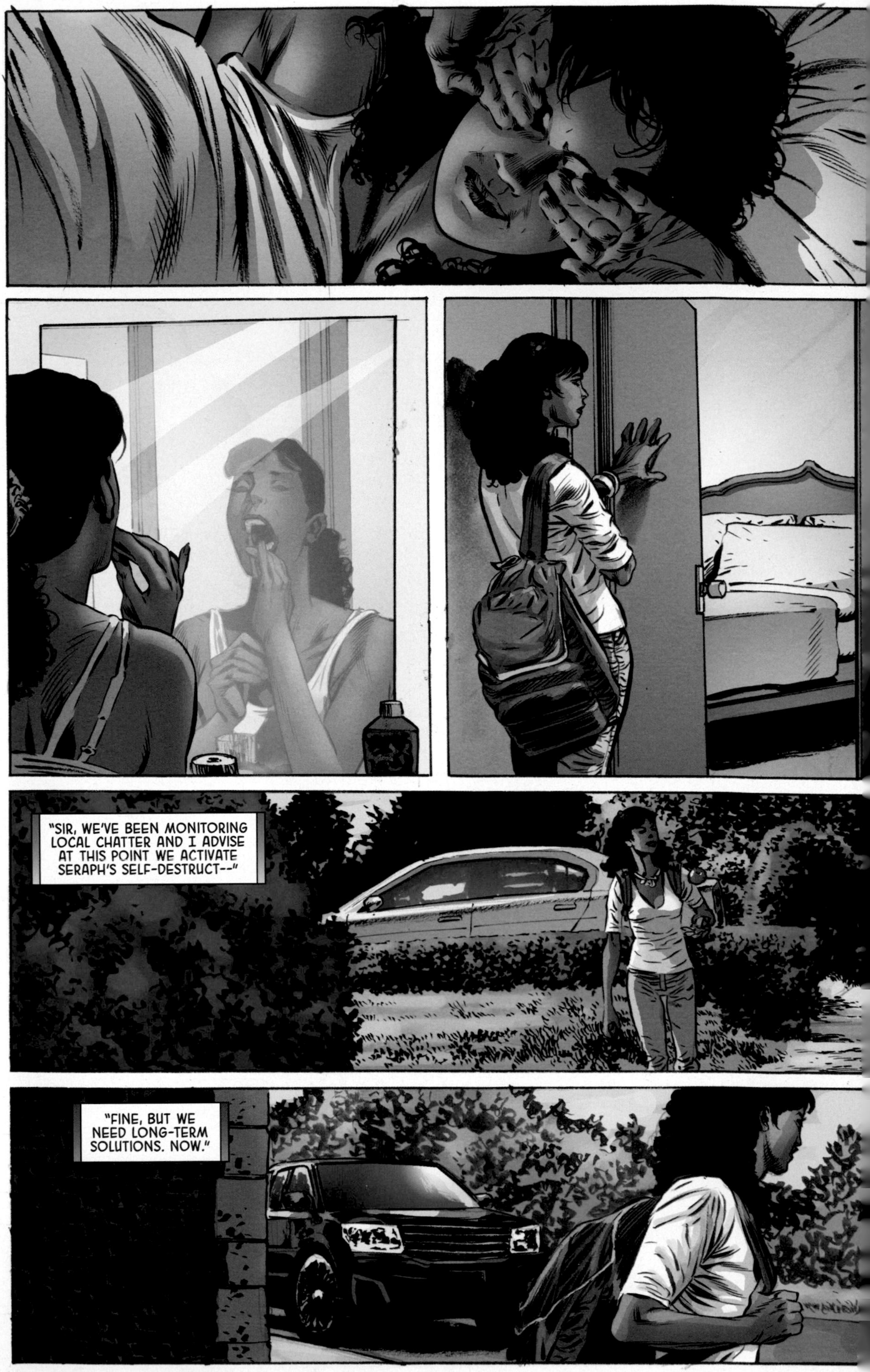
"SIR, WE'VE BEEN MONITORING LOCAL CHATTER AND I ADVISE AT THIS POINT WE ACTIVATE SERAPH'S SELF-DESTRUCT--"
"FINE, BUT WE NEED LONG-TERM SOLUTIONS. NOW."

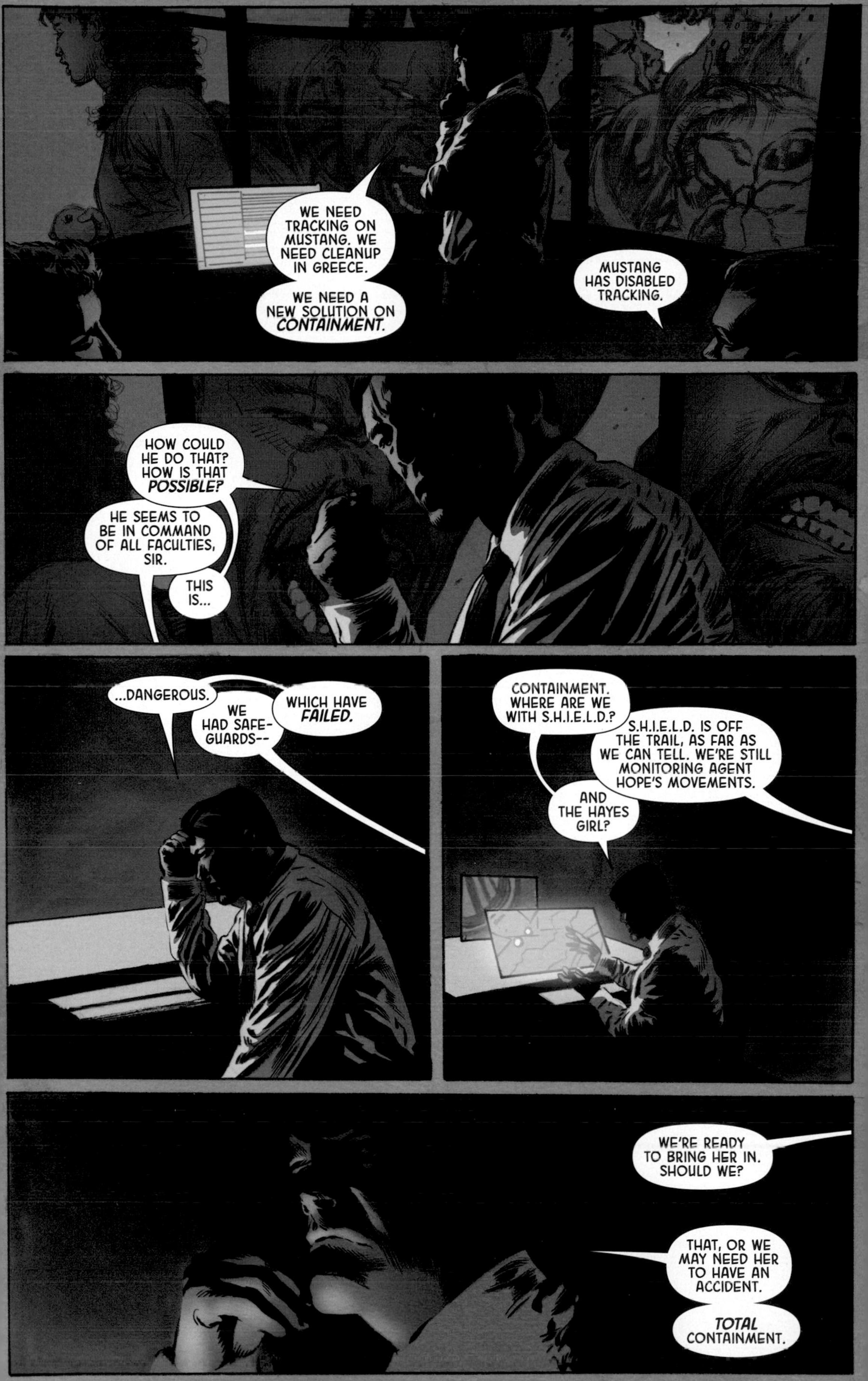
WE NEED TRACKING ON MUSTANG. WE NEED CLEANUP IN GREECE.
WE NEED A NEW SOLUTION ON *CONTAINMENT*.
MUSTANG HAS DISABLED TRACKING.
HOW COULD HE DO THAT? HOW IS THAT *POSSIBLE?*
HE SEEMS TO BE IN COMMAND OF ALL FACULTIES, SIR.
THIS IS...
...DANGEROUS.
WE HAD SAFE-GUARDS--
WHICH HAVE *FAILED.*
CONTAINMENT. WHERE ARE WE WITH S.H.I.E.L.D.?
S.H.I.E.L.D. IS OFF THE TRAIL, AS FAR AS WE CAN TELL. WE'RE STILL MONITORING AGENT HOPE'S MOVEMENTS.
AND THE HAYES GIRL?
WE'RE READY TO BRING HER IN. SHOULD WE?
THAT, OR WE MAY NEED HER TO HAVE AN ACCIDENT.
TOTAL CONTAINMENT.

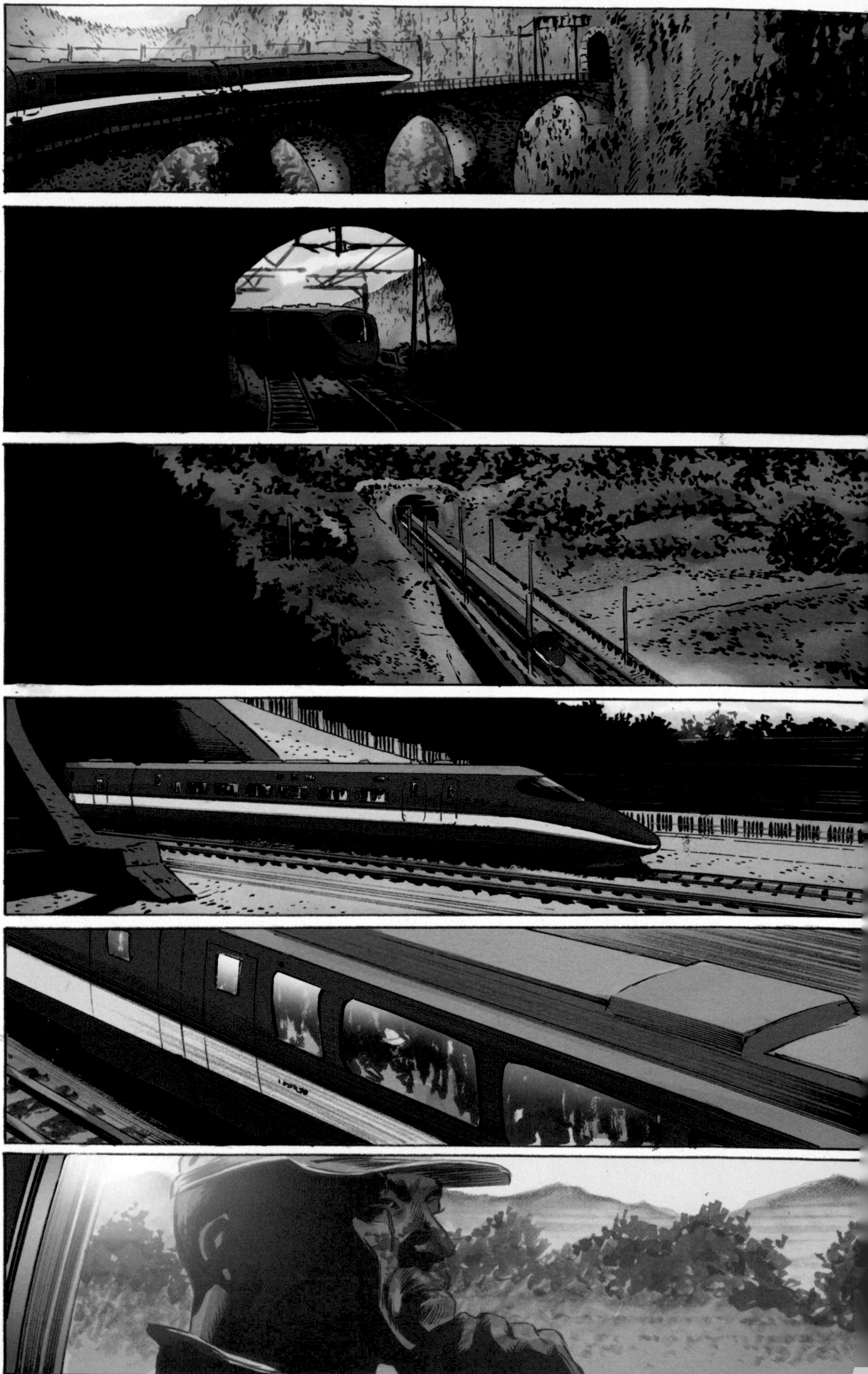

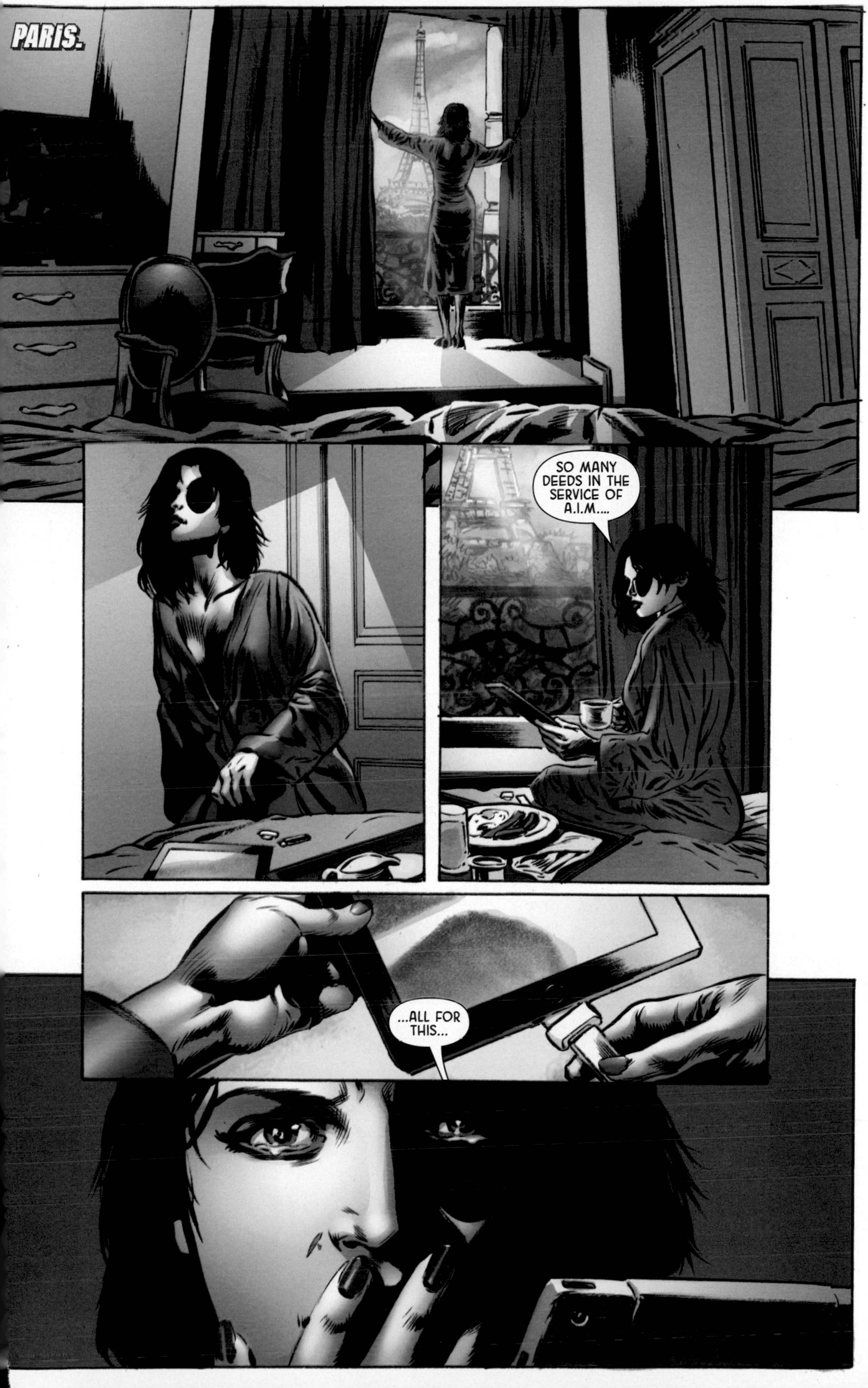
PARIS.
SO MANY DEEDS IN THE SERVICE OF A.I.M....
...ALL FOR THIS...

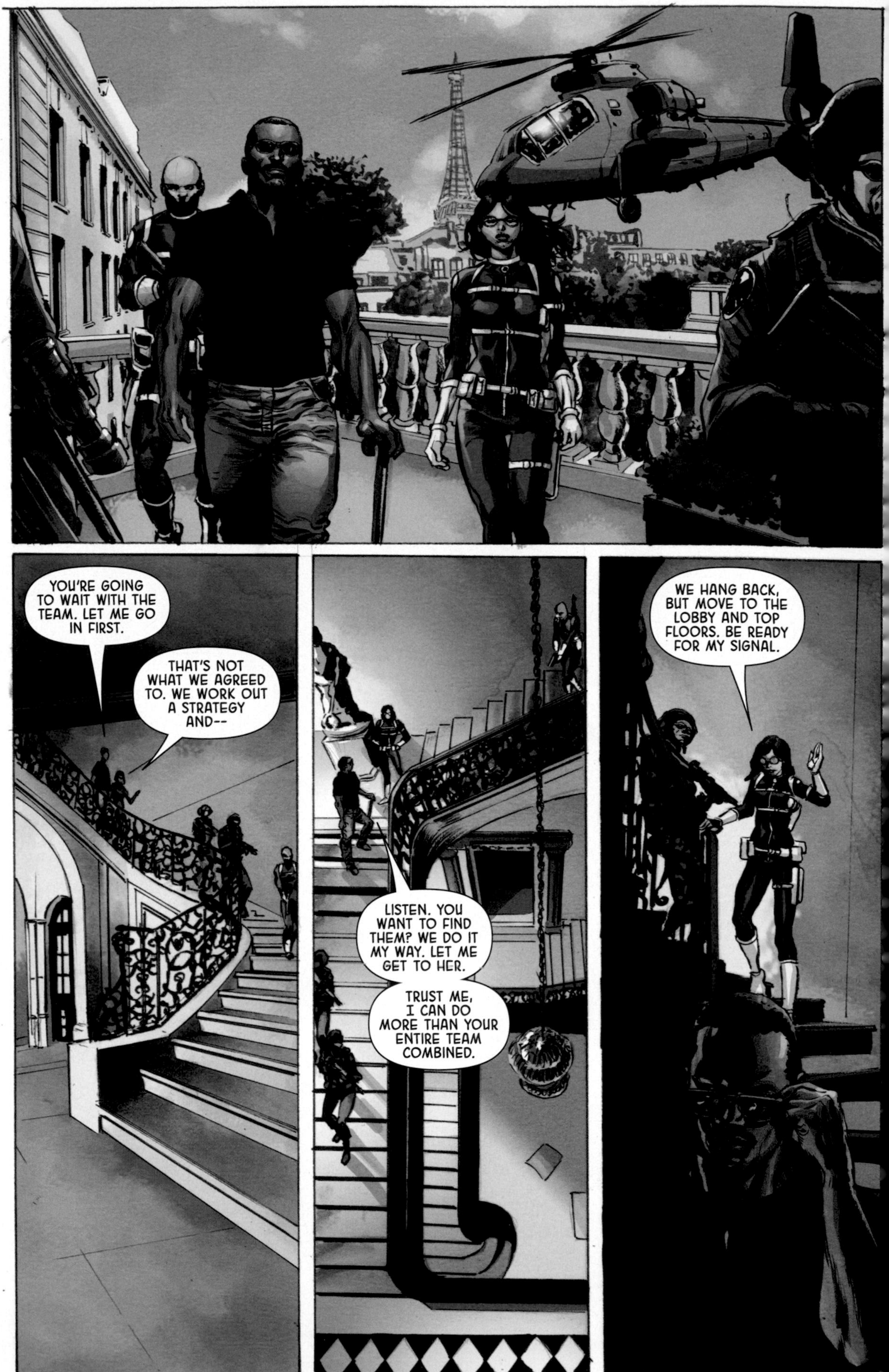
YOU'RE GOING TO WAIT WITH THE TEAM. LET ME GO IN FIRST.
THAT'S NOT WHAT WE AGREED TO. WE WORK OUT A STRATEGY AND--
LISTEN. YOU WANT TO FIND THEM? WE DO IT MY WAY. LET ME GET TO HER.
TRUST ME, I CAN DO MORE THAN YOUR ENTIRE TEAM COMBINED.
WE HANG BACK, BUT MOVE TO THE LOBBY AND TOP FLOORS. BE READY FOR MY SIGNAL.

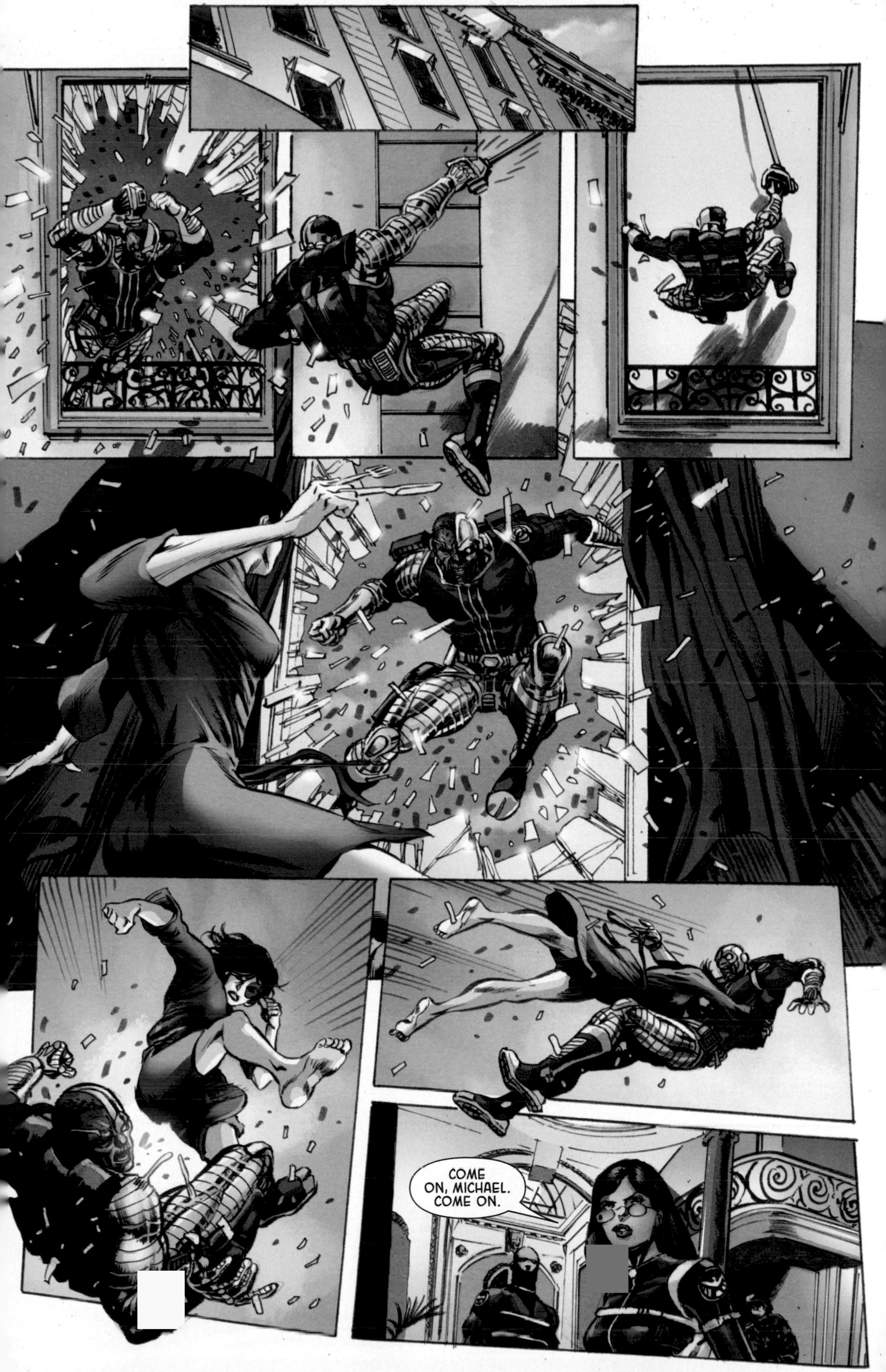
COME ON, MICHAEL. COME ON.

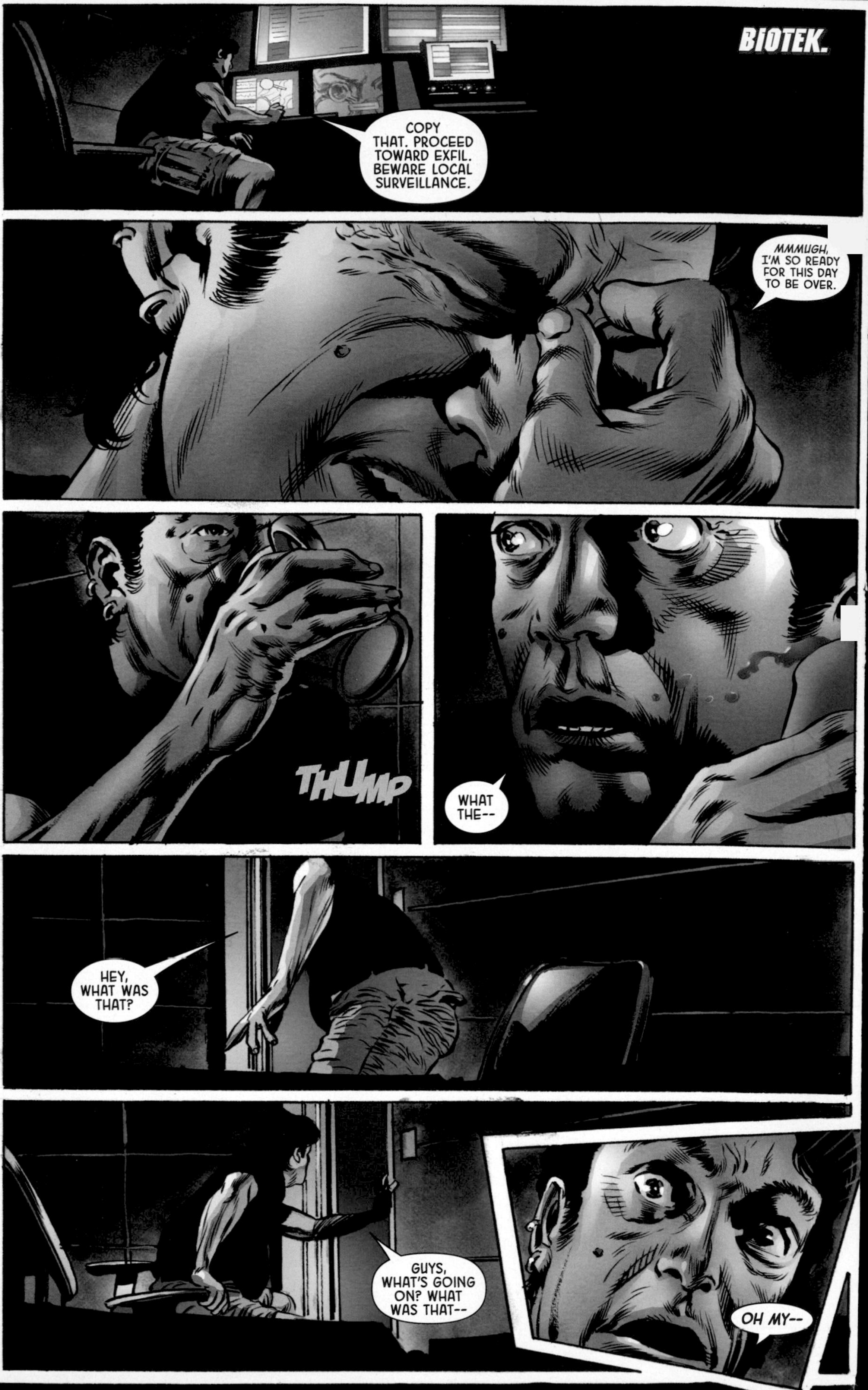
BIOTEK.
COPY THAT. PROCEED TOWARD EXFIL. BEWARE LOCAL SURVEILLANCE.
MMMUGH, I'M SO READY FOR THIS DAY TO BE OVER.
THUMP
WHAT THE--
HEY, WHAT WAS THAT?
GUYS, WHAT'S GOING ON? WHAT WAS THAT--
OH MY--

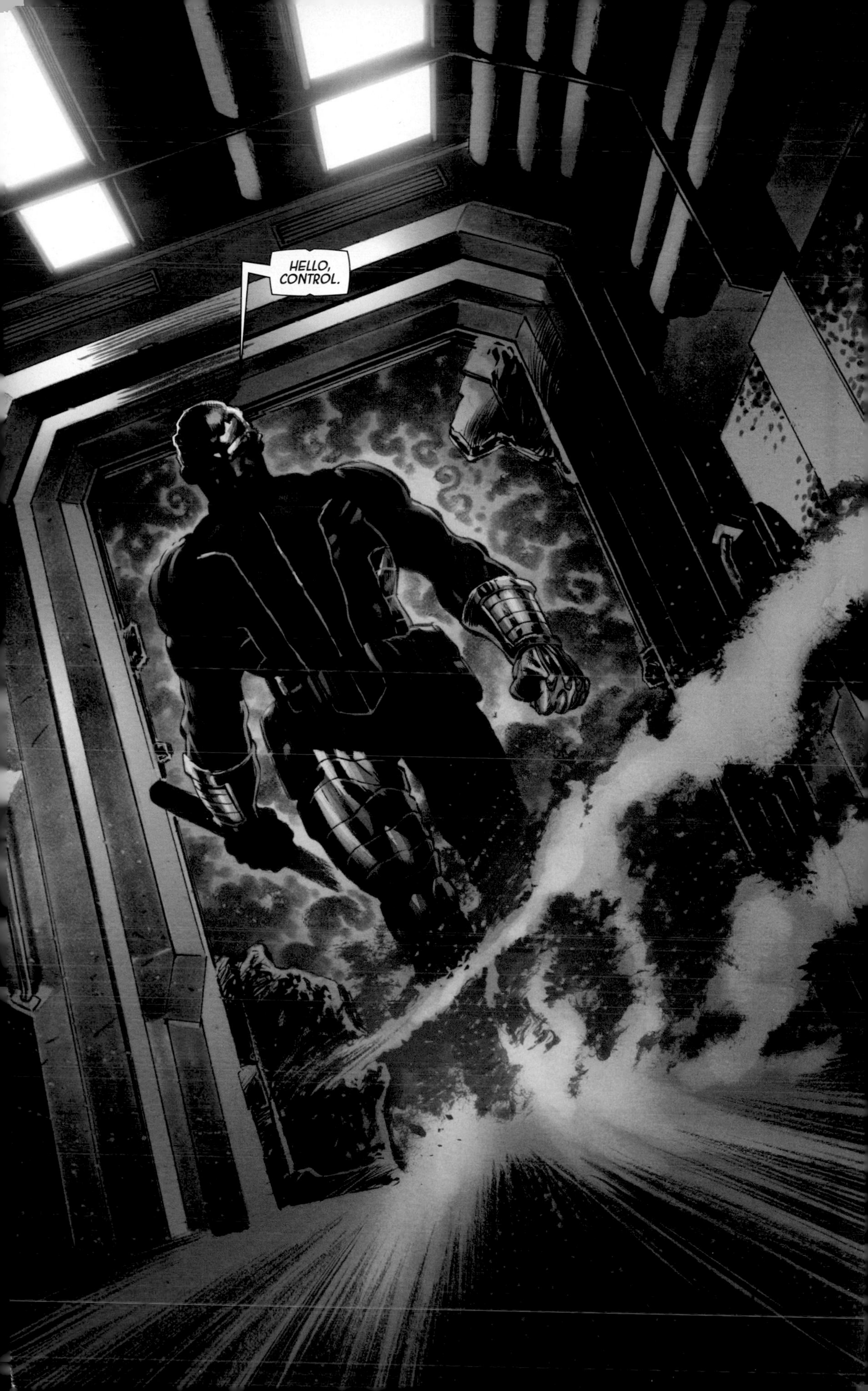
HELLO, CONTROL.

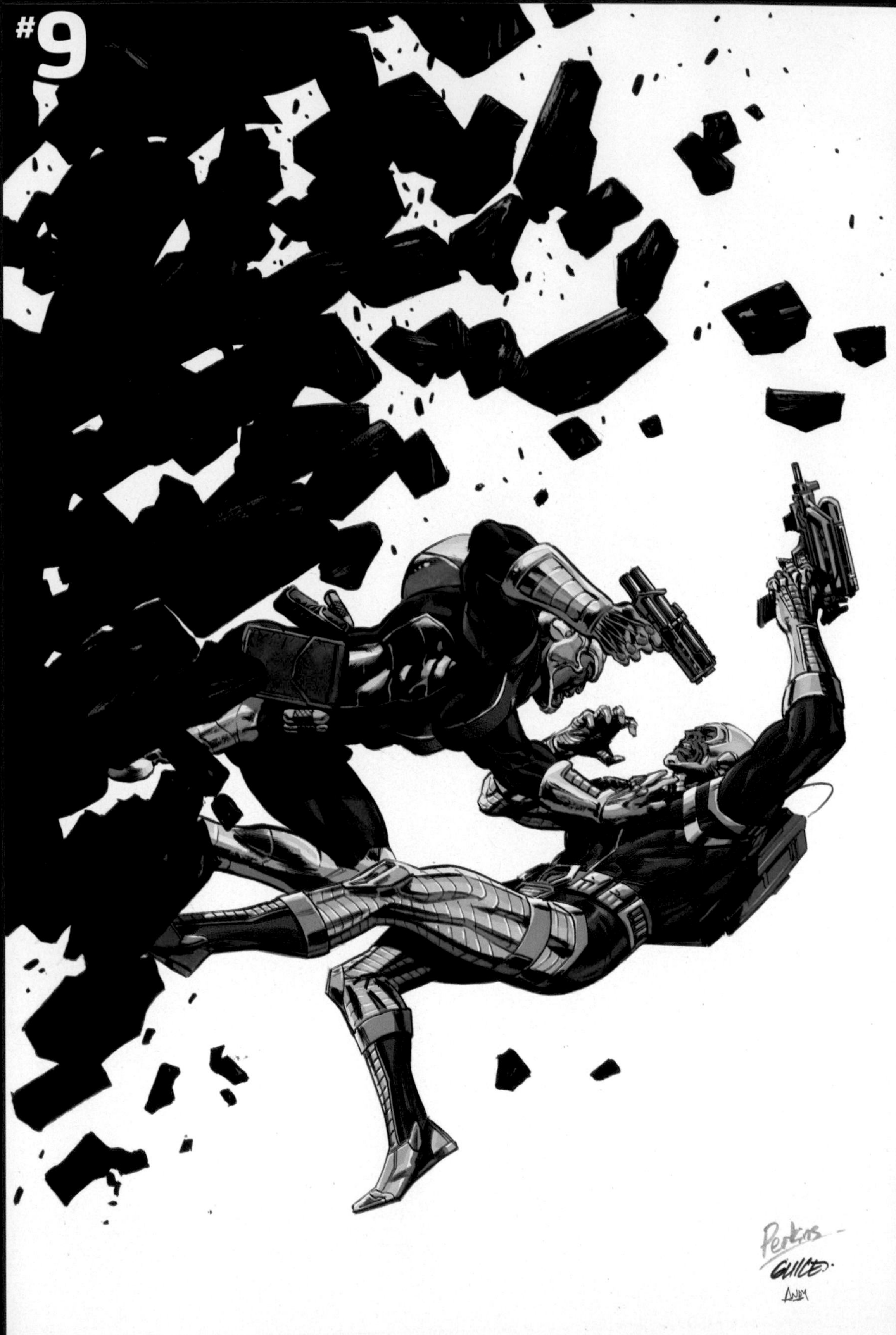
#9
Perkins
GUICE
ANDY

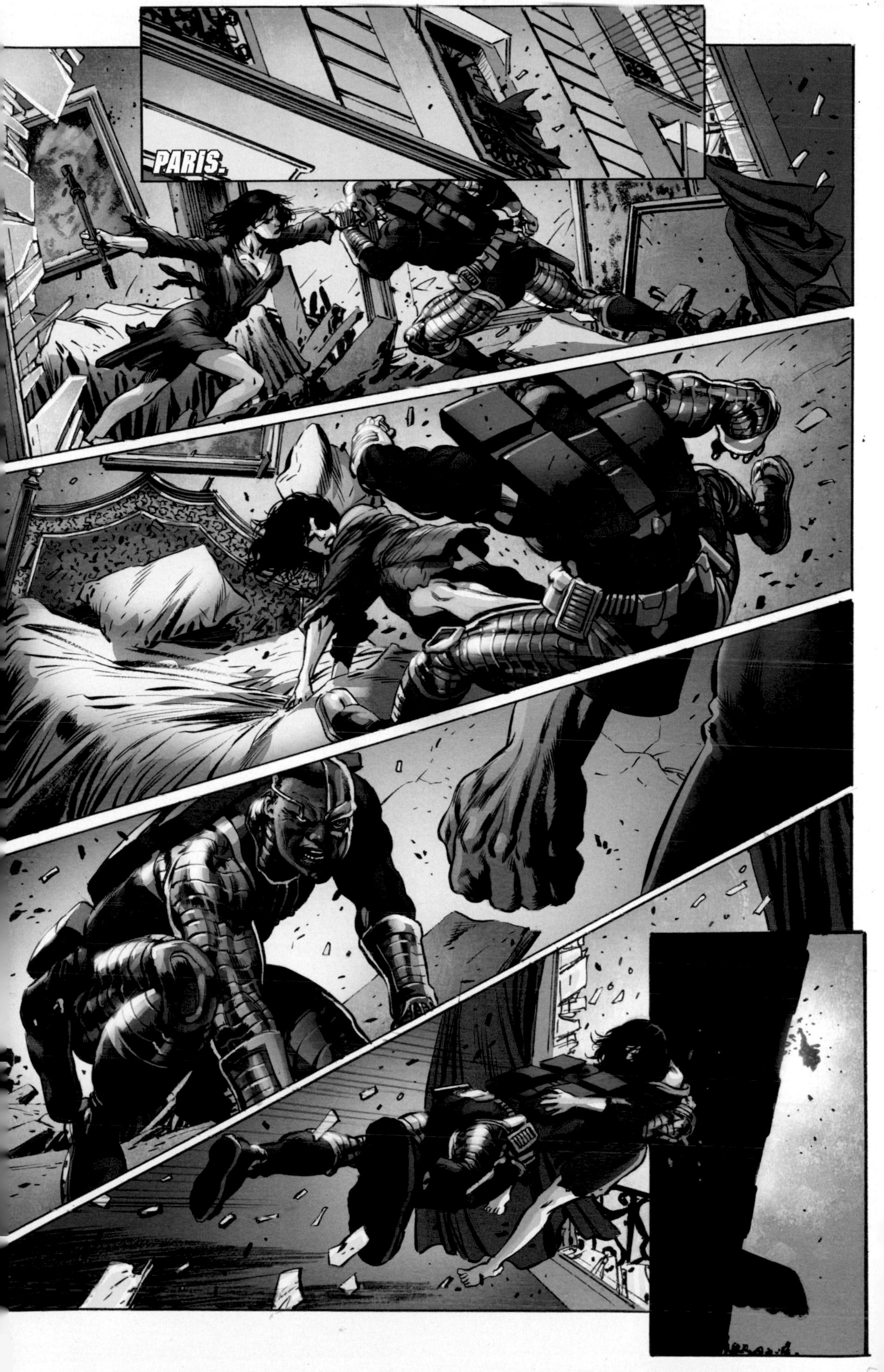
PARIS.

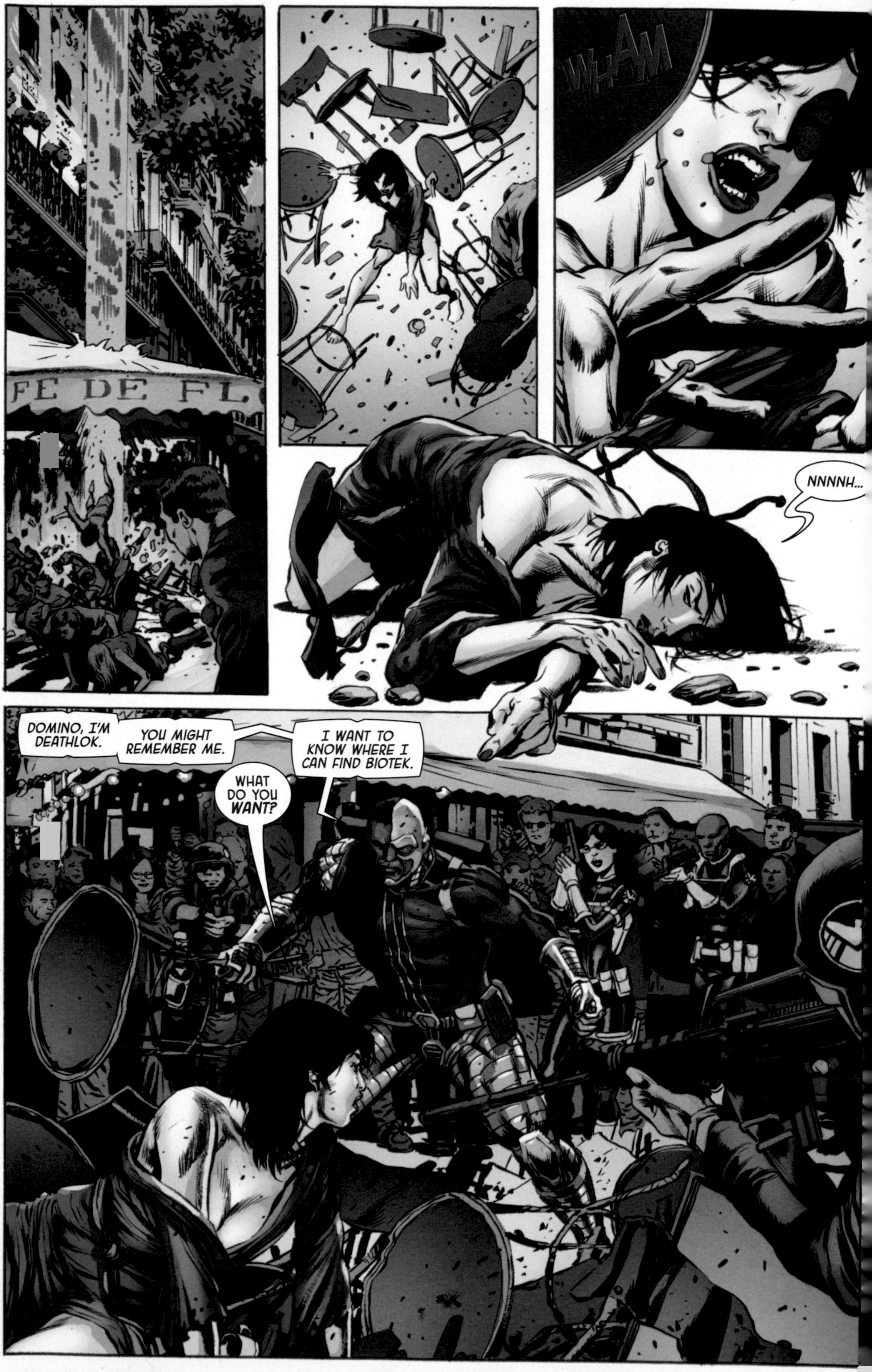
WHAM
FE DE FL
NNNNH...
DOMINO, I'M DEATHLOK.
YOU MIGHT REMEMBER ME.
WHAT DO YOU WANT?
I WANT TO KNOW WHERE I CAN FIND BIOTEK.

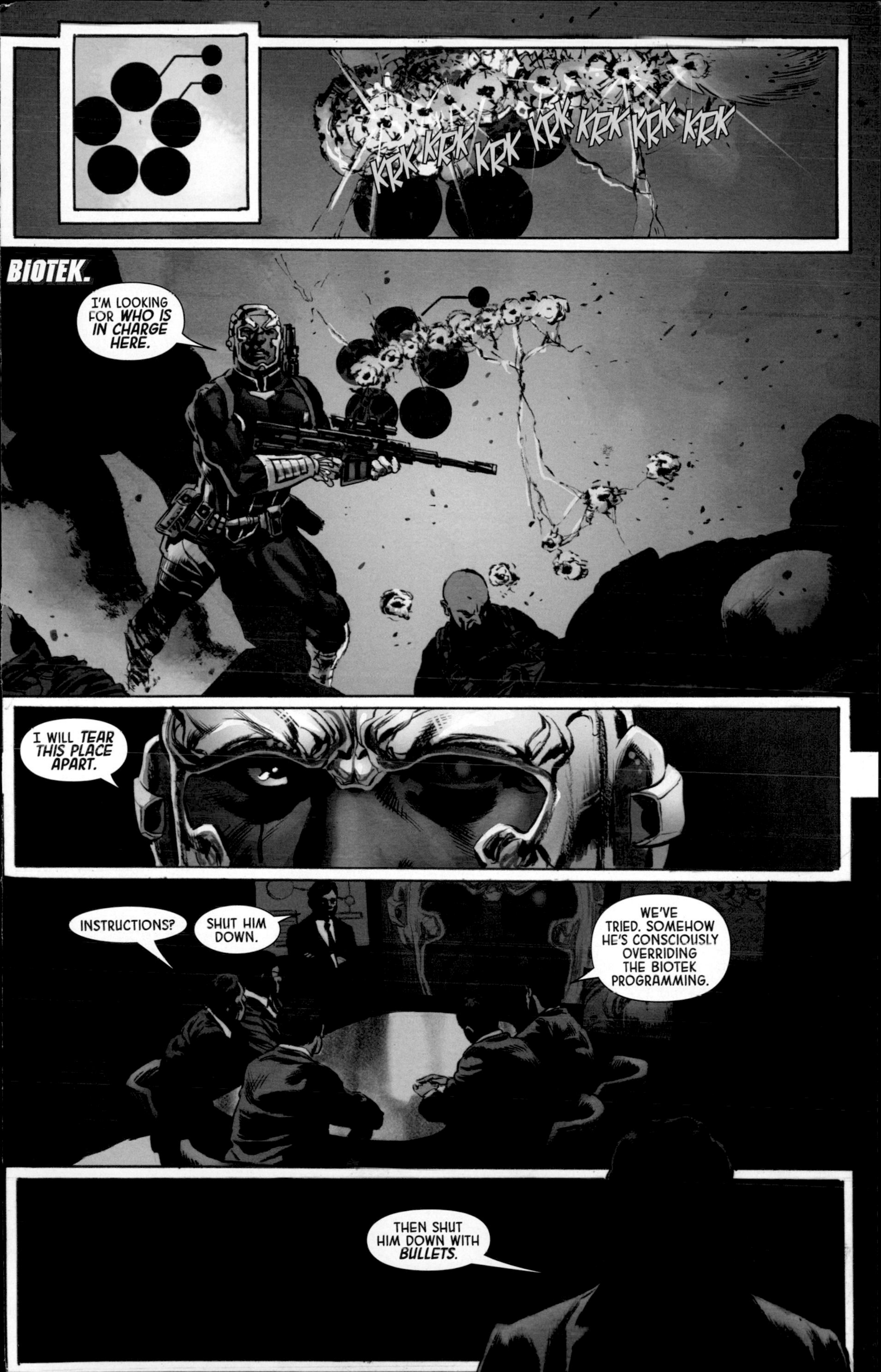
KRK KRK KRK KRK KRK KRK KRK
BIOTEK.
I'M LOOKING FOR WHO IS IN CHARGE HERE.
I WILL TEAR THIS PLACE APART.
INSTRUCTIONS?
SHUT HIM DOWN.
WE'VE TRIED. SOMEHOW HE'S CONSCIOUSLY OVERRIDING THE BIOTEK PROGRAMMING.
THEN SHUT HIM DOWN WITH BULLETS.

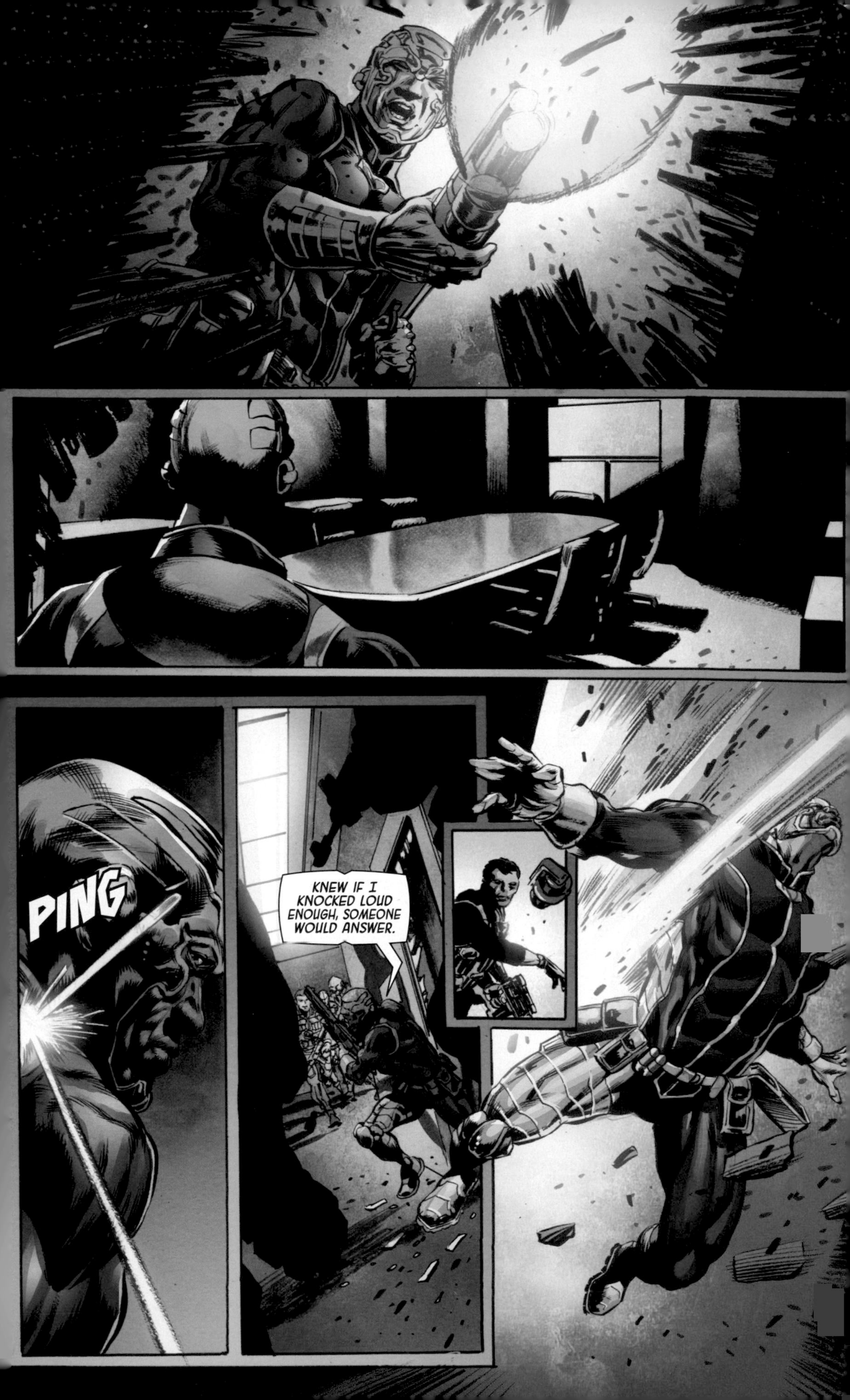
PING
KNEW IF I KNOCKED LOUD ENOUGH, SOMEONE WOULD ANSWER.

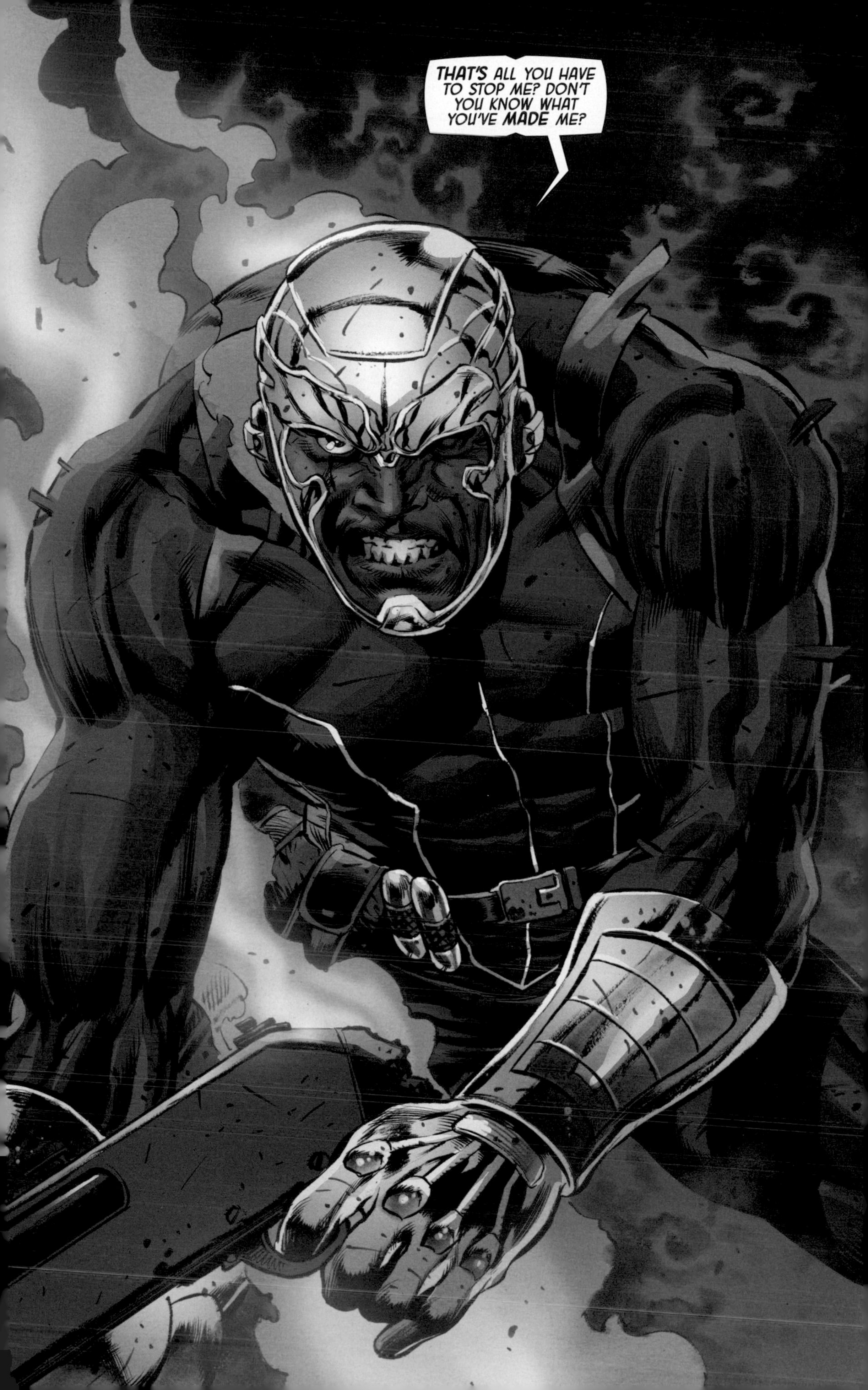
THAT'S ALL YOU HAVE TO STOP ME? DON'T YOU KNOW WHAT YOU'VE MADE ME?

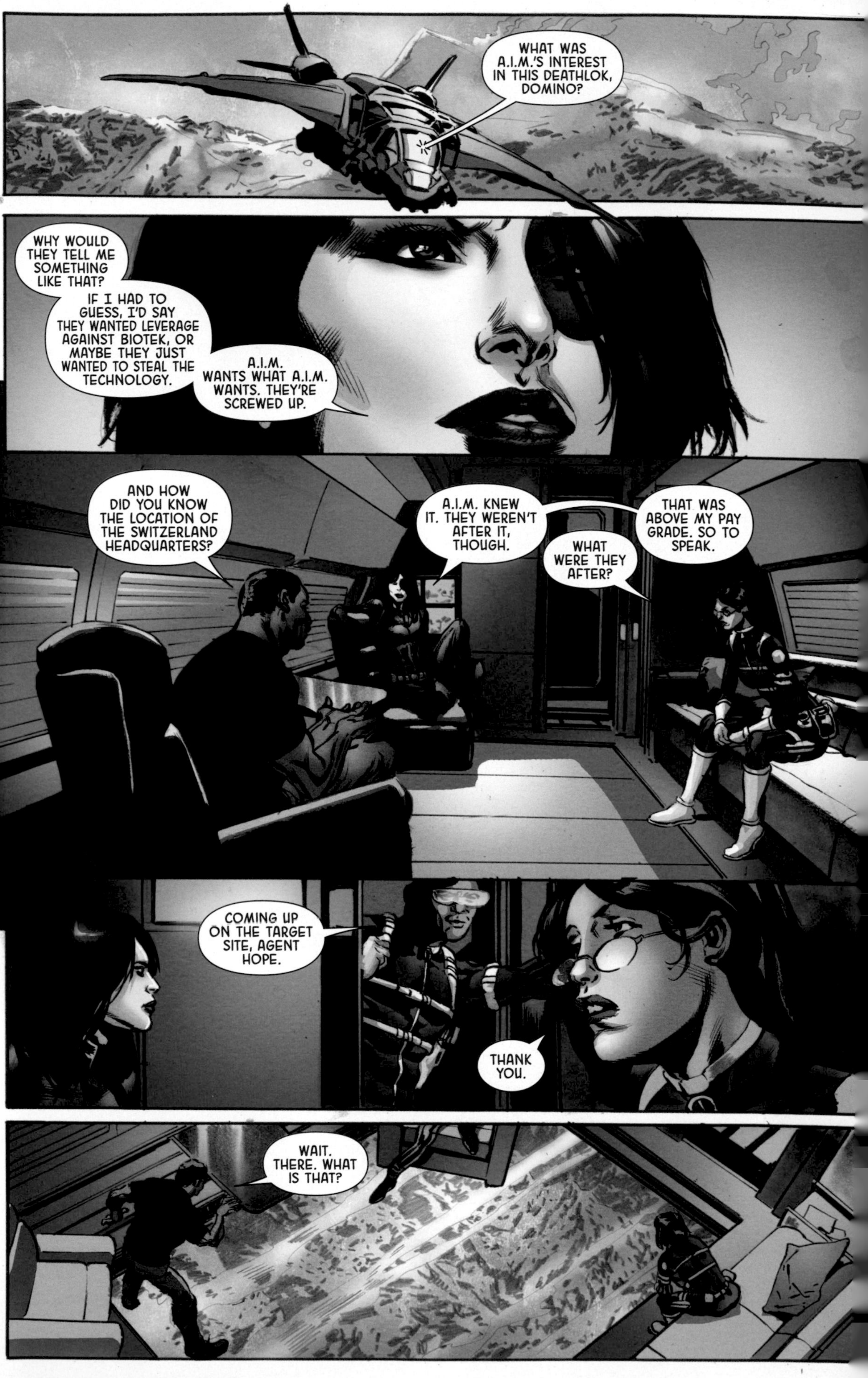
WHAT WAS A.I.M.'S INTEREST IN THIS DEATHLOK, DOMINO?
WHY WOULD THEY TELL ME SOMETHING LIKE THAT?
IF I HAD TO GUESS, I'D SAY THEY WANTED LEVERAGE AGAINST BIOTEK, OR MAYBE THEY JUST WANTED TO STEAL THE TECHNOLOGY.
A.I.M. WANTS WHAT A.I.M. WANTS. THEY'RE SCREWED UP.
AND HOW DID YOU KNOW THE LOCATION OF THE SWITZERLAND HEADQUARTERS?
A.I.M. KNEW IT. THEY WEREN'T AFTER IT, THOUGH.
WHAT WERE THEY AFTER?
THAT WAS ABOVE MY PAY GRADE. SO TO SPEAK.
COMING UP ON THE TARGET SITE, AGENT HOPE.
THANK YOU.
WAIT. THERE. WHAT IS THAT?

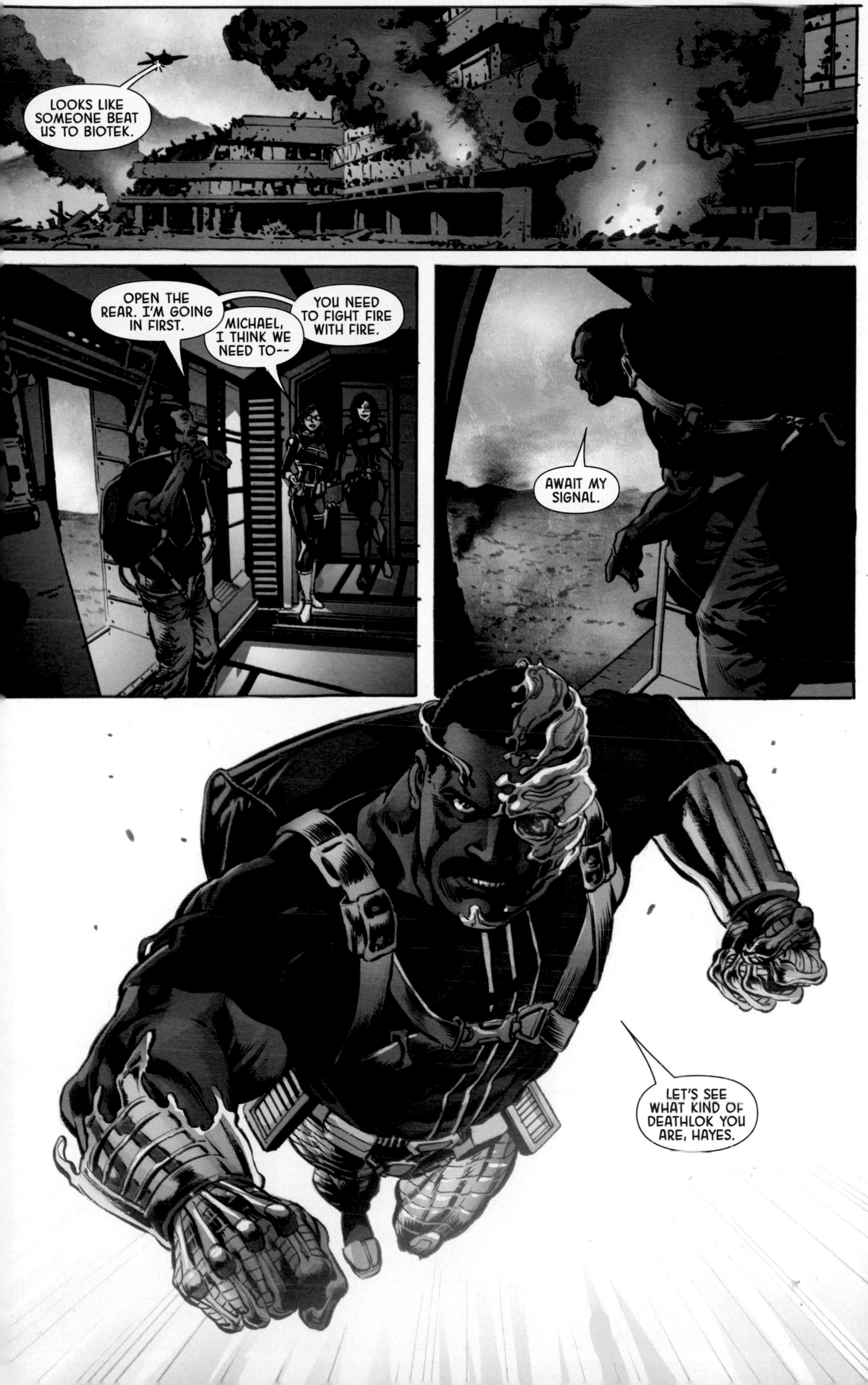
LOOKS LIKE SOMEONE BEAT US TO BIOTEK.
OPEN THE REAR. I'M GOING IN FIRST.
MICHAEL, I THINK WE NEED TO--
YOU NEED TO FIGHT FIRE WITH FIRE.
AWAIT MY SIGNAL.
LET'S SEE WHAT KIND OF DEATHLOK YOU ARE, HAYES.

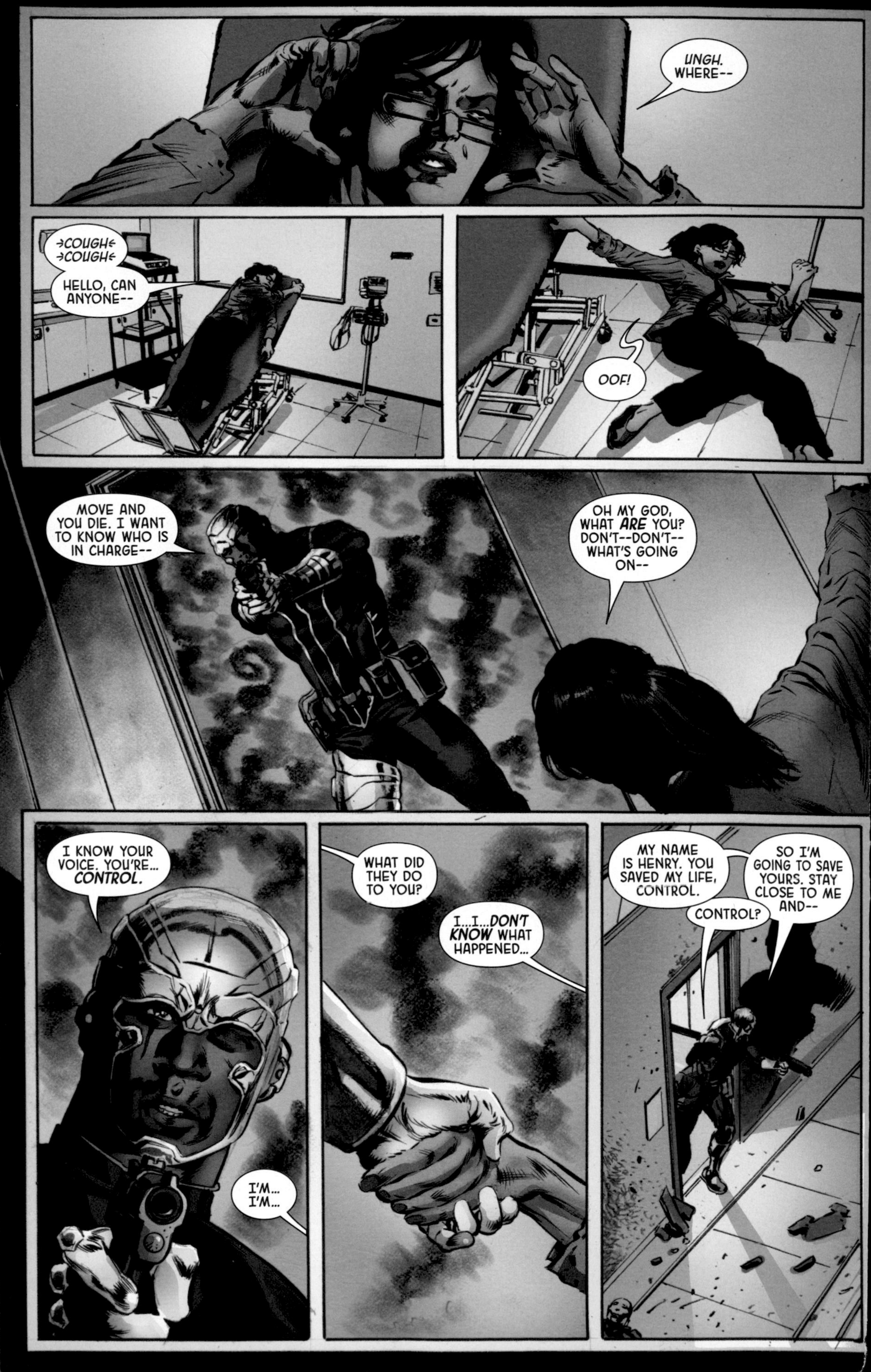
UNGH. WHERE--
→COUGH← →COUGH←
HELLO, CAN ANYONE--
OOF!
MOVE AND YOU DIE. I WANT TO KNOW WHO IS IN CHARGE--
OH MY GOD, WHAT ARE YOU? DON'T--DON'T--WHAT'S GOING ON--
I KNOW YOUR VOICE. YOU'RE... CONTROL.
I'M... I'M...
WHAT DID THEY DO TO YOU?
I...I...DON'T KNOW WHAT HAPPENED...
MY NAME IS HENRY. YOU SAVED MY LIFE, CONTROL.
SO I'M GOING TO SAVE YOURS. STAY CLOSE TO ME AND--
CONTROL?

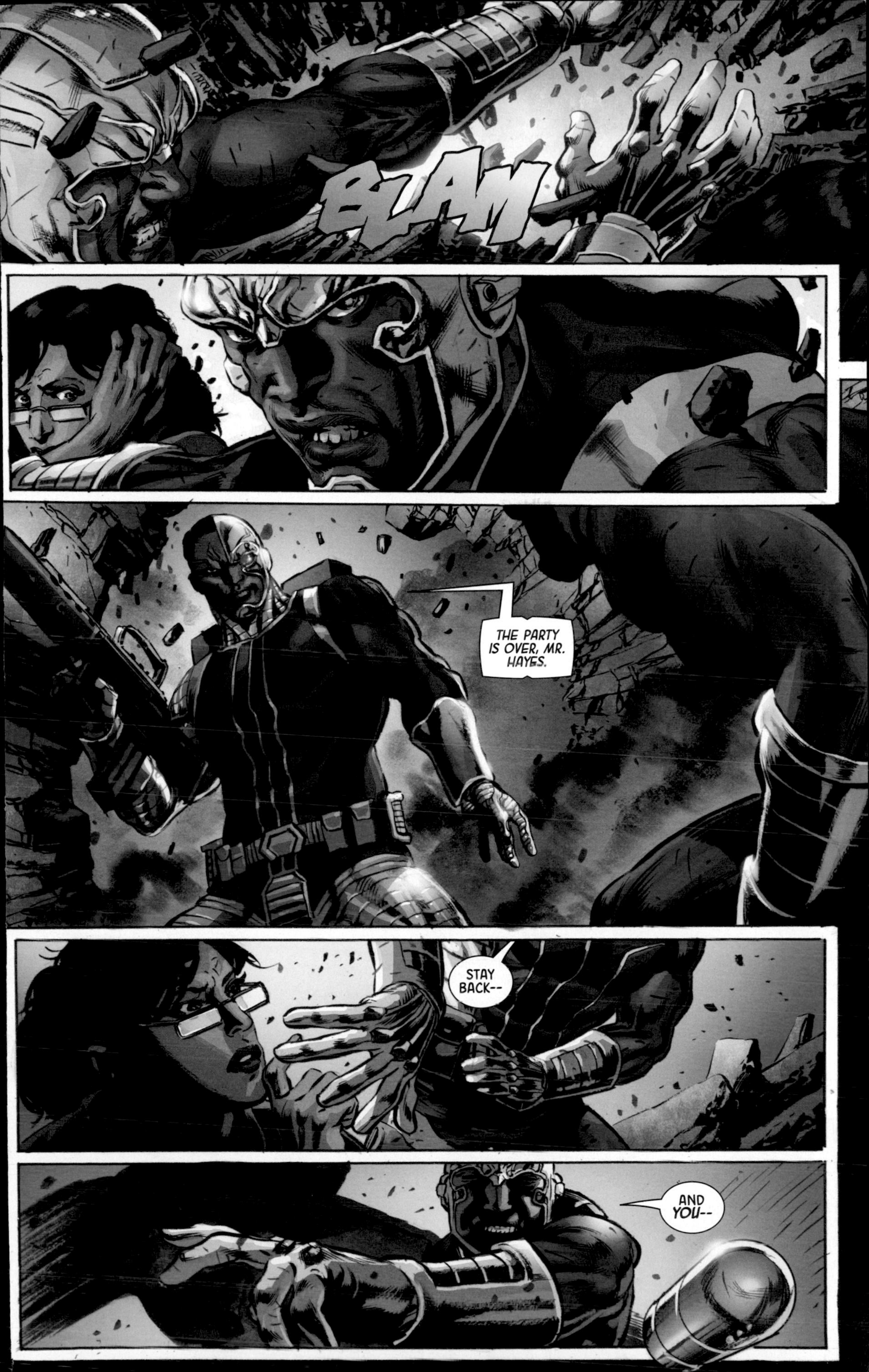
BLAM
THE PARTY IS OVER, MR. HAYES.
STAY BACK--
AND YOU--

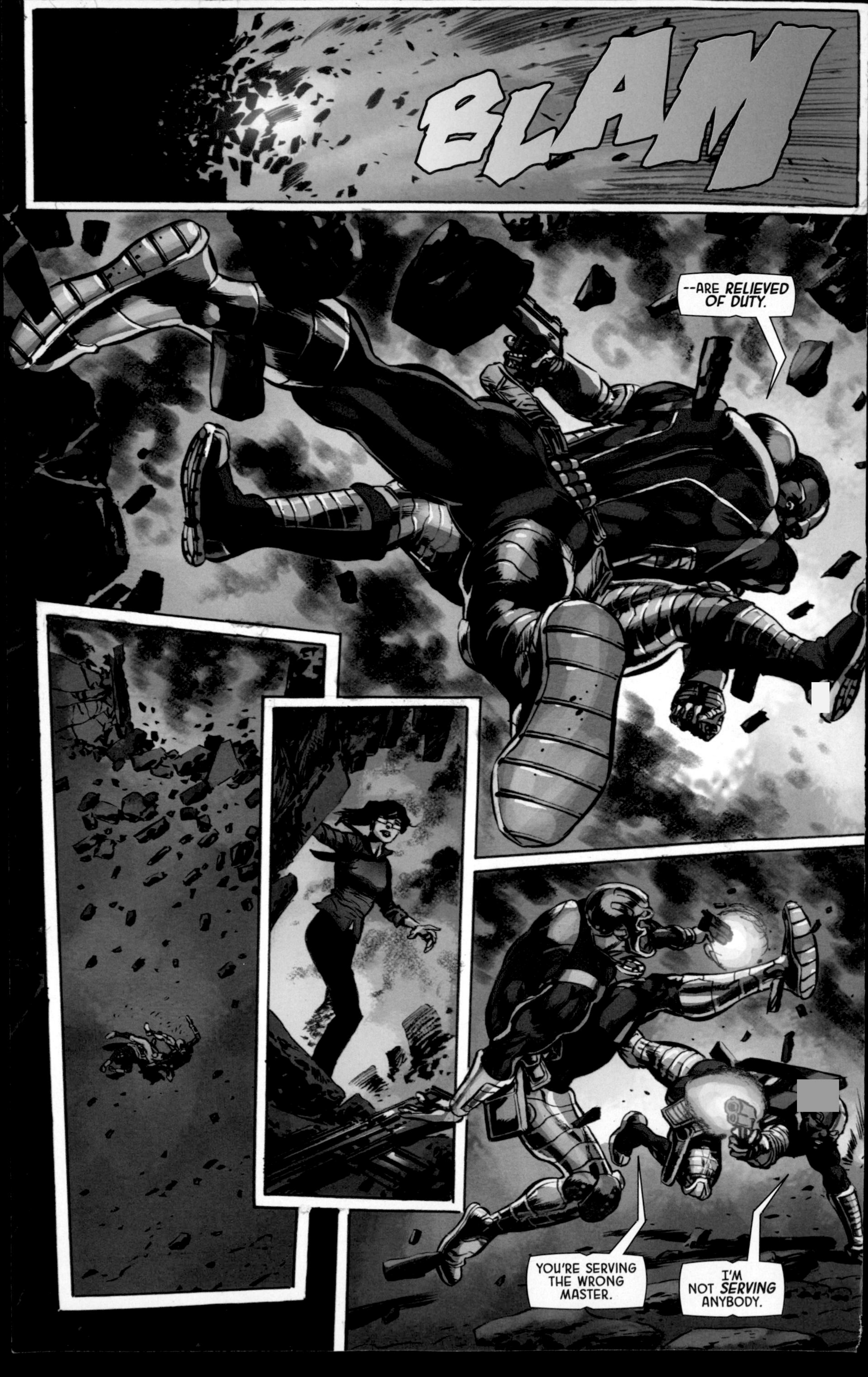
BLAM
--ARE RELIEVED OF DUTY.
YOU'RE SERVING THE WRONG MASTER.
I'M NOT SERVING ANYBODY.

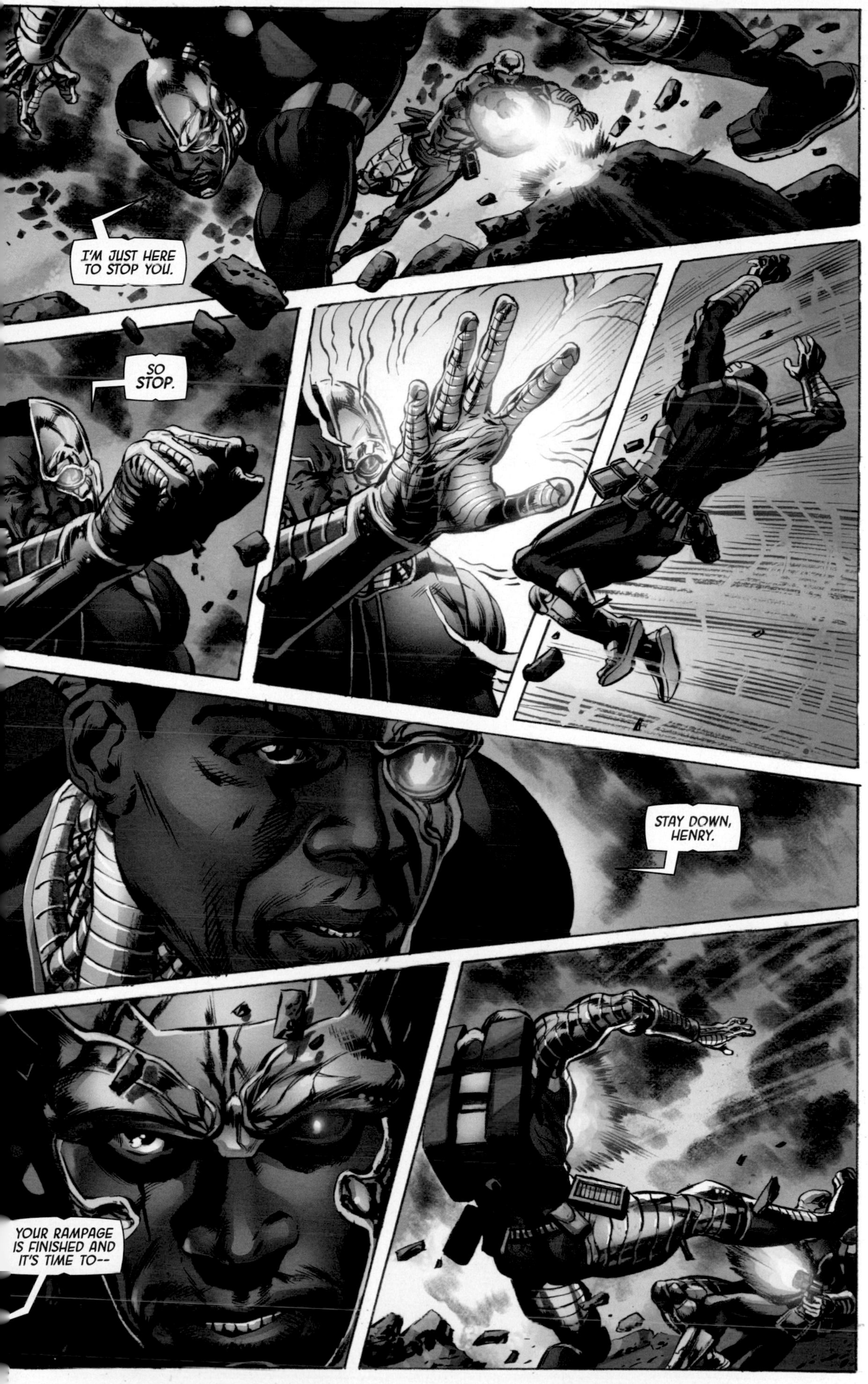
I'M JUST HERE TO STOP YOU.
SO STOP.
STAY DOWN, HENRY.
YOUR RAMPAGE IS FINISHED AND IT'S TIME TO--

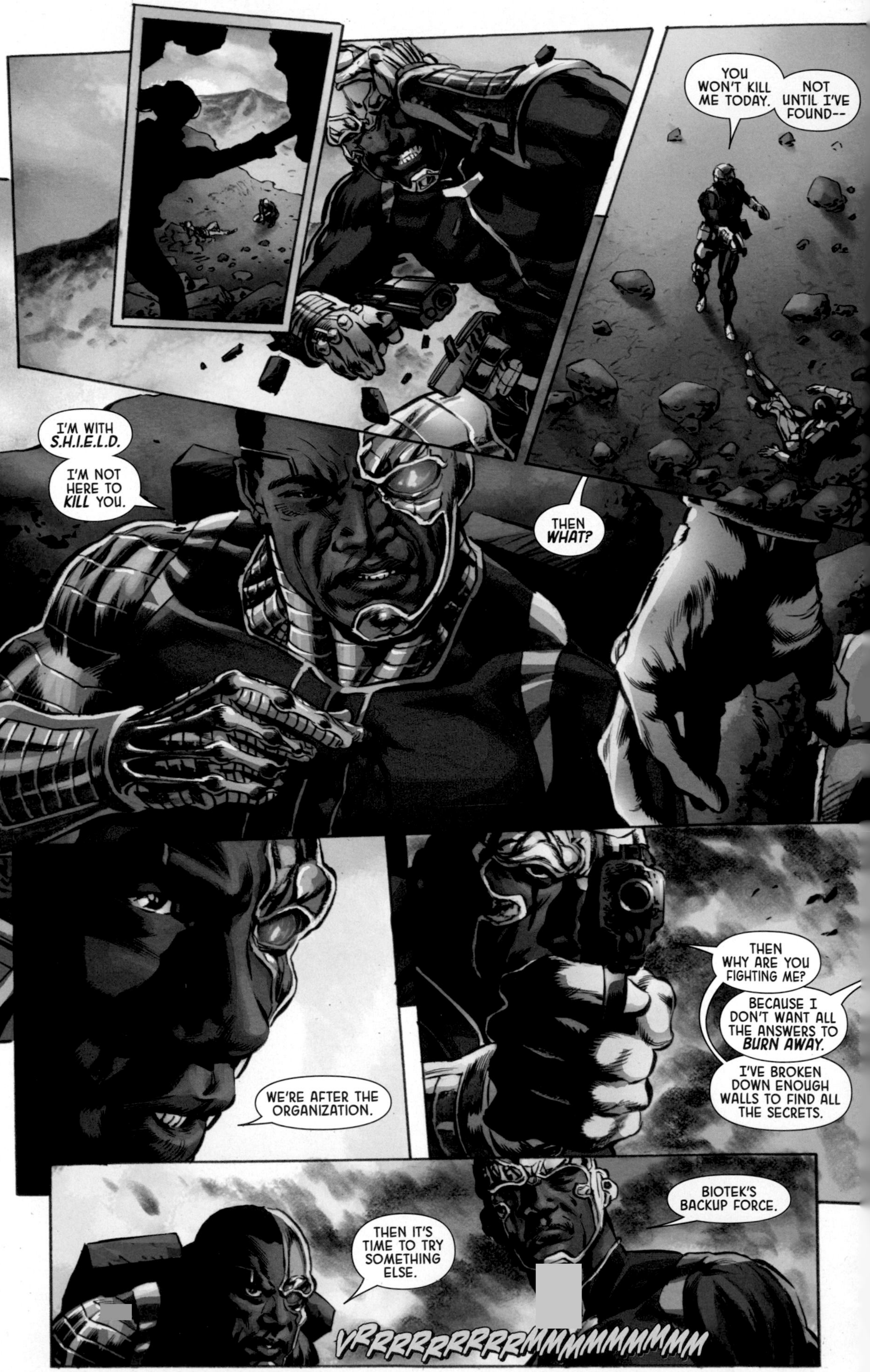
YOU WON'T KILL ME TODAY.
NOT UNTIL I'VE FOUND--
I'M WITH *S.H.I.E.L.D.*
I'M NOT HERE TO *KILL* YOU.
THEN *WHAT?*
WE'RE AFTER THE ORGANIZATION.
THEN WHY ARE YOU FIGHTING ME?
BECAUSE I DON'T WANT ALL THE ANSWERS TO *BURN AWAY.*
I'VE BROKEN DOWN ENOUGH WALLS TO FIND ALL THE SECRETS.
THEN IT'S TIME TO TRY SOMETHING ELSE.
BIOTEK'S BACKUP FORCE.
VRRRRRRRRRMMMMMMMMM

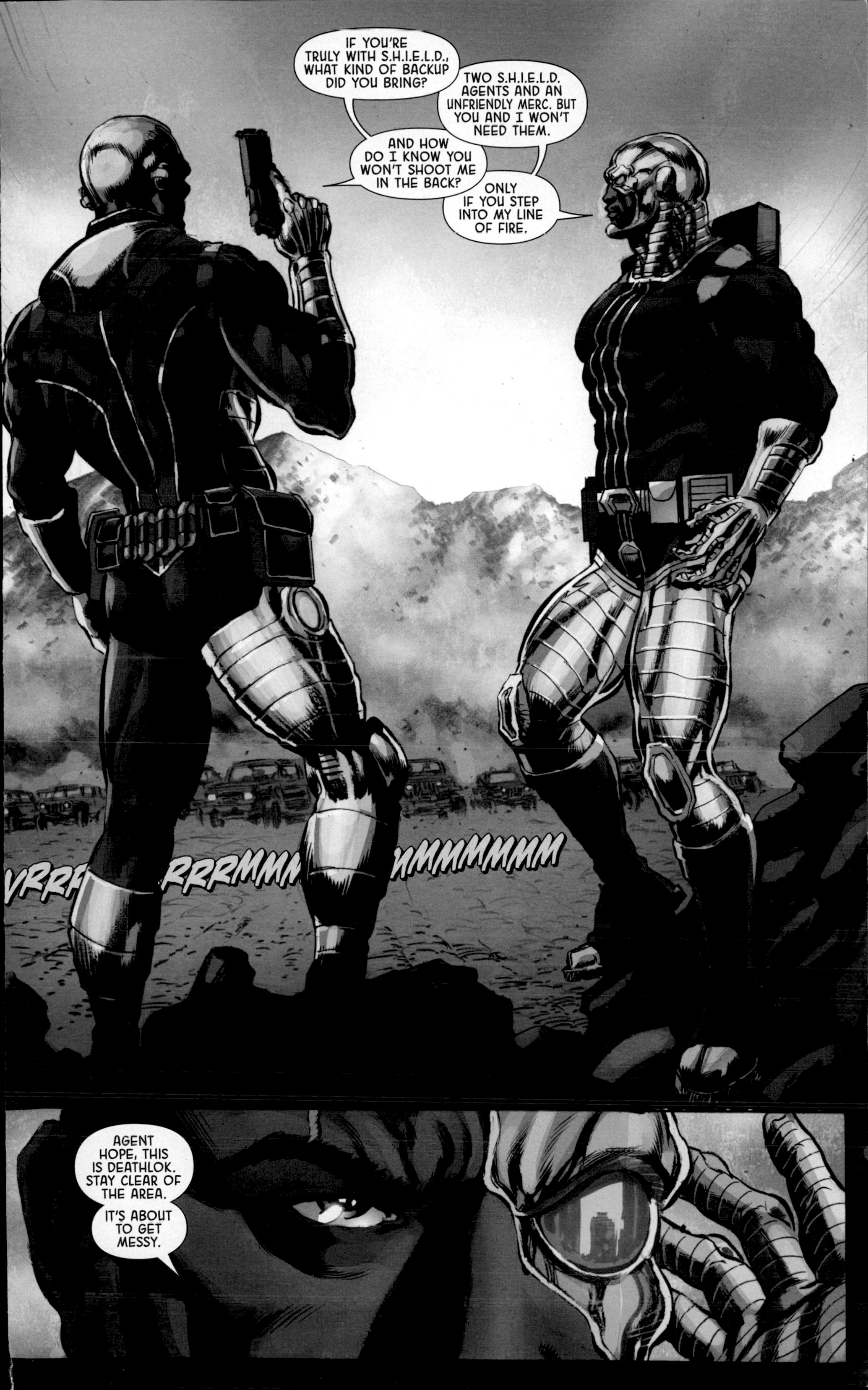
IF YOU'RE TRULY WITH S.H.I.E.L.D., WHAT KIND OF BACKUP DID YOU BRING?
TWO S.H.I.E.L.D. AGENTS AND AN UNFRIENDLY MERC. BUT YOU AND I WON'T NEED THEM.
AND HOW DO I KNOW YOU WON'T SHOOT ME IN THE BACK?
ONLY IF YOU STEP INTO MY LINE OF FIRE.
VRRRRRRRMMMMMMMMMMMMM
AGENT HOPE, THIS IS DEATHLOK. STAY CLEAR OF THE AREA.
IT'S ABOUT TO GET MESSY.

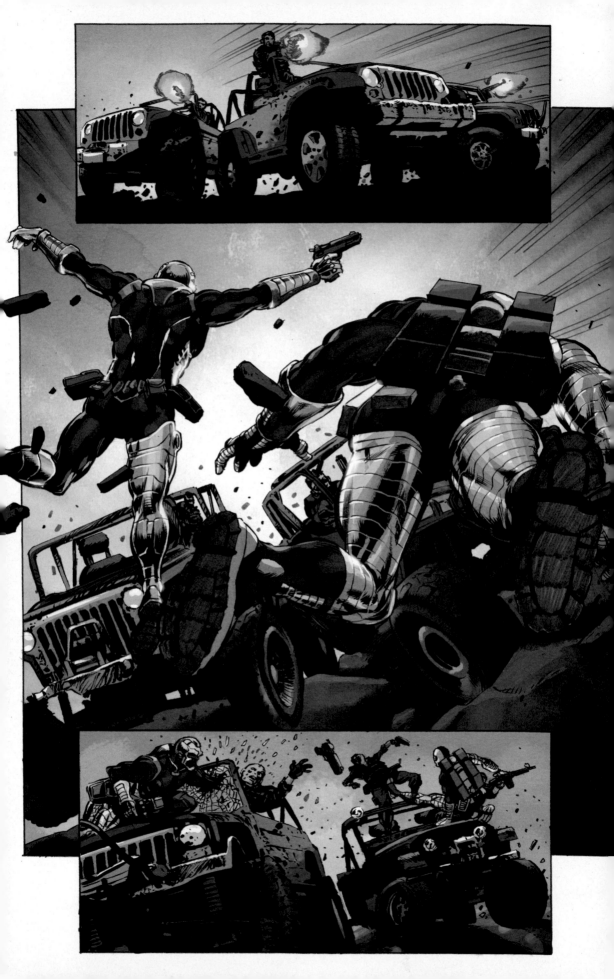

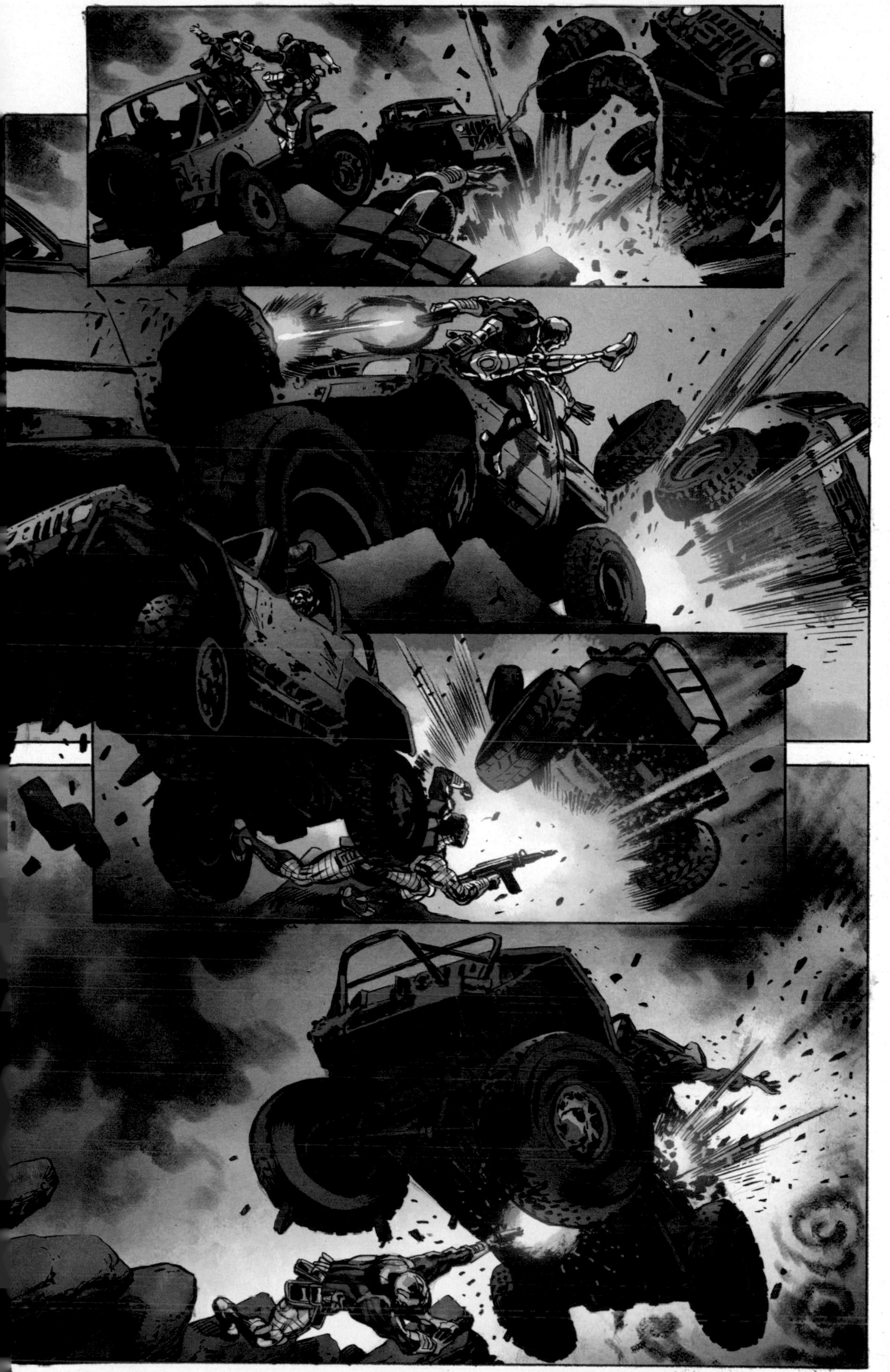

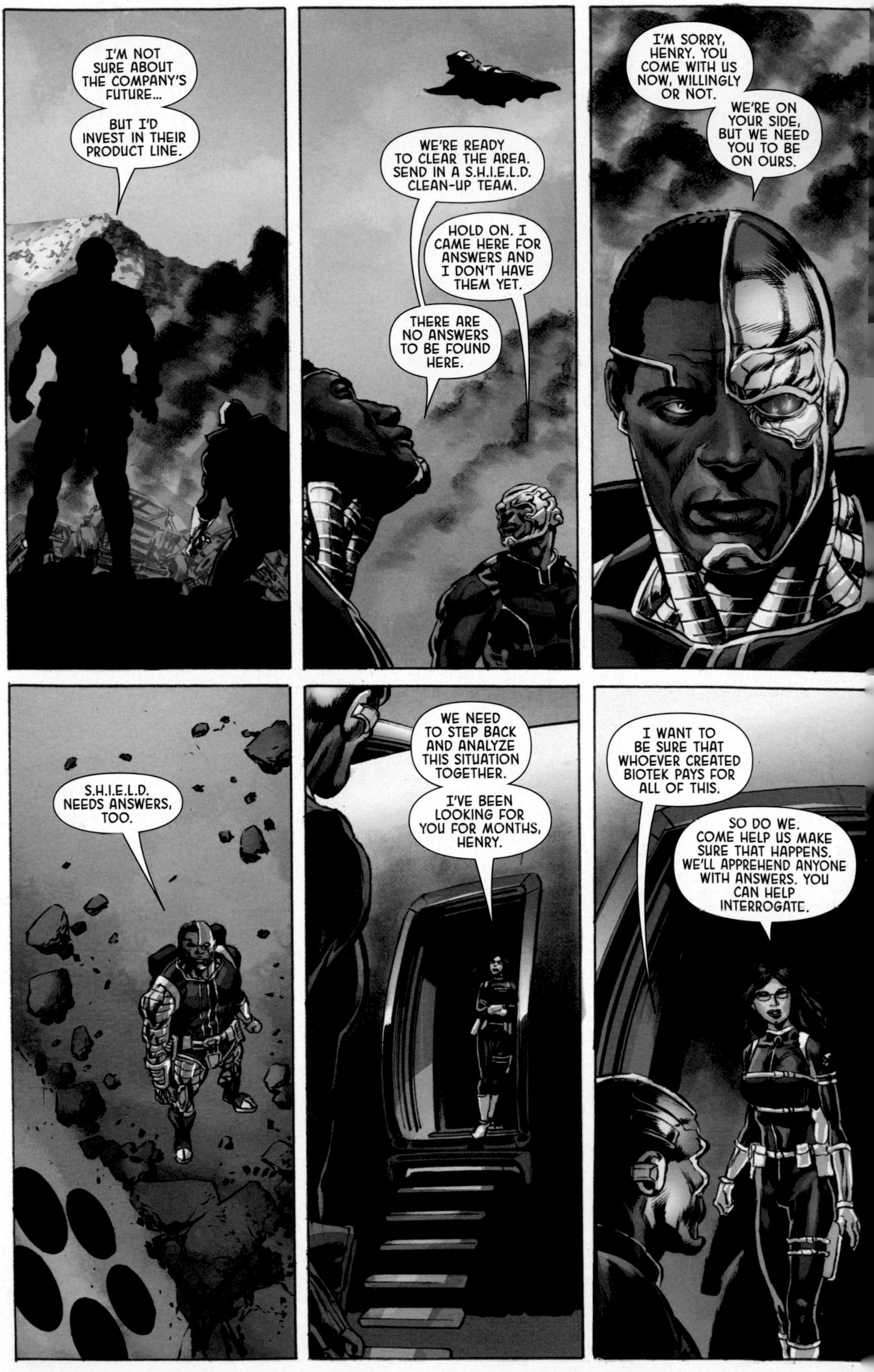
I'M NOT SURE ABOUT THE COMPANY'S FUTURE...
BUT I'D INVEST IN THEIR PRODUCT LINE.
WE'RE READY TO CLEAR THE AREA. SEND IN A S.H.I.E.L.D. CLEAN-UP TEAM.
HOLD ON. I CAME HERE FOR ANSWERS AND I DON'T HAVE THEM YET.
THERE ARE NO ANSWERS TO BE FOUND HERE.
I'M SORRY, HENRY. YOU COME WITH US NOW, WILLINGLY OR NOT.
WE'RE ON YOUR SIDE, BUT WE NEED YOU TO BE ON OURS.
S.H.I.E.L.D. NEEDS ANSWERS, TOO.
WE NEED TO STEP BACK AND ANALYZE THIS SITUATION TOGETHER.
I'VE BEEN LOOKING FOR YOU FOR MONTHS, HENRY.
I WANT TO BE SURE THAT WHOEVER CREATED BIOTEK PAYS FOR ALL OF THIS.
SO DO WE. COME HELP US MAKE SURE THAT HAPPENS. WE'LL APPREHEND ANYONE WITH ANSWERS. YOU CAN HELP INTERROGATE.

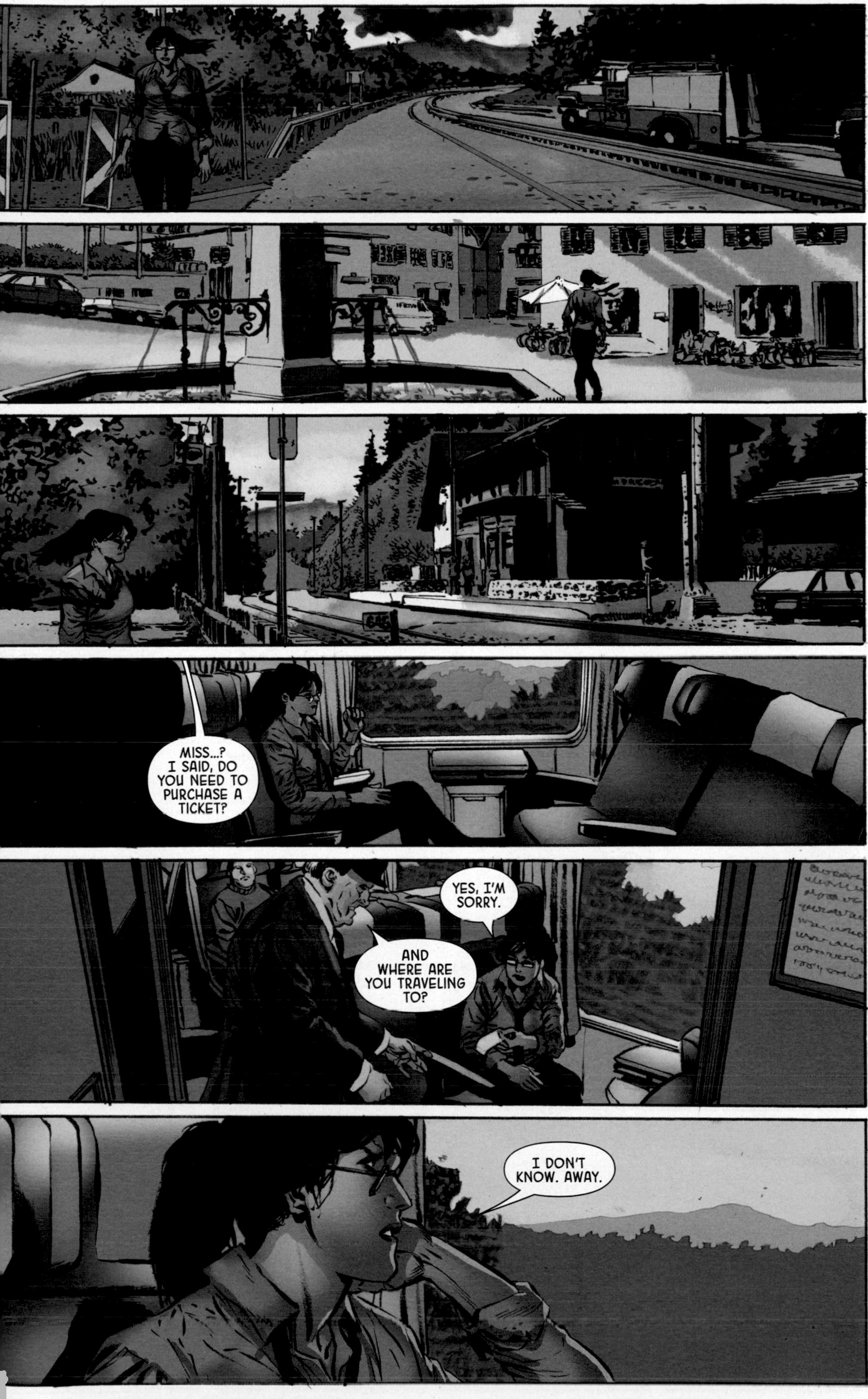
MISS...? I SAID, DO YOU NEED TO PURCHASE A TICKET?
YES, I'M SORRY.
AND WHERE ARE YOU TRAVELING TO?
I DON'T KNOW. AWAY.

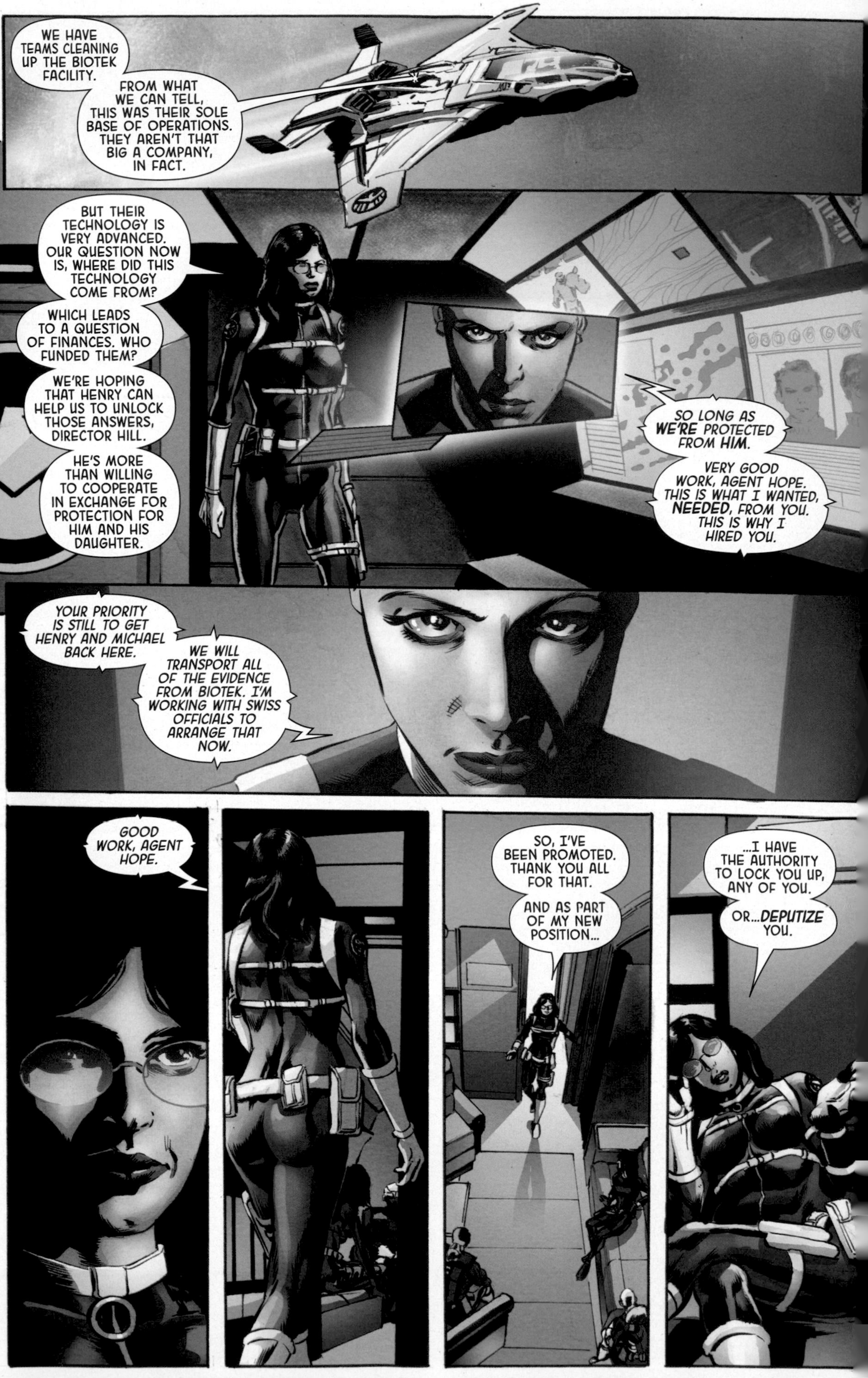
WE HAVE TEAMS CLEANING UP THE BIOTEK FACILITY.
FROM WHAT WE CAN TELL, THIS WAS THEIR SOLE BASE OF OPERATIONS. THEY AREN'T THAT BIG A COMPANY, IN FACT.
BUT THEIR TECHNOLOGY IS VERY ADVANCED. OUR QUESTION NOW IS, WHERE DID THIS TECHNOLOGY COME FROM?
WHICH LEADS TO A QUESTION OF FINANCES. WHO FUNDED THEM?
WE'RE HOPING THAT HENRY CAN HELP US TO UNLOCK THOSE ANSWERS, DIRECTOR HILL.
HE'S MORE THAN WILLING TO COOPERATE IN EXCHANGE FOR PROTECTION FOR HIM AND HIS DAUGHTER.
SO LONG AS WE'RE PROTECTED FROM HIM.
VERY GOOD WORK, AGENT HOPE. THIS IS WHAT I WANTED, NEEDED, FROM YOU. THIS IS WHY I HIRED YOU.
YOUR PRIORITY IS STILL TO GET HENRY AND MICHAEL BACK HERE.
WE WILL TRANSPORT ALL OF THE EVIDENCE FROM BIOTEK. I'M WORKING WITH SWISS OFFICIALS TO ARRANGE THAT NOW.
GOOD WORK, AGENT HOPE.
SO, I'VE BEEN PROMOTED. THANK YOU ALL FOR THAT.
AND AS PART OF MY NEW POSITION...
...I HAVE THE AUTHORITY TO LOCK YOU UP, ANY OF YOU.
OR...DEPUTIZE YOU.

SO TO START THIS PROCESS, I NEED YOU ALL TO TELL ME EVERYTHING YOU KNOW.

EVERYTHING ABOUT BIOTEK.

STARTING WITH YOU, DOMINO.

TELL ME ANYTHING I DON'T KNOW ALREADY.

HENRY...

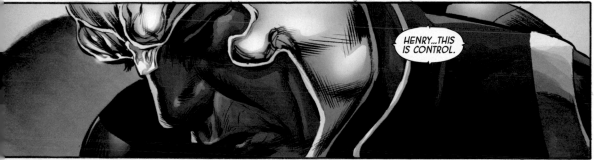

HENRY...THIS IS CONTROL.

CAN YOU HEAR ME, HENRY?

YOU CAUSED QUITE A MESS TODAY, HENRY.

BUT, HENRY, IF YOU WANT YOUR DAUGHTER TO LIVE ANOTHER 30 SECONDS...

...YOU'LL DO EXACTLY WHAT WE TELL YOU TO DO NEXT. DO YOU UNDERSTAND, HENRY?

... YES.

"YES," WHAT?

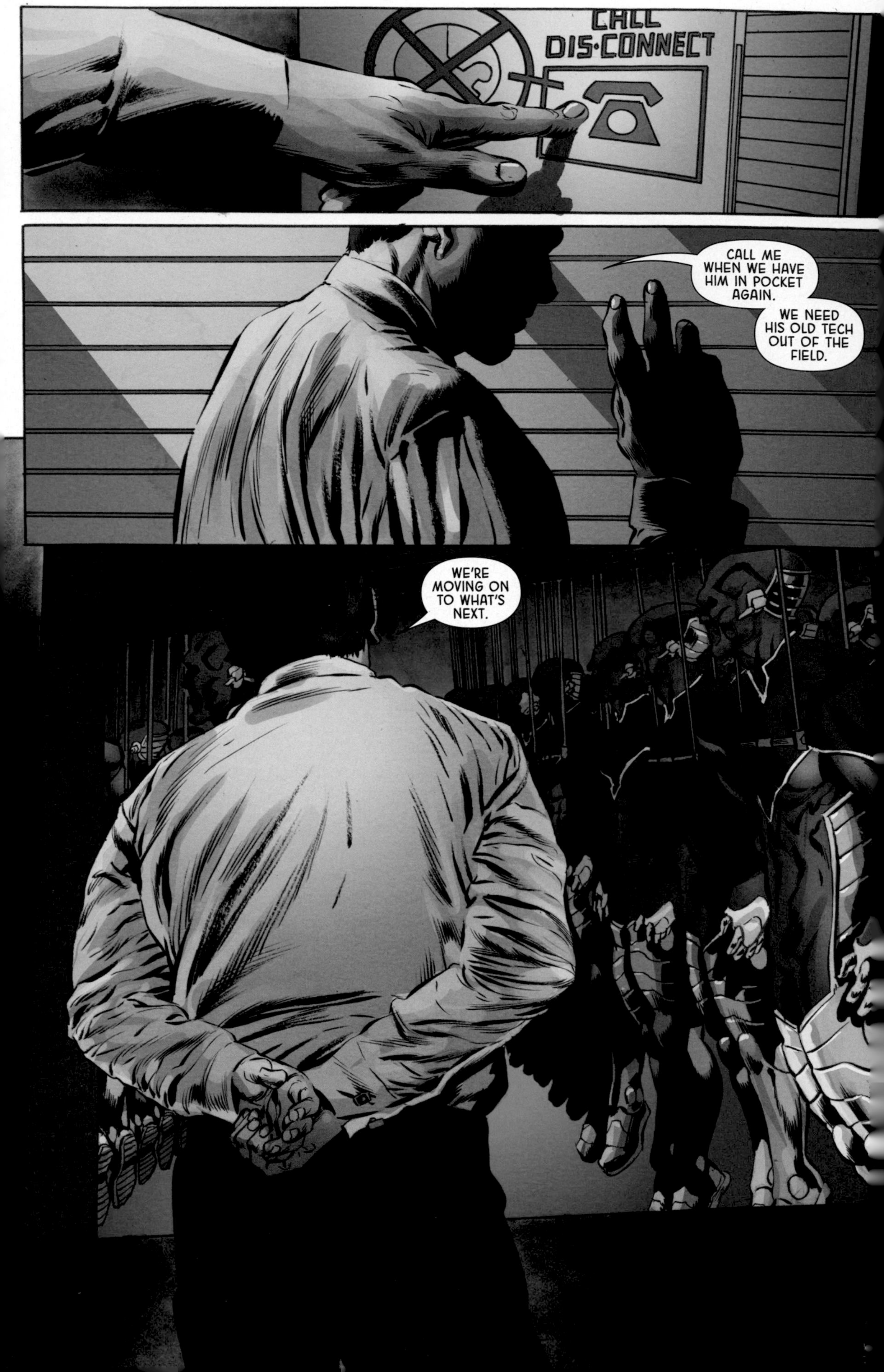
CALL DIS·CONNECT
CALL ME WHEN WE HAVE HIM IN POCKET AGAIN.
WE NEED HIS OLD TECH OUT OF THE FIELD.
WE'RE MOVING ON TO WHAT'S NEXT.

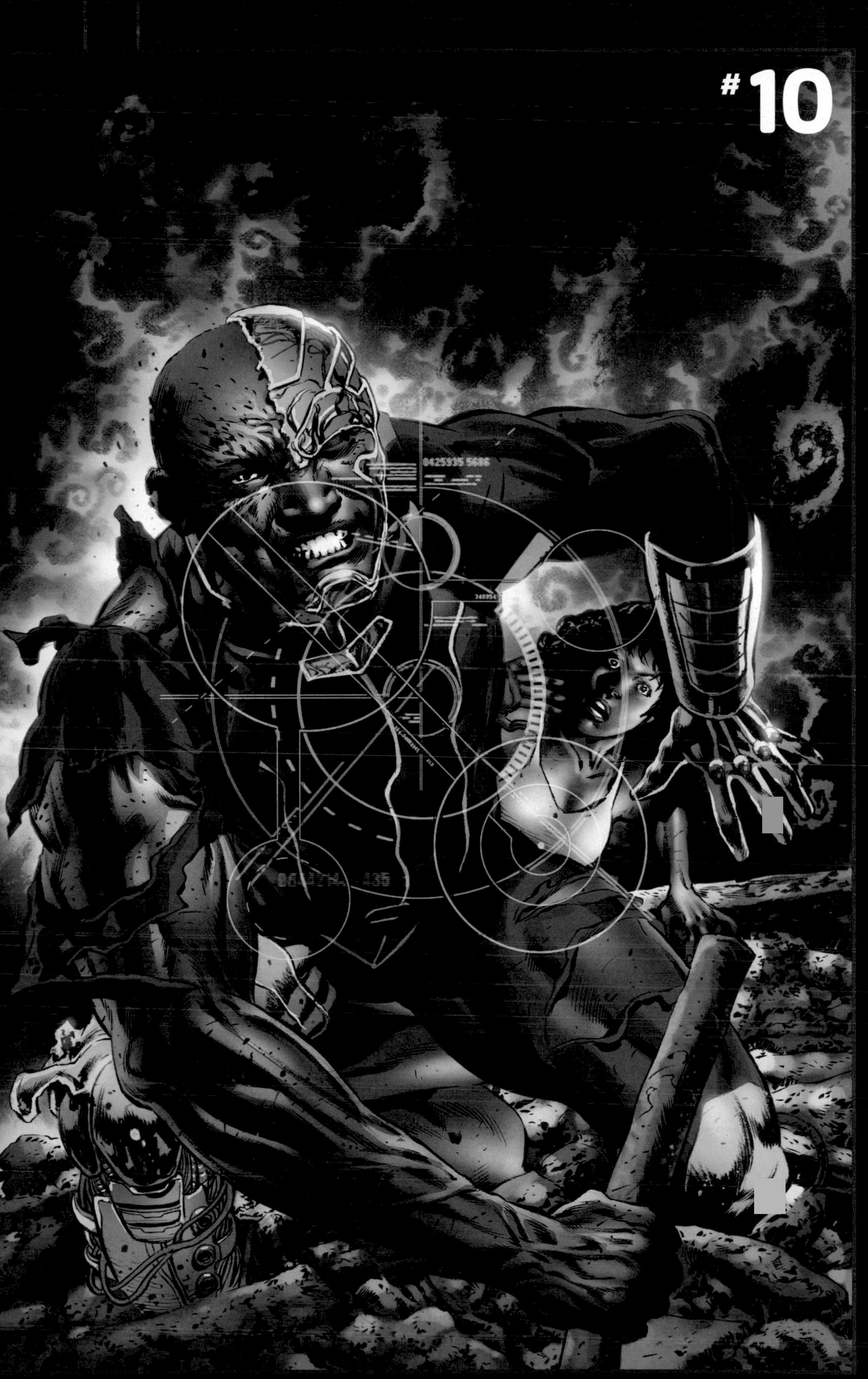
#10

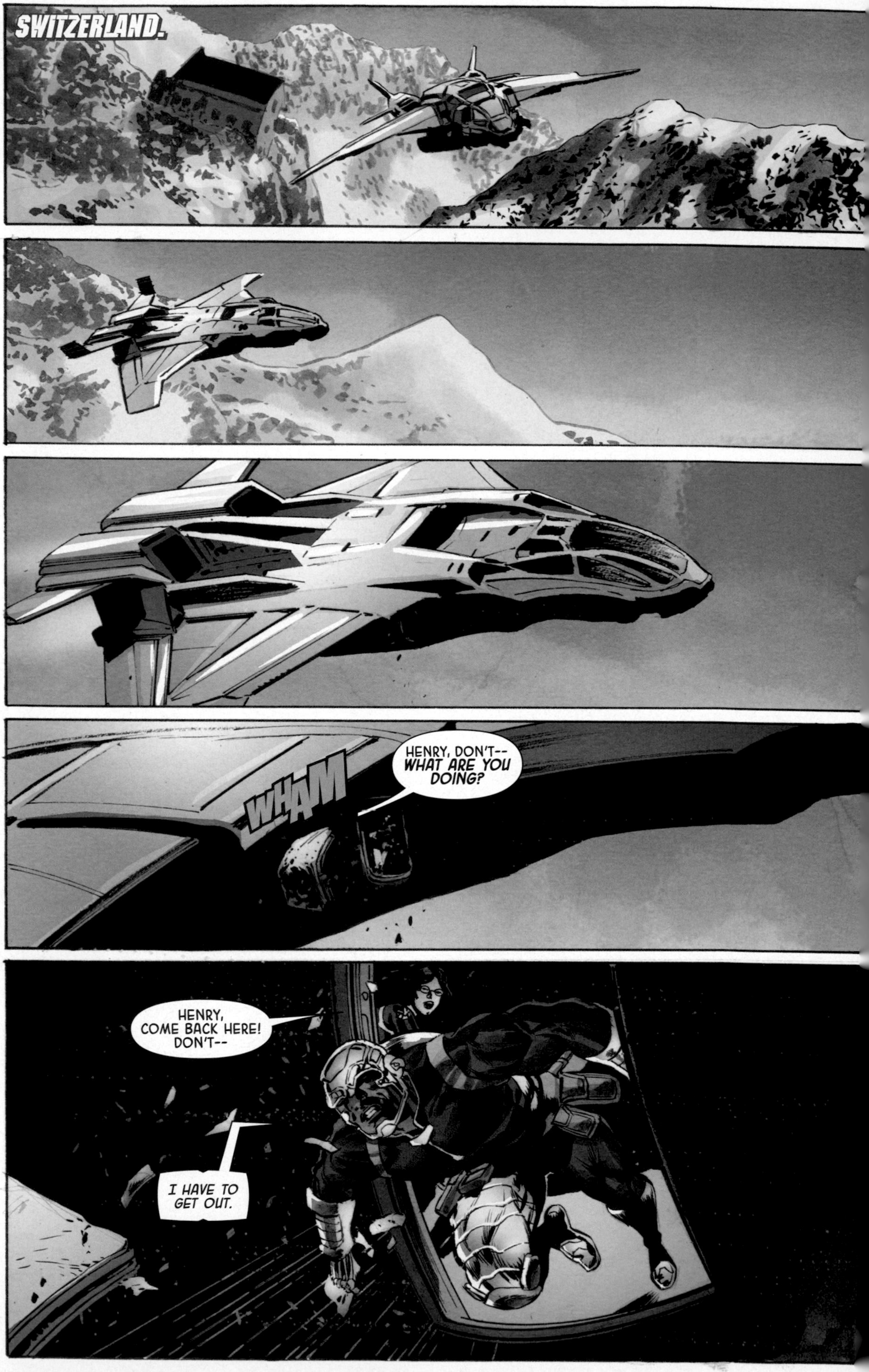
SWITZERLAND.
WHAM
HENRY, DON'T-- WHAT ARE YOU DOING?
HENRY, COME BACK HERE! DON'T--
I HAVE TO GET OUT.

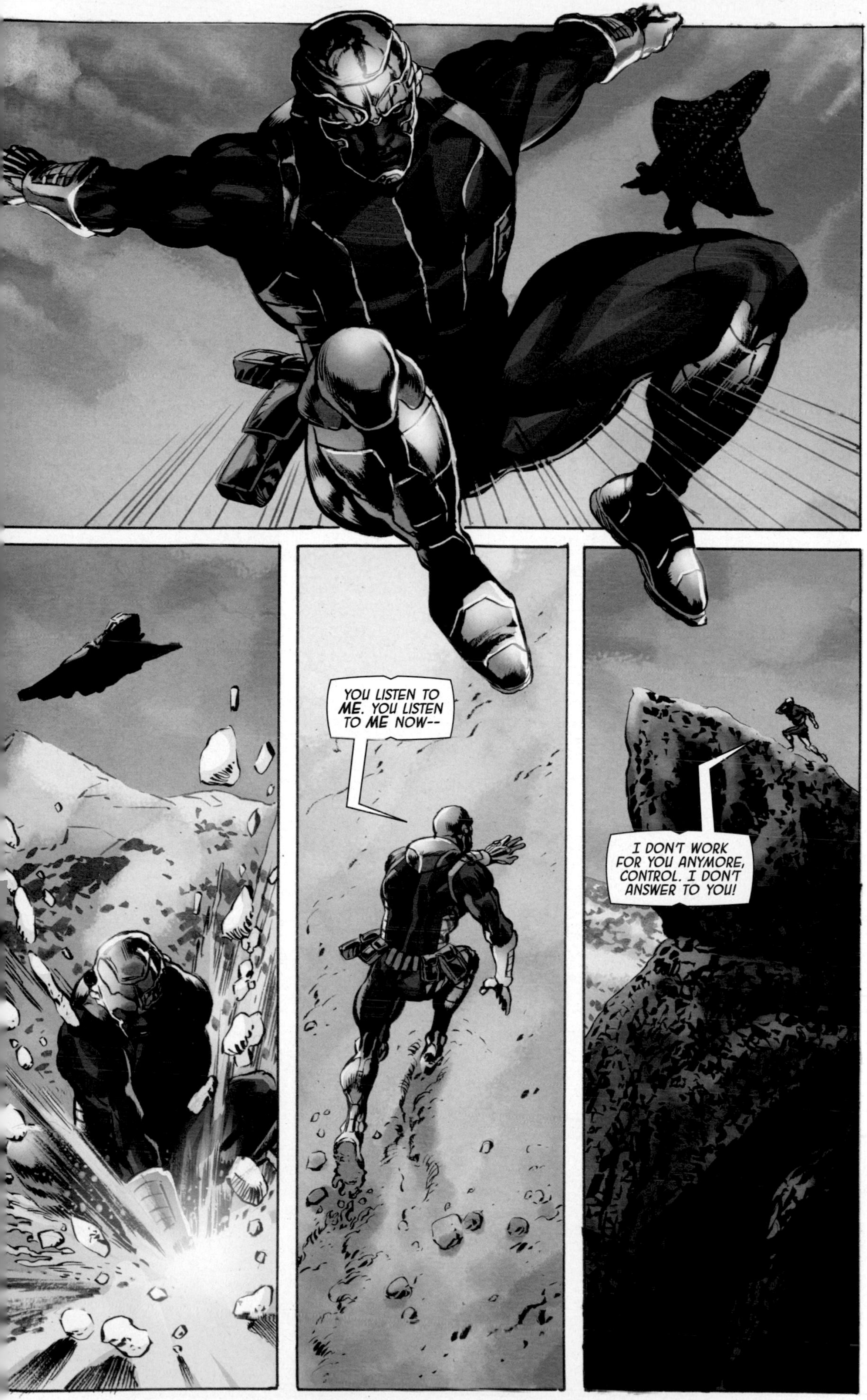
YOU LISTEN TO ME. YOU LISTEN TO ME NOW--
I DON'T WORK FOR YOU ANYMORE, CONTROL. I DON'T ANSWER TO YOU!

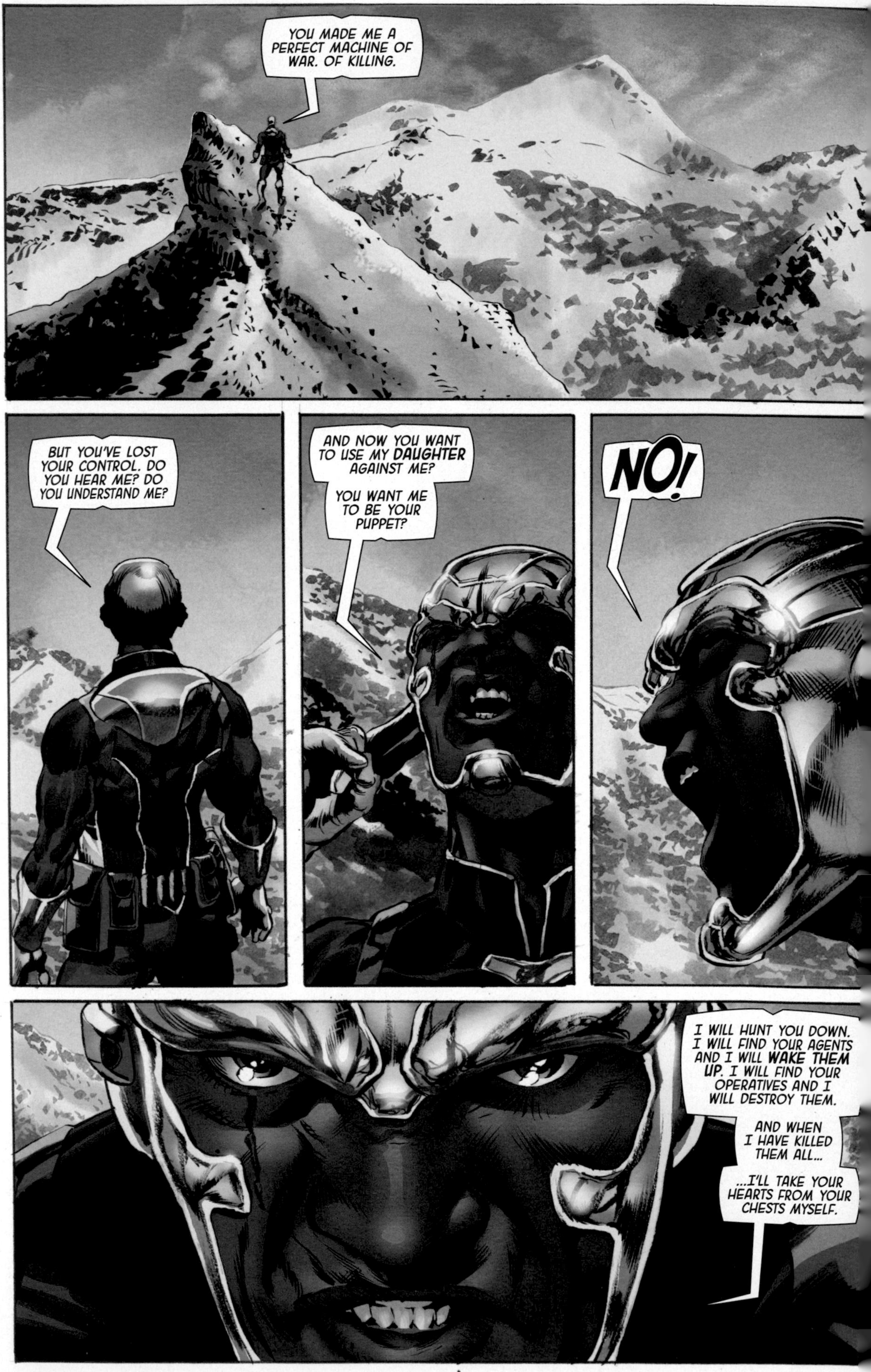
YOU MADE ME A PERFECT MACHINE OF WAR. OF KILLING.
BUT YOU'VE LOST YOUR CONTROL. DO YOU HEAR ME? DO YOU UNDERSTAND ME?
AND NOW YOU WANT TO USE MY DAUGHTER AGAINST ME?
YOU WANT ME TO BE YOUR PUPPET?
NO!
I WILL HUNT YOU DOWN. I WILL FIND YOUR AGENTS AND I WILL WAKE THEM UP. I WILL FIND YOUR OPERATIVES AND I WILL DESTROY THEM.
AND WHEN I HAVE KILLED THEM ALL...
...I'LL TAKE YOUR HEARTS FROM YOUR CHESTS MYSELF.

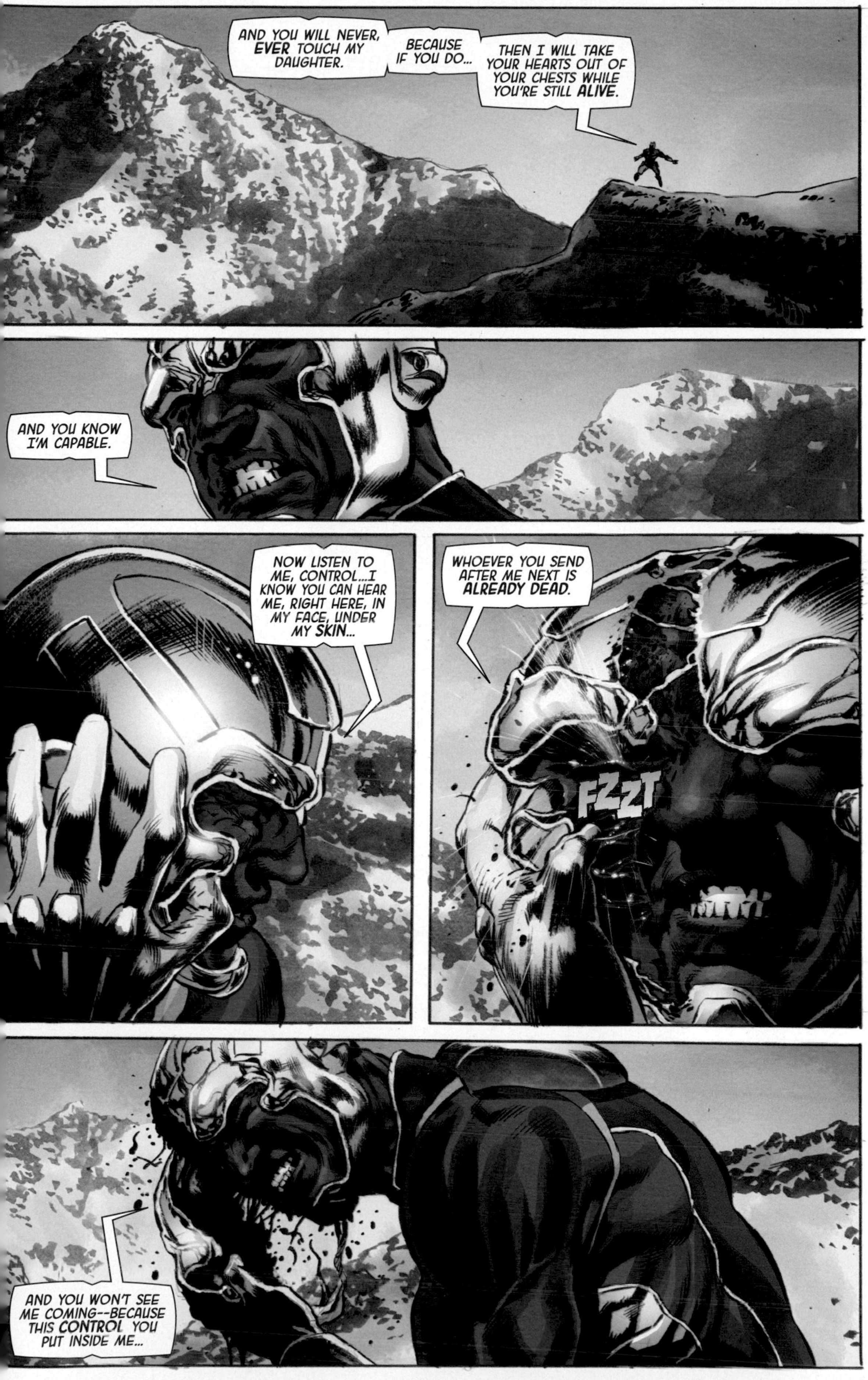
AND YOU WILL NEVER, EVER TOUCH MY DAUGHTER.
BECAUSE IF YOU DO...
THEN I WILL TAKE YOUR HEARTS OUT OF YOUR CHESTS WHILE YOU'RE STILL ALIVE.
AND YOU KNOW I'M CAPABLE.
NOW LISTEN TO ME, CONTROL...I KNOW YOU CAN HEAR ME, RIGHT HERE, IN MY FACE, UNDER MY SKIN...
WHOEVER YOU SEND AFTER ME NEXT IS ALREADY DEAD.
FZZT
AND YOU WON'T SEE ME COMING--BECAUSE THIS CONTROL YOU PUT INSIDE ME...

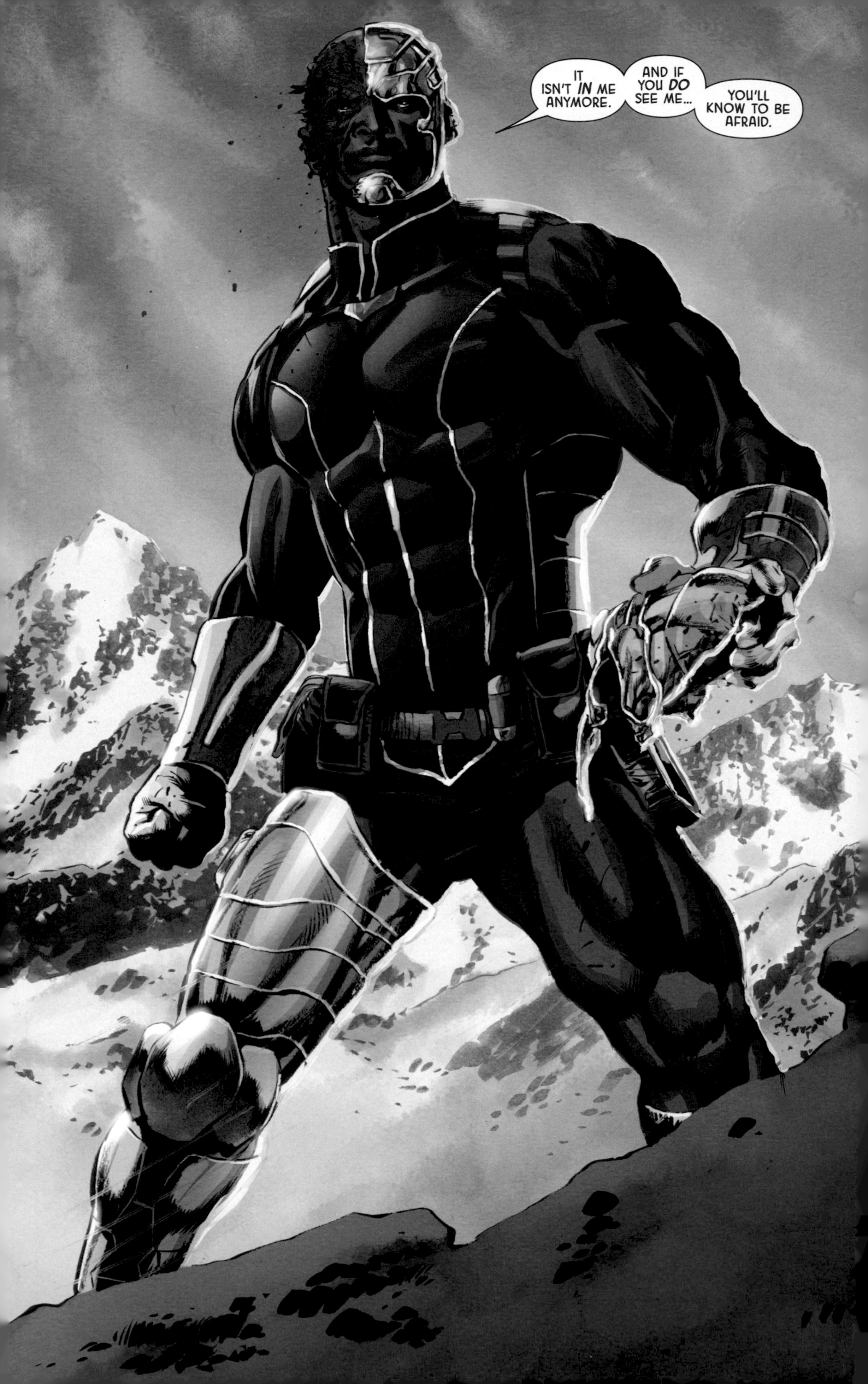
IT ISN'T IN ME ANYMORE.
AND IF YOU DO SEE ME...
YOU'LL KNOW TO BE AFRAID.

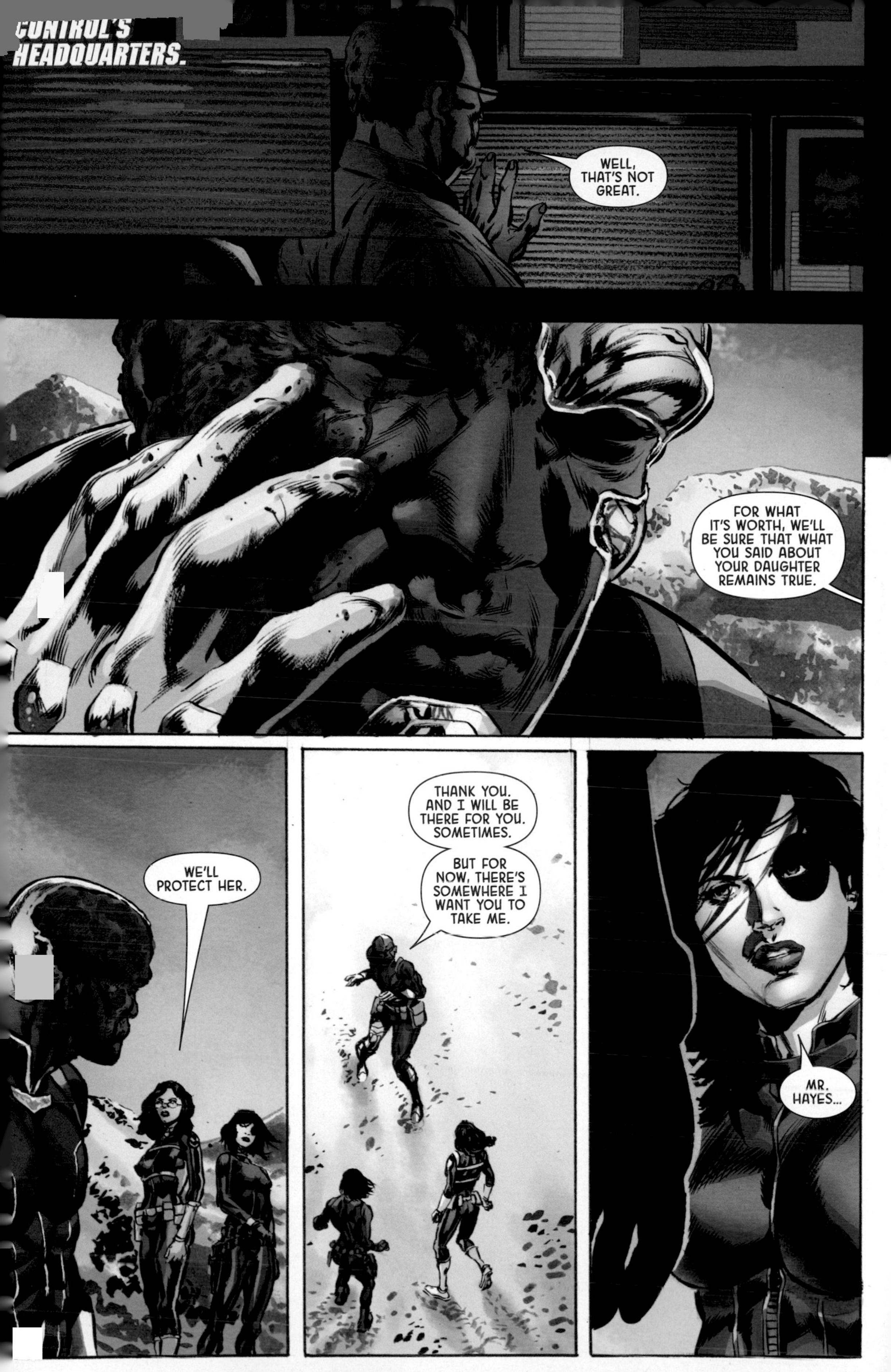
CONTROL'S HEADQUARTERS.
WELL, THAT'S NOT GREAT.
FOR WHAT IT'S WORTH, WE'LL BE SURE THAT WHAT YOU SAID ABOUT YOUR DAUGHTER REMAINS TRUE.
WE'LL PROTECT HER.
THANK YOU. AND I WILL BE THERE FOR YOU. SOMETIMES.
BUT FOR NOW, THERE'S SOMEWHERE I WANT YOU TO TAKE ME.
MR. HAYES...

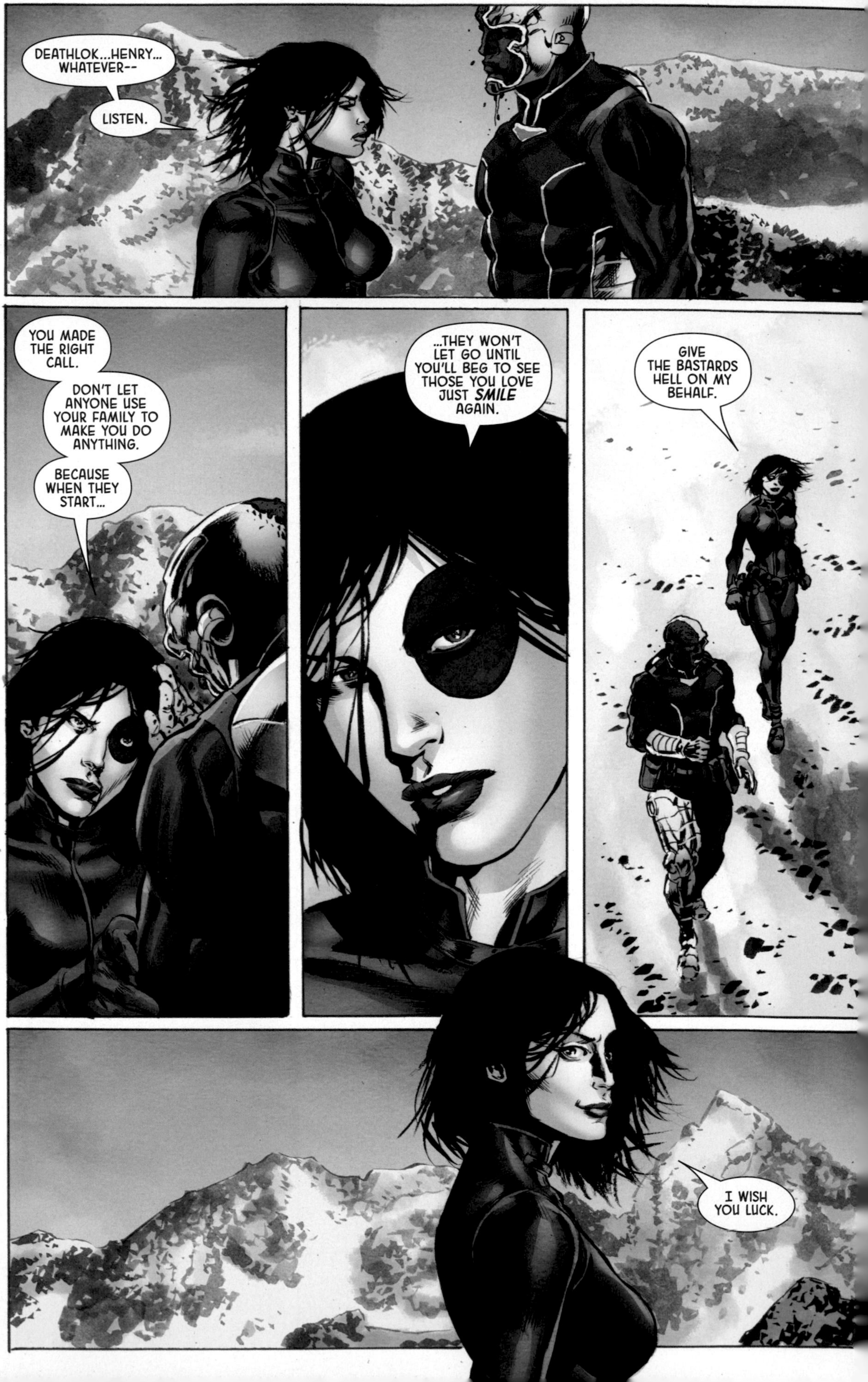
DEATHLOK...HENRY... WHATEVER--
LISTEN.
YOU MADE THE RIGHT CALL.
DON'T LET ANYONE USE YOUR FAMILY TO MAKE YOU DO ANYTHING.
BECAUSE WHEN THEY START...
...THEY WON'T LET GO UNTIL YOU'LL BEG TO SEE THOSE YOU LOVE JUST *SMILE* AGAIN.
GIVE THE BASTARDS HELL ON MY BEHALF.
I WISH YOU LUCK.

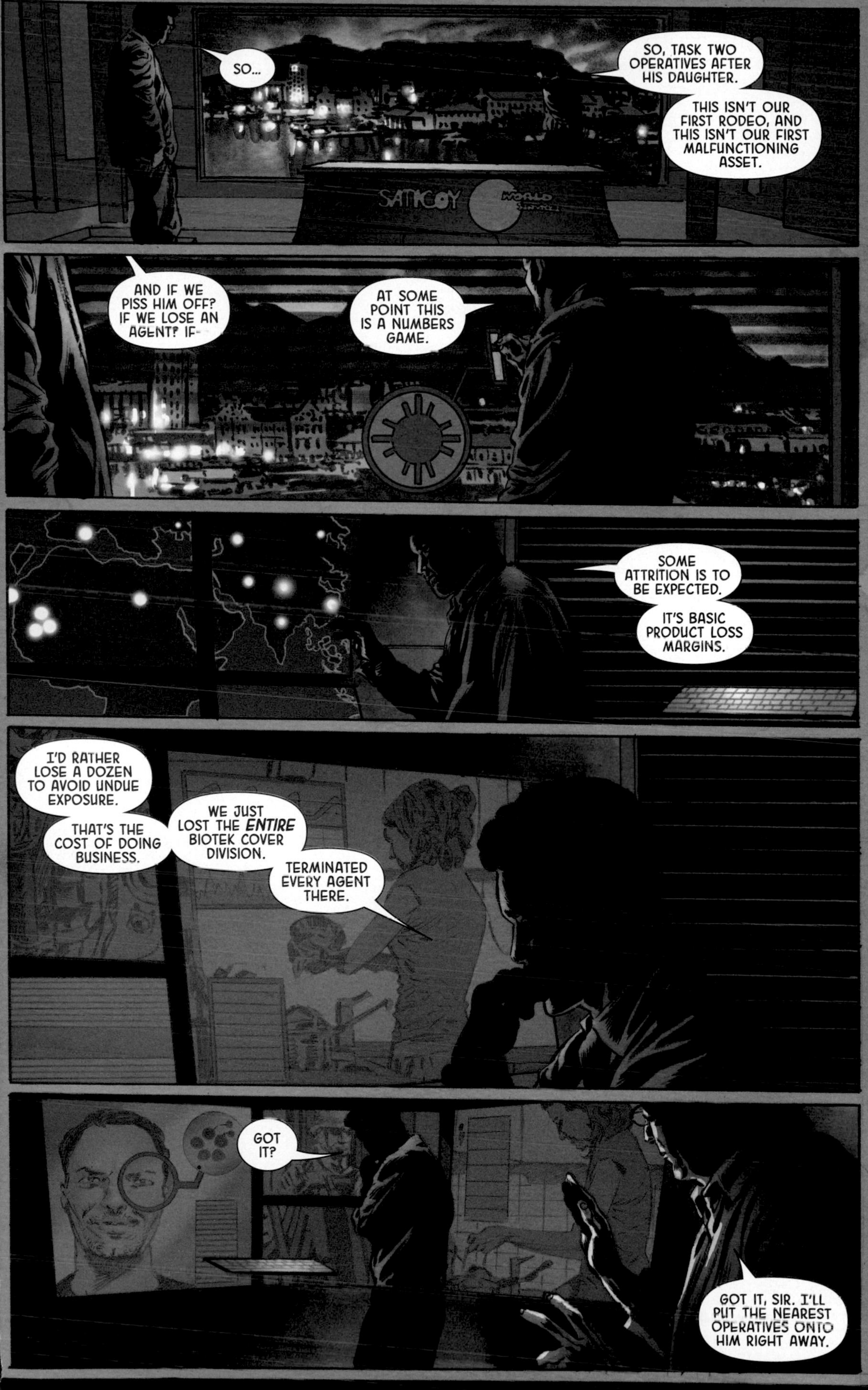
SO...
SO, TASK TWO OPERATIVES AFTER HIS DAUGHTER.
THIS ISN'T OUR FIRST RODEO, AND THIS ISN'T OUR FIRST MALFUNCTIONING ASSET.
SATICOY
AND IF WE PISS HIM OFF? IF WE LOSE AN AGENT? IF-
AT SOME POINT THIS IS A NUMBERS GAME.
SOME ATTRITION IS TO BE EXPECTED.
IT'S BASIC PRODUCT LOSS MARGINS.
I'D RATHER LOSE A DOZEN TO AVOID UNDUE EXPOSURE.
THAT'S THE COST OF DOING BUSINESS.
WE JUST LOST THE *ENTIRE* BIOTEK COVER DIVISION.
TERMINATED EVERY AGENT THERE.
GOT IT?
GOT IT, SIR. I'LL PUT THE NEAREST OPERATIVES ONTO HIM RIGHT AWAY.

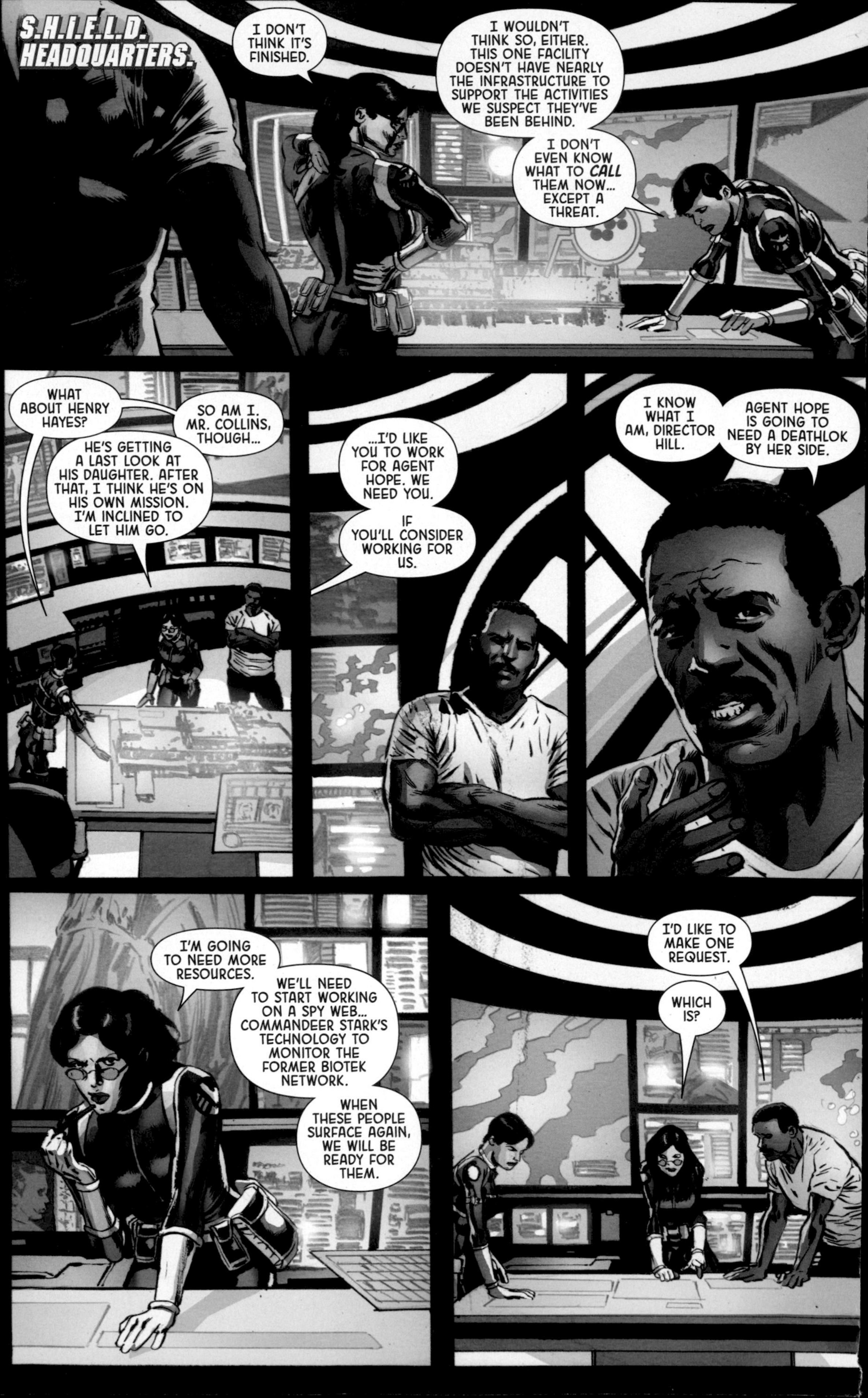
S.H.I.E.L.D. HEADQUARTERS.
I DON'T THINK IT'S FINISHED.
I WOULDN'T THINK SO, EITHER. THIS ONE FACILITY DOESN'T HAVE NEARLY THE INFRASTRUCTURE TO SUPPORT THE ACTIVITIES WE SUSPECT THEY'VE BEEN BEHIND.
I DON'T EVEN KNOW WHAT TO CALL THEM NOW... EXCEPT A THREAT.
WHAT ABOUT HENRY HAYES?
HE'S GETTING A LAST LOOK AT HIS DAUGHTER. AFTER THAT, I THINK HE'S ON HIS OWN MISSION. I'M INCLINED TO LET HIM GO.
SO AM I. MR. COLLINS, THOUGH...
...I'D LIKE YOU TO WORK FOR AGENT HOPE. WE NEED YOU.
IF YOU'LL CONSIDER WORKING FOR US.
I KNOW WHAT I AM, DIRECTOR HILL.
AGENT HOPE IS GOING TO NEED A DEATHLOK BY HER SIDE.
I'M GOING TO NEED MORE RESOURCES.
WE'LL NEED TO START WORKING ON A SPY WEB... COMMANDEER STARK'S TECHNOLOGY TO MONITOR THE FORMER BIOTEK NETWORK.
WHEN THESE PEOPLE SURFACE AGAIN, WE WILL BE READY FOR THEM.
I'D LIKE TO MAKE ONE REQUEST.
WHICH IS?

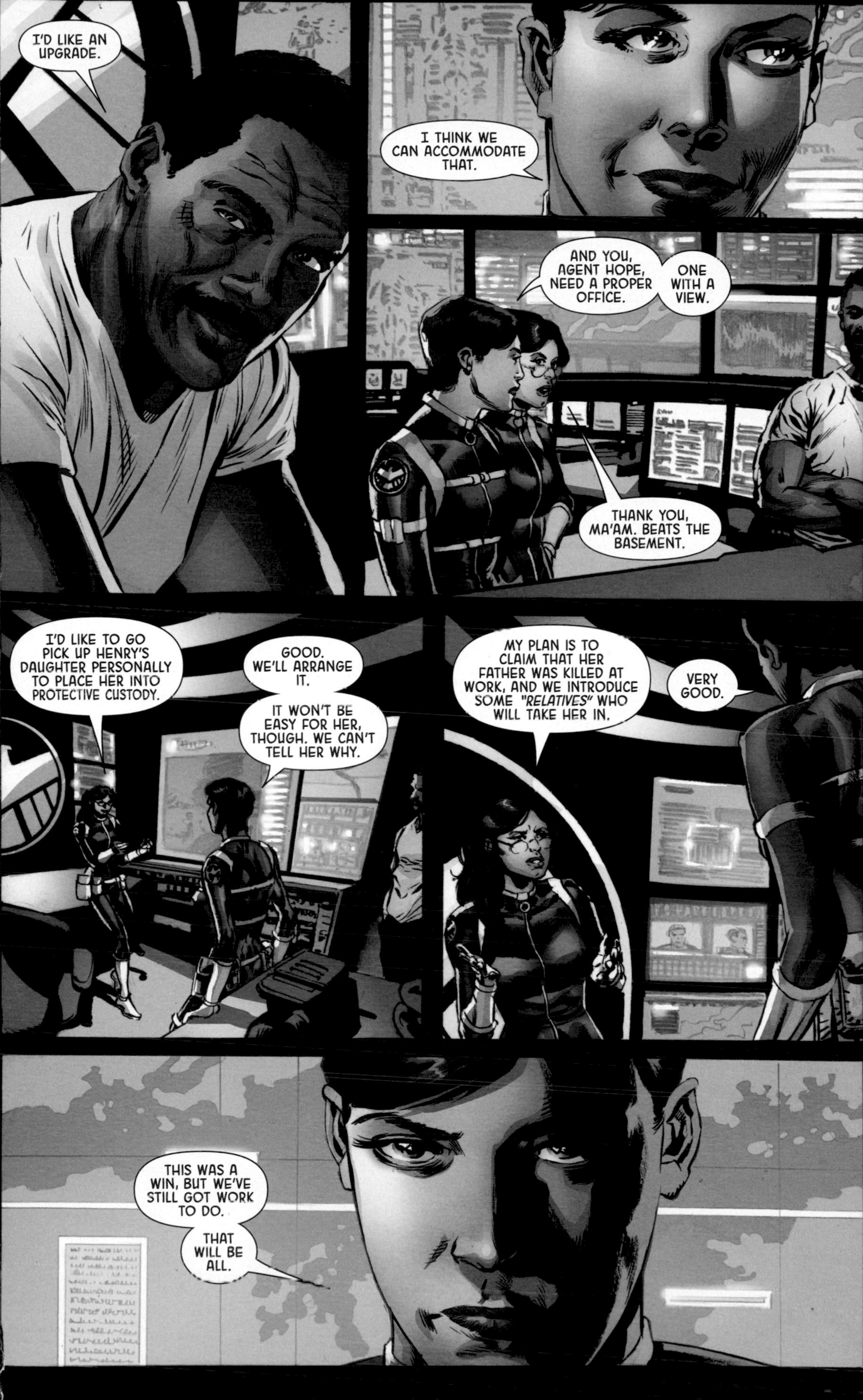
I'D LIKE AN UPGRADE.
I THINK WE CAN ACCOMMODATE THAT.
AND YOU, AGENT HOPE, NEED A PROPER OFFICE.
ONE WITH A VIEW.
THANK YOU, MA'AM. BEATS THE BASEMENT.
I'D LIKE TO GO PICK UP HENRY'S DAUGHTER PERSONALLY TO PLACE HER INTO PROTECTIVE CUSTODY.
GOOD. WE'LL ARRANGE IT.
IT WON'T BE EASY FOR HER, THOUGH. WE CAN'T TELL HER WHY.
MY PLAN IS TO CLAIM THAT HER FATHER WAS KILLED AT WORK, AND WE INTRODUCE SOME "RELATIVES" WHO WILL TAKE HER IN.
VERY GOOD.
THIS WAS A WIN, BUT WE'VE STILL GOT WORK TO DO.
THAT WILL BE ALL.

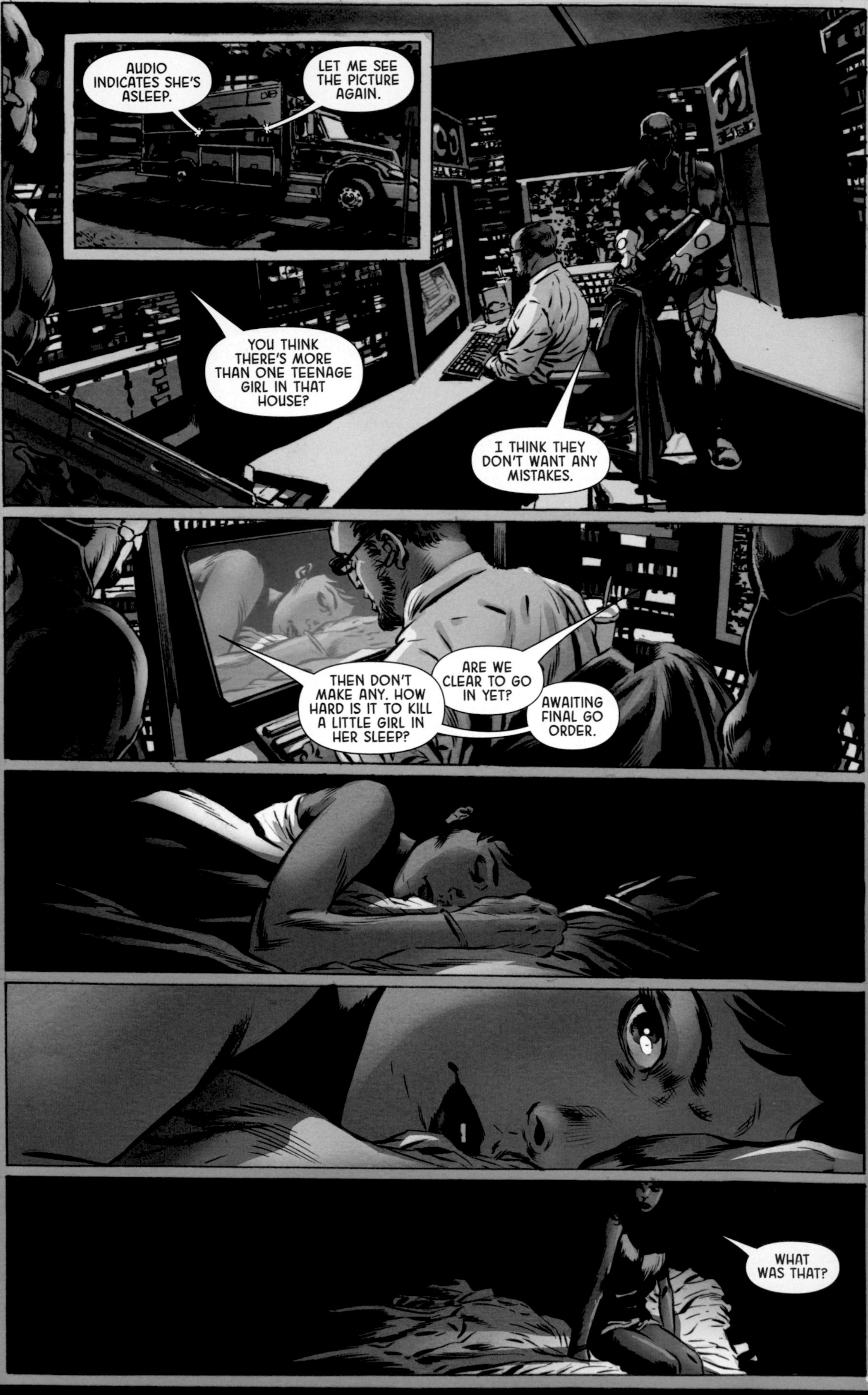
AUDIO INDICATES SHE'S ASLEEP.
LET ME SEE THE PICTURE AGAIN.
YOU THINK THERE'S MORE THAN ONE TEENAGE GIRL IN THAT HOUSE?
I THINK THEY DON'T WANT ANY MISTAKES.
THEN DON'T MAKE ANY. HOW HARD IS IT TO KILL A LITTLE GIRL IN HER SLEEP?
ARE WE CLEAR TO GO IN YET?
AWAITING FINAL GO ORDER.
WHAT WAS THAT?

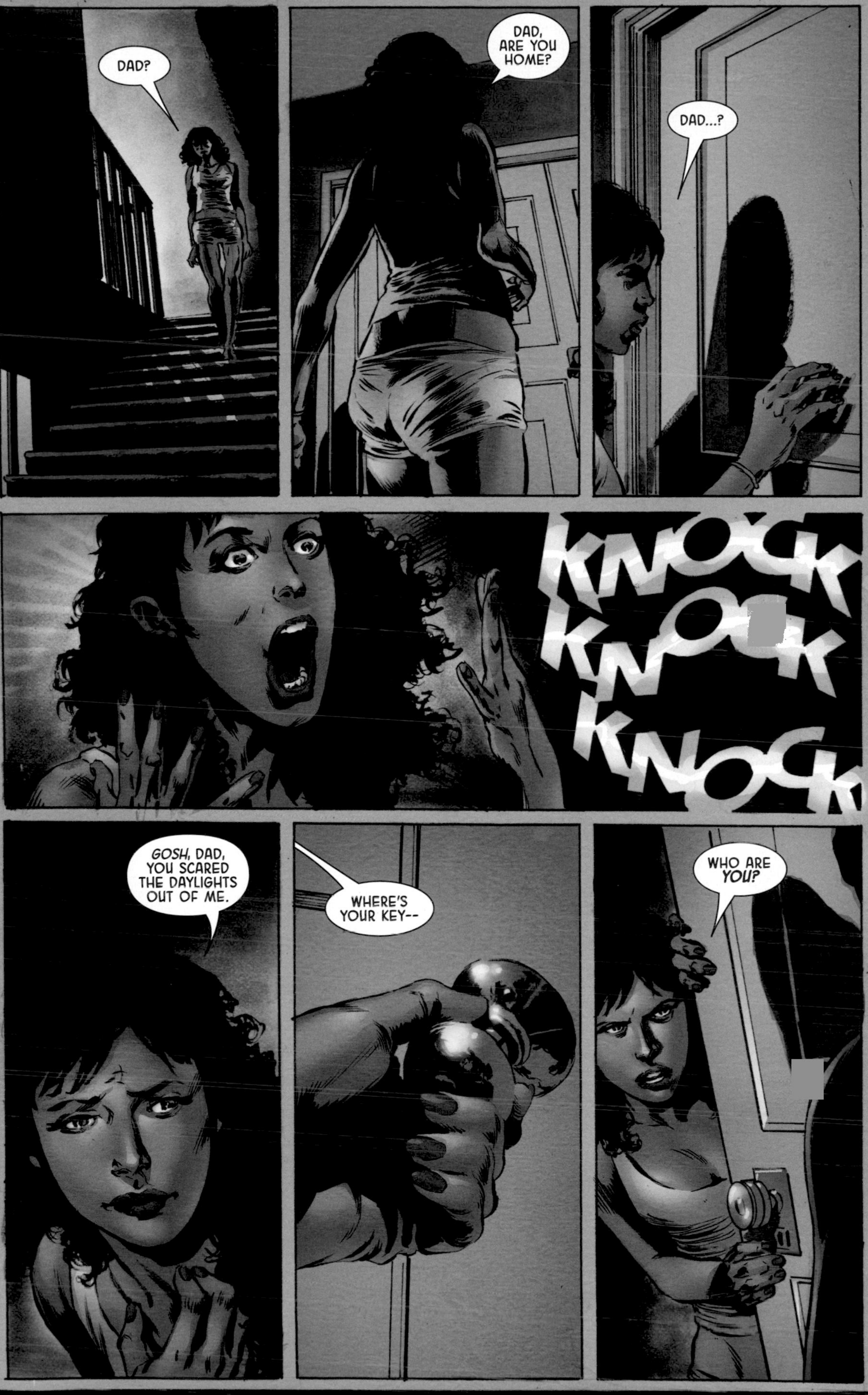
DAD?
DAD, ARE YOU HOME?
DAD...?
KNOCK
KNOCK
KNOCK
GOSH, DAD, YOU SCARED THE DAYLIGHTS OUT OF ME.
WHERE'S YOUR KEY--
WHO ARE *YOU?*

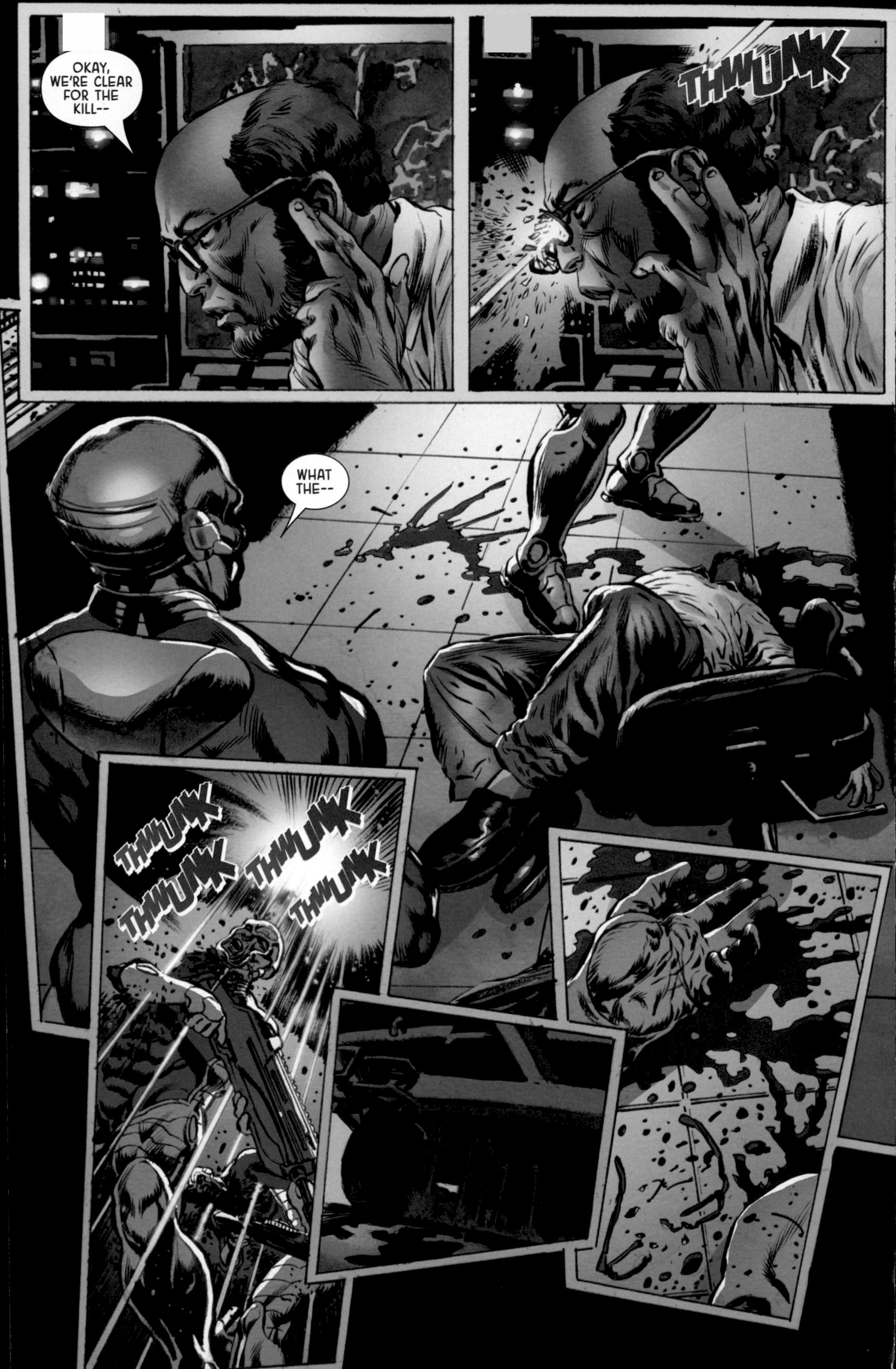
OKAY, WE'RE CLEAR FOR THE KILL--
THWUNK
WHAT THE--
THWUNK
THWUNK
THWUNK
THWUNK

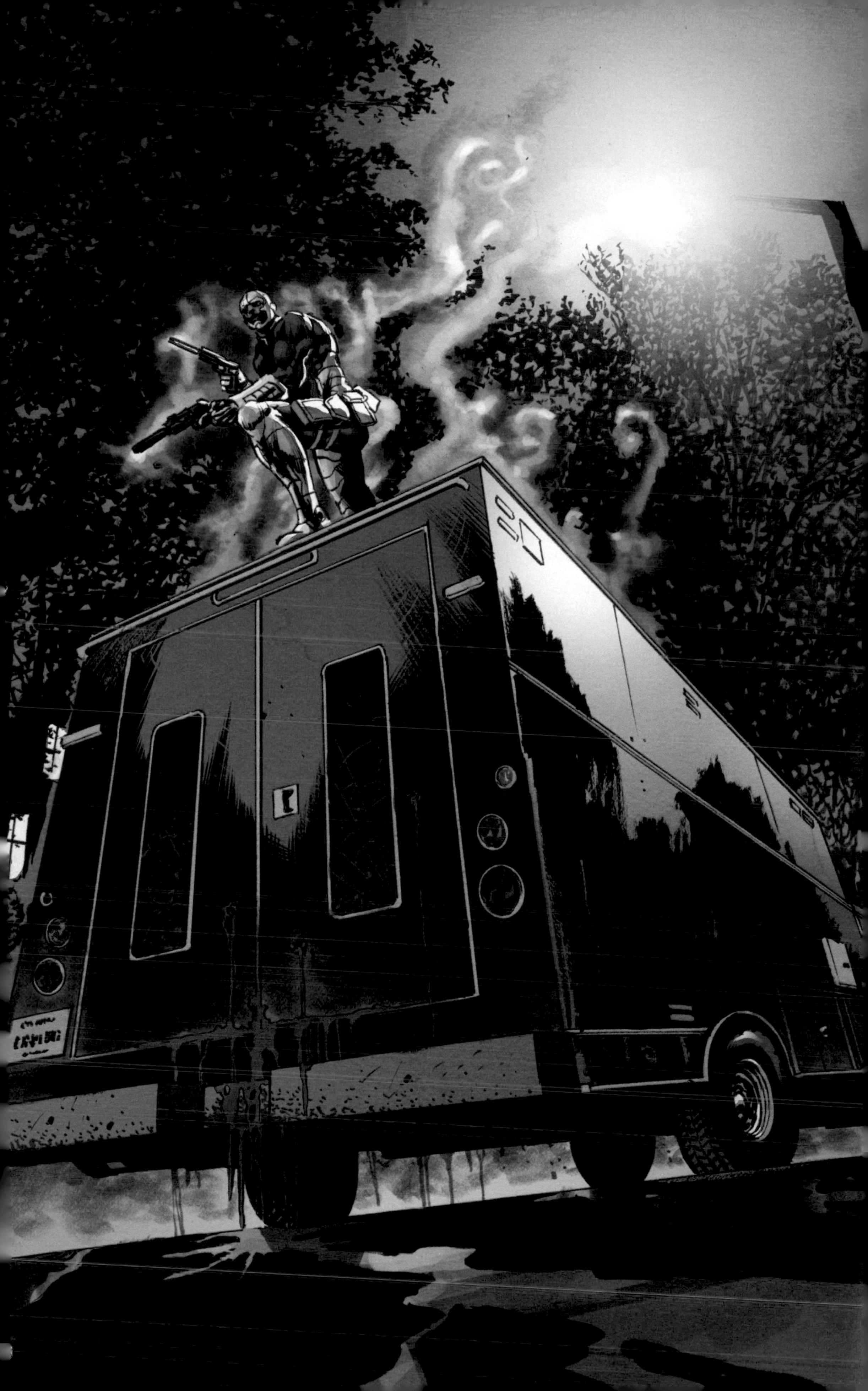

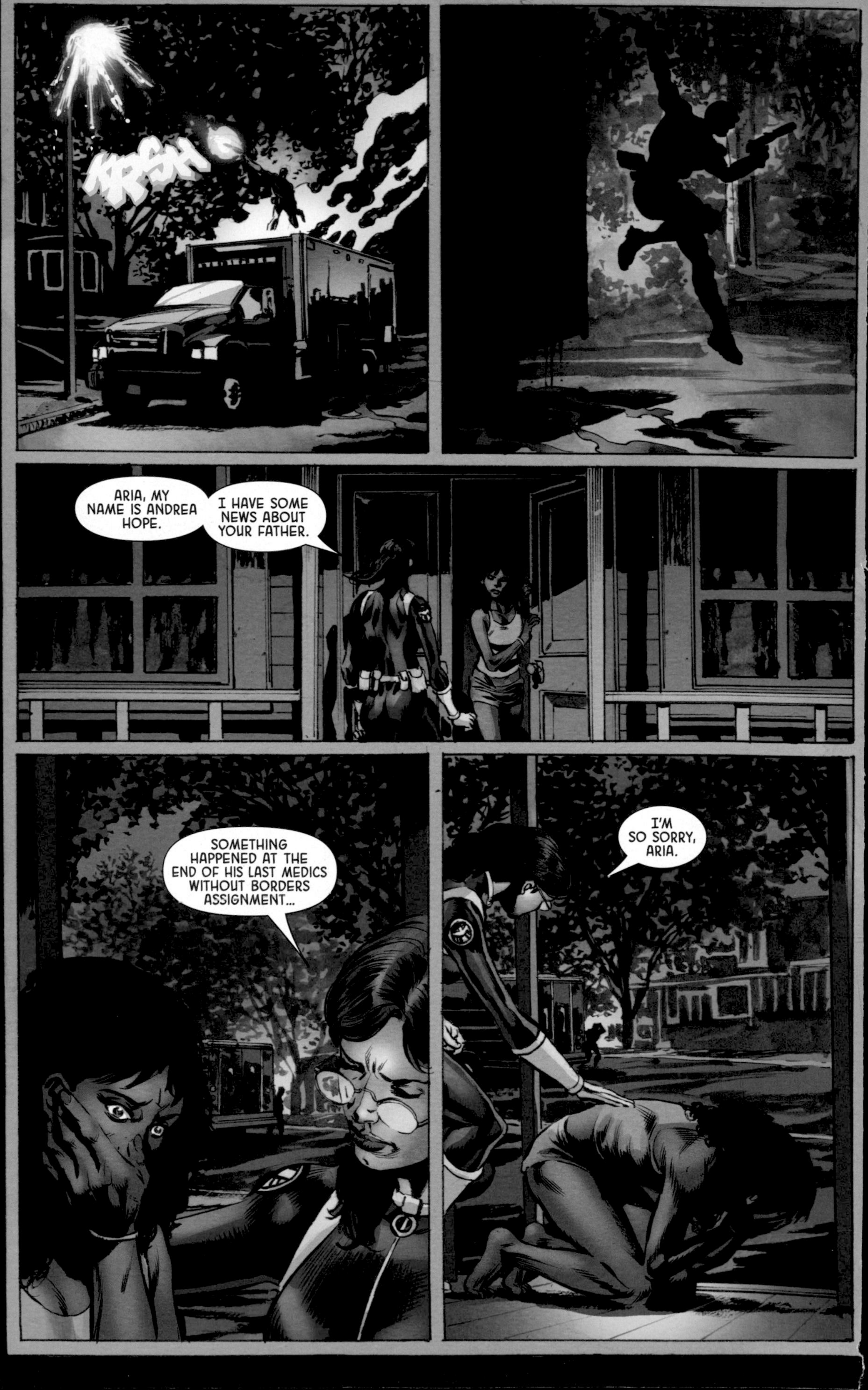
KRSH
ARIA, MY NAME IS ANDREA HOPE.
I HAVE SOME NEWS ABOUT YOUR FATHER.
SOMETHING HAPPENED AT THE END OF HIS LAST MEDICS WITHOUT BORDERS ASSIGNMENT...
I'M SO SORRY, ARIA.

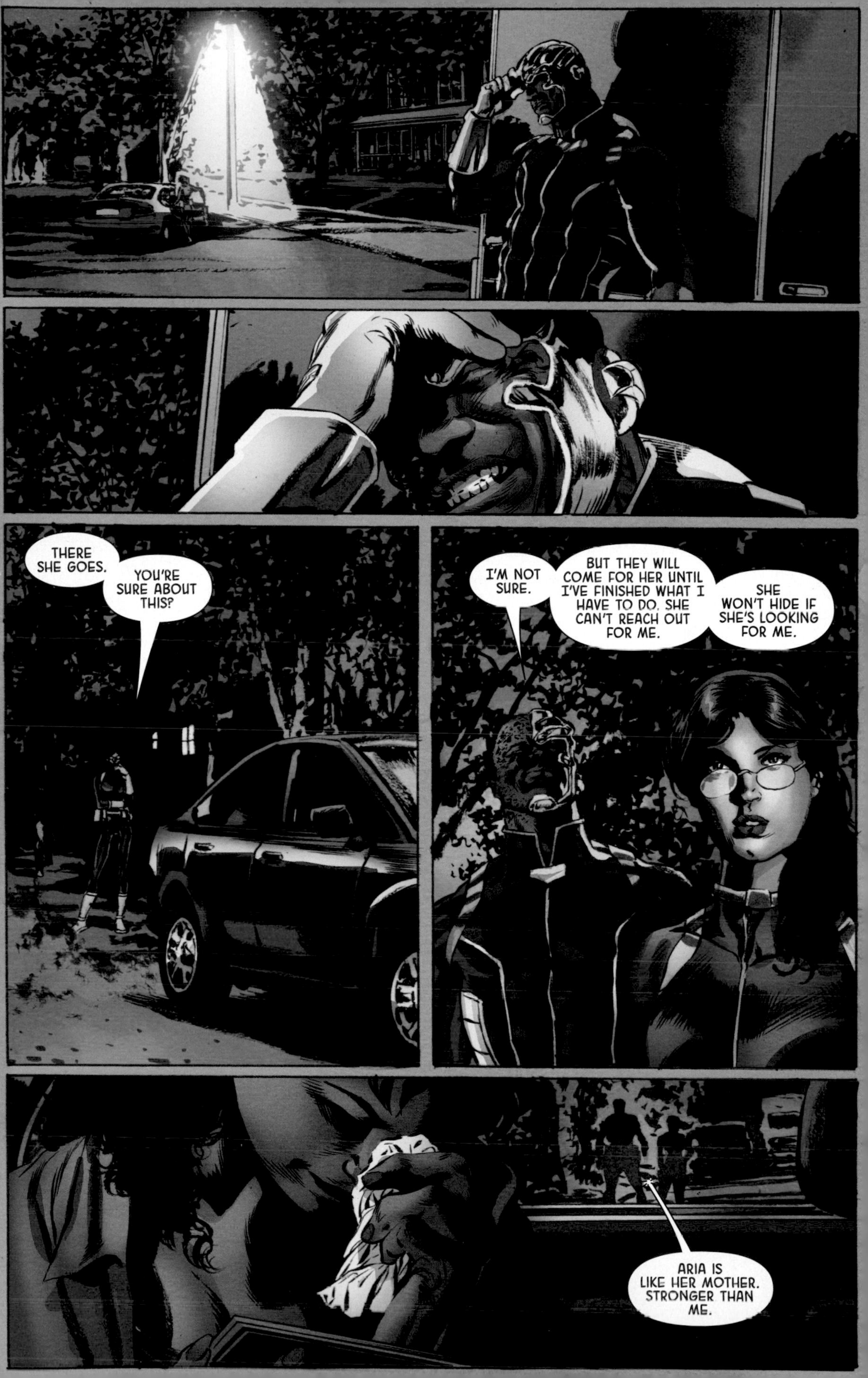
THERE SHE GOES.
YOU'RE SURE ABOUT THIS?
I'M NOT SURE.
BUT THEY WILL COME FOR HER UNTIL I'VE FINISHED WHAT I HAVE TO DO. SHE CAN'T REACH OUT FOR ME.
SHE WON'T HIDE IF SHE'S LOOKING FOR ME.
ARIA IS LIKE HER MOTHER. STRONGER THAN ME.

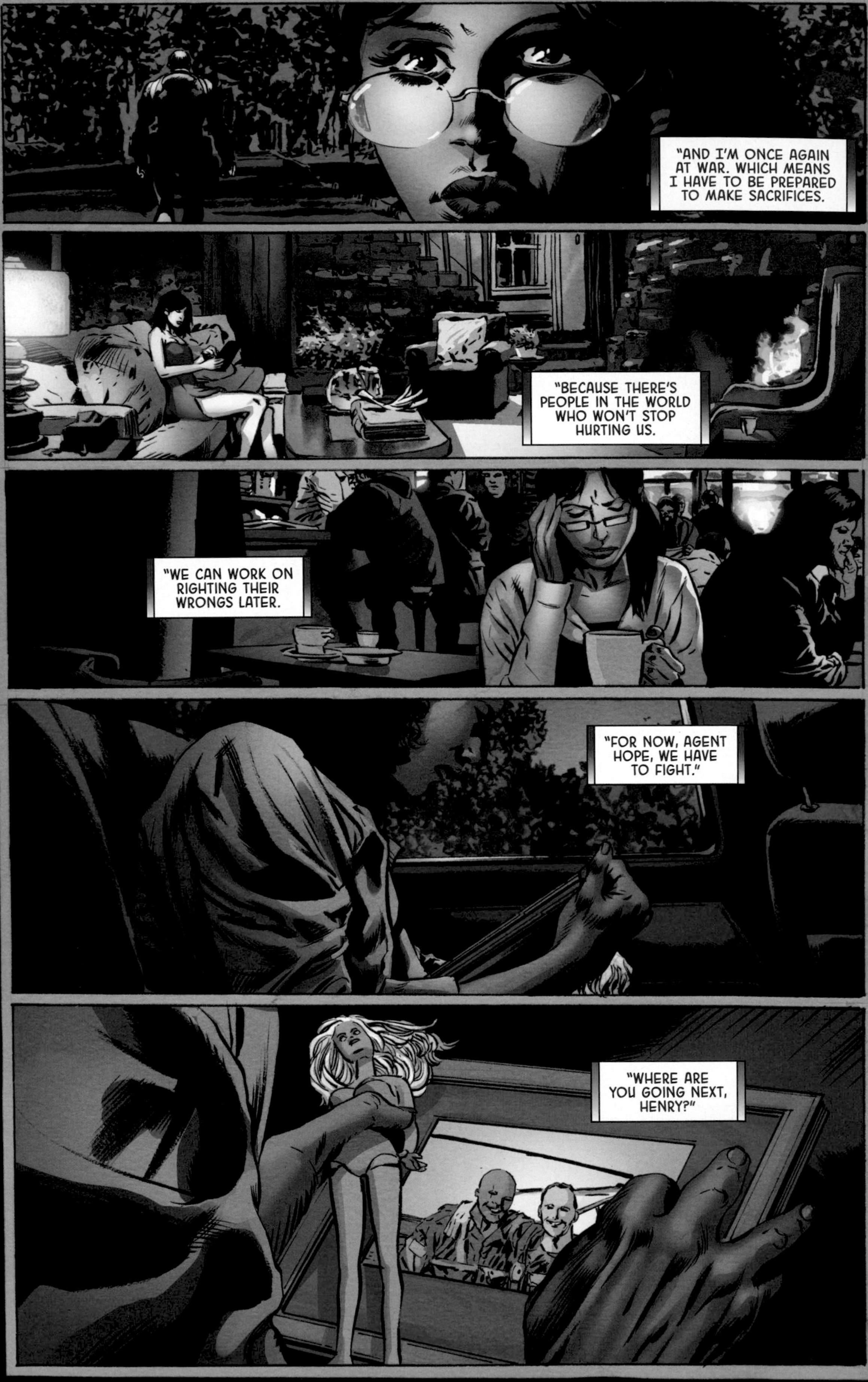
"AND I'M ONCE AGAIN AT WAR. WHICH MEANS I HAVE TO BE PREPARED TO MAKE SACRIFICES.
"BECAUSE THERE'S PEOPLE IN THE WORLD WHO WON'T STOP HURTING US.
"WE CAN WORK ON RIGHTING THEIR WRONGS LATER.
"FOR NOW, AGENT HOPE, WE HAVE TO FIGHT."
"WHERE ARE YOU GOING NEXT, HENRY?"

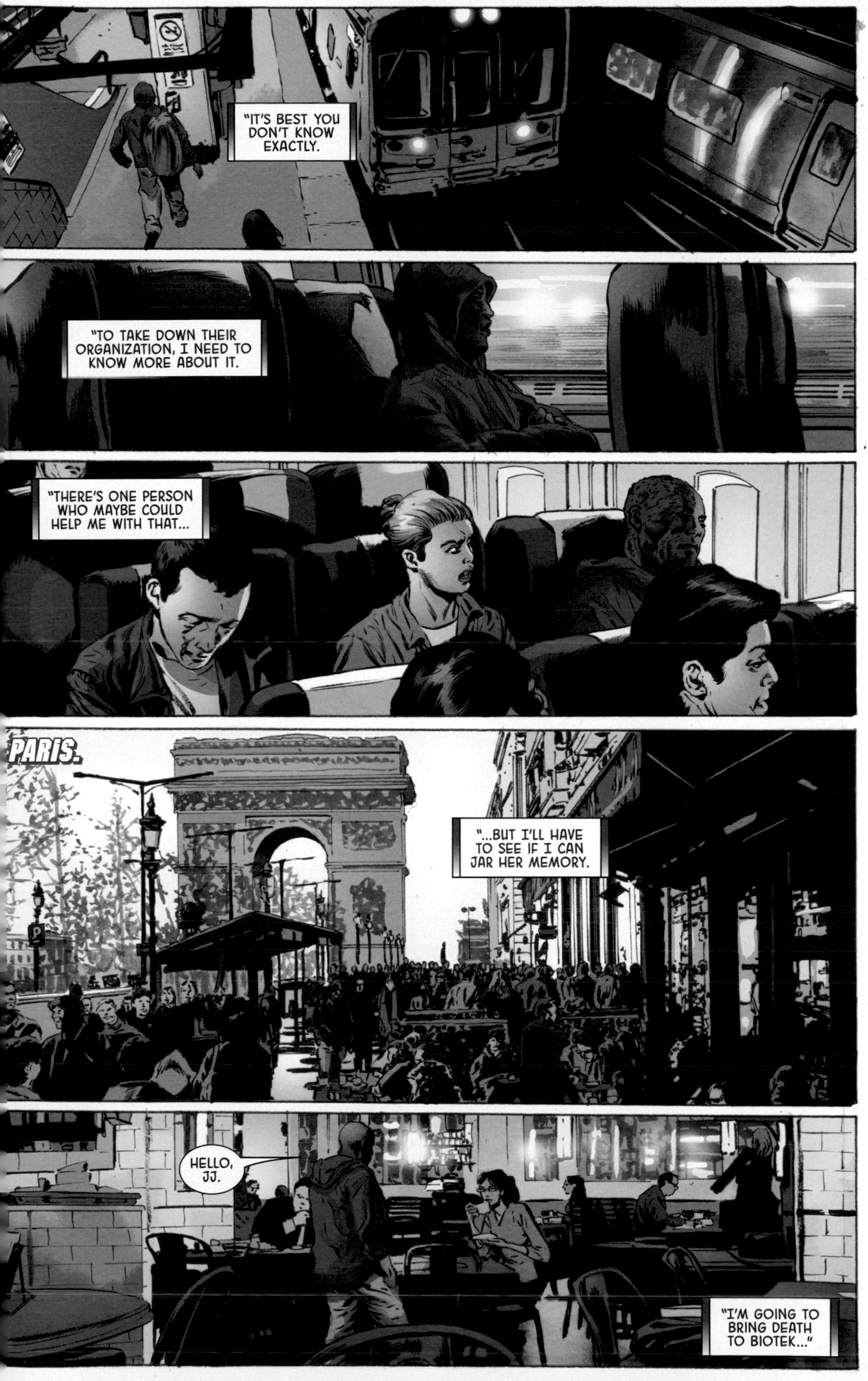
"IT'S BEST YOU DON'T KNOW EXACTLY.
"TO TAKE DOWN THEIR ORGANIZATION, I NEED TO KNOW MORE ABOUT IT.
"THERE'S ONE PERSON WHO MAYBE COULD HELP ME WITH THAT...
PARIS.
"...BUT I'LL HAVE TO SEE IF I CAN JAR HER MEMORY.
HELLO, JJ.
"I'M GOING TO BRING DEATH TO BIOTEK..."

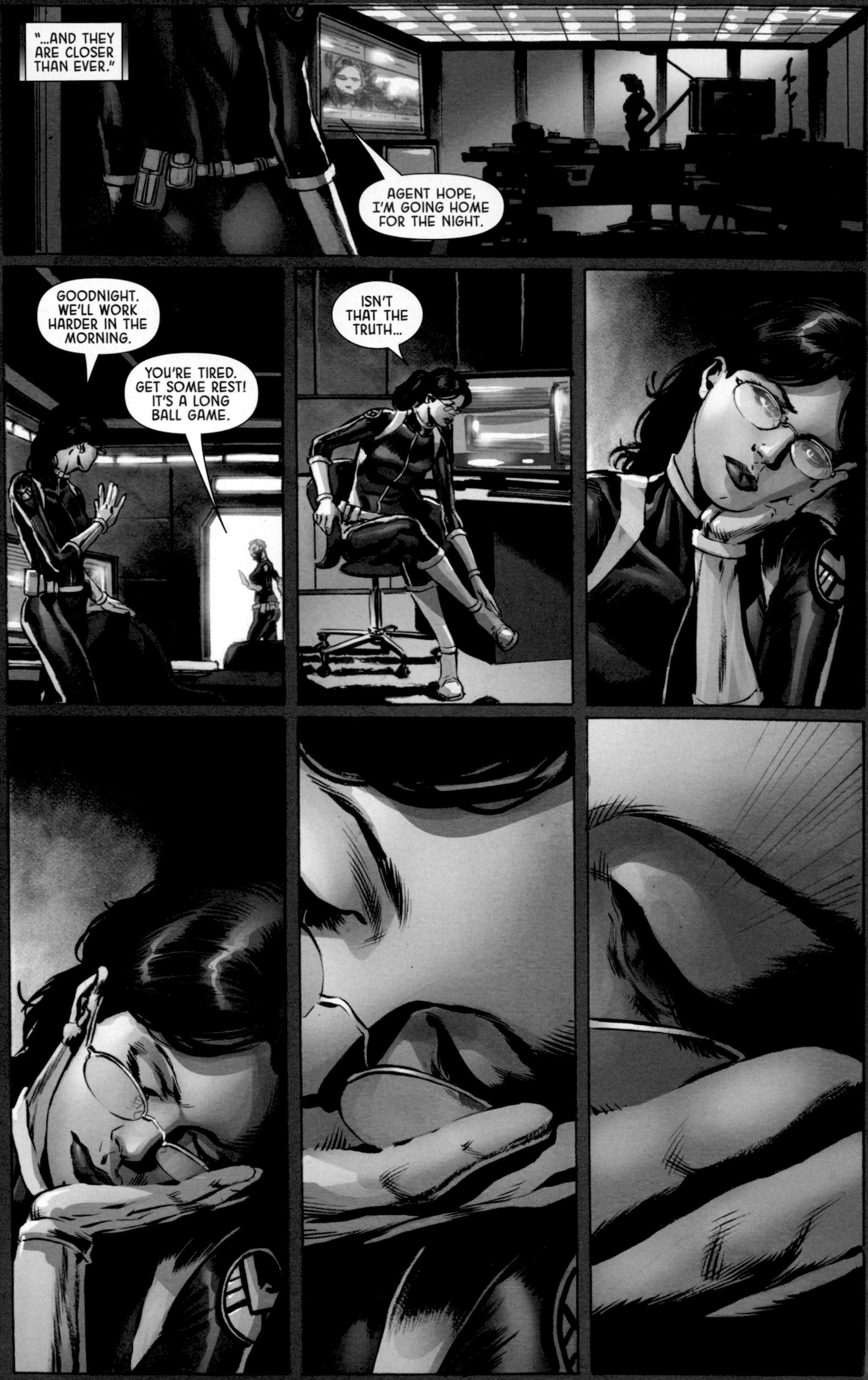
"...AND THEY ARE CLOSER THAN EVER."
AGENT HOPE, I'M GOING HOME FOR THE NIGHT.
GOODNIGHT. WE'LL WORK HARDER IN THE MORNING.
YOU'RE TIRED. GET SOME REST! IT'S A LONG BALL GAME.
ISN'T THAT THE TRUTH...

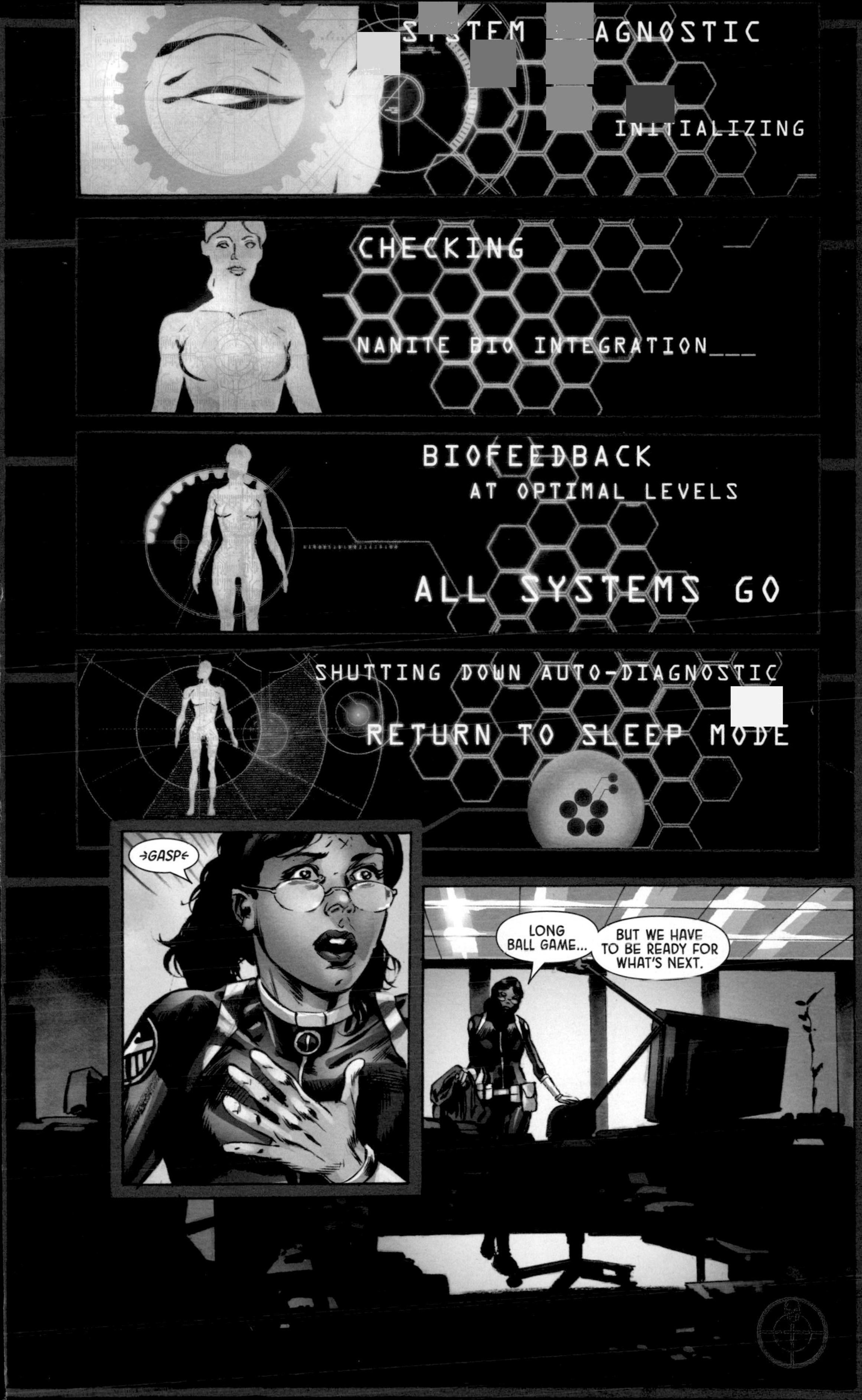
SYSTEM DIAGNOSTIC
INITIALIZING
CHECKING
NANITE BIO INTEGRATION___
BIOFEEDBACK
AT OPTIMAL LEVELS
ALL SYSTEMS GO
SHUTTING DOWN AUTO-DIAGNOSTIC
RETURN TO SLEEP MODE
GASP
LONG BALL GAME...
BUT WE HAVE TO BE READY FOR WHAT'S NEXT.

>>> **DEATHLOK #6, PAGE 6** ORIGINAL ART BY MIKE PERKINS

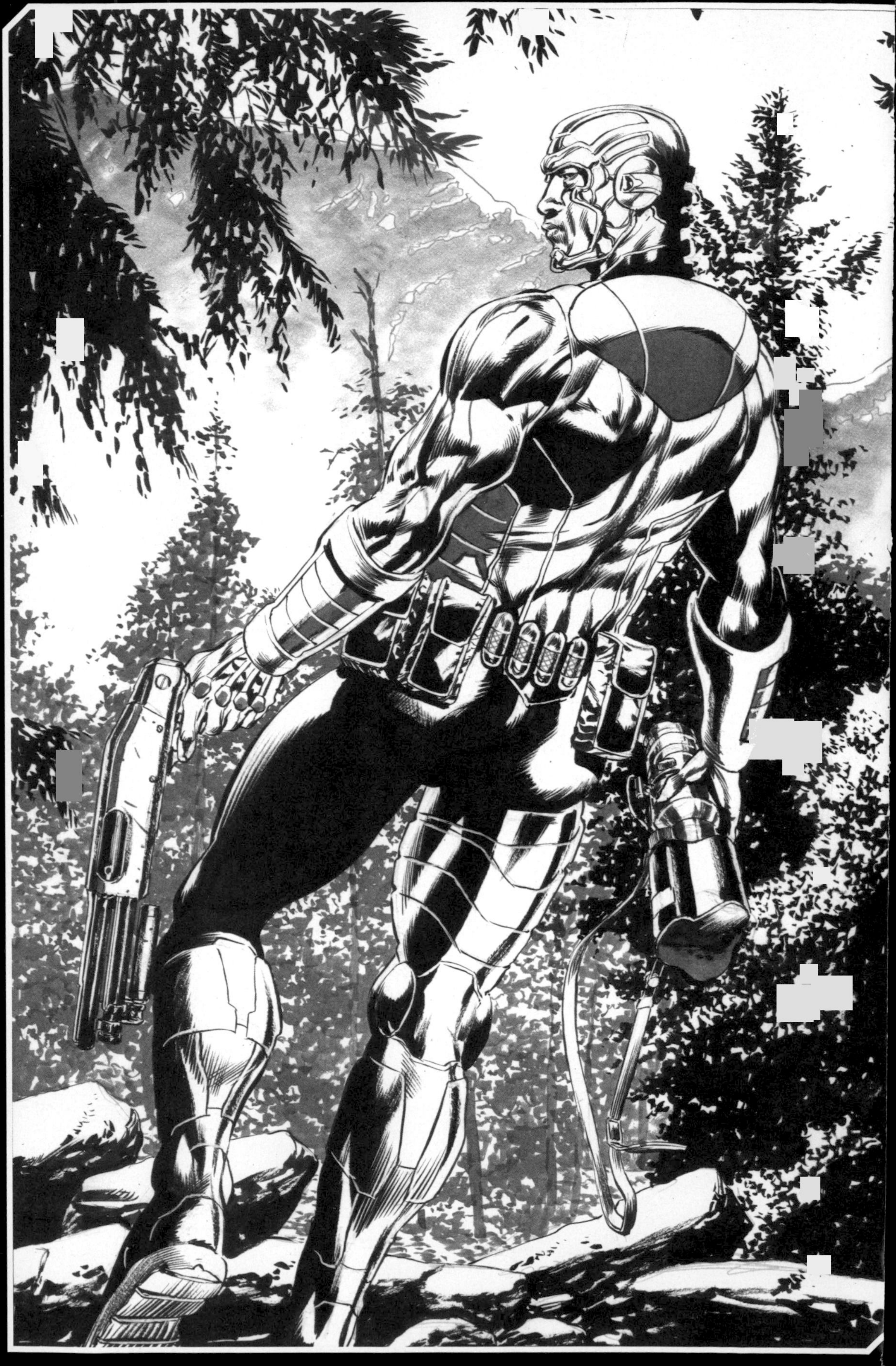

>>> **DEATHLOK #7, PAGE 2** ORIGINAL ART BY MIKE PERKINS

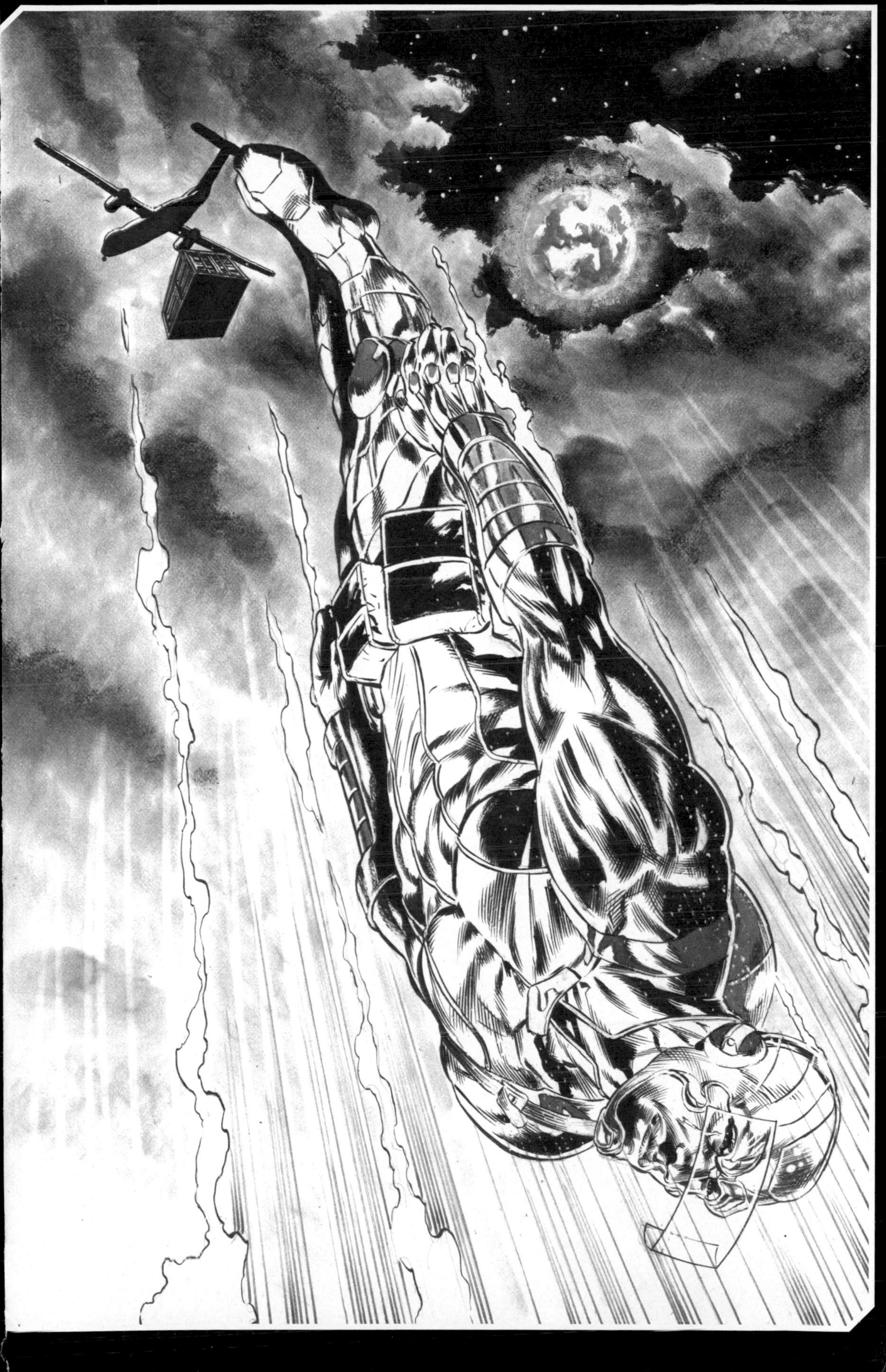

>>> **DEATHLOK #7, PAGE 20** ORIGINAL ART BY MIKE PERKINS

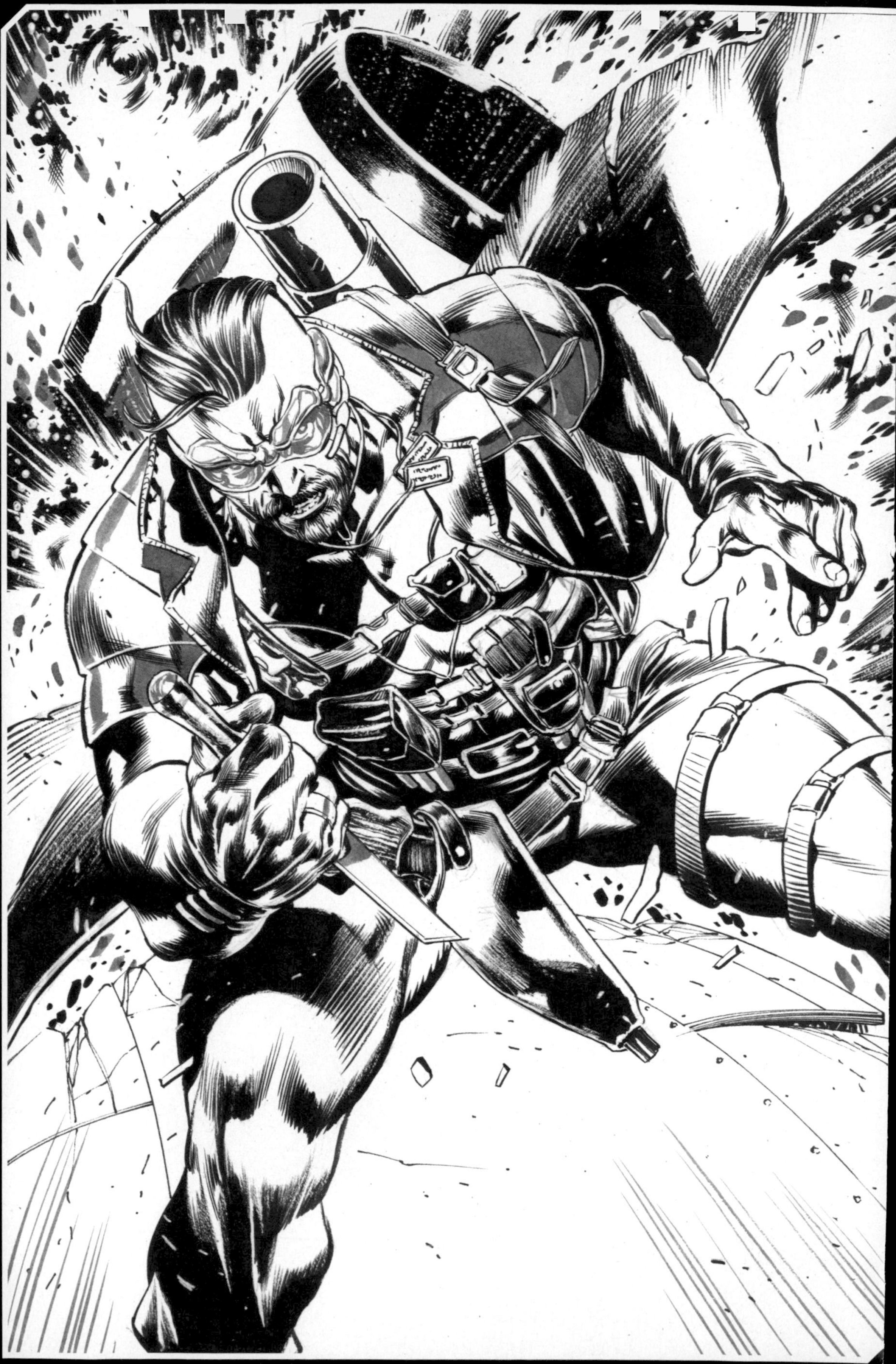